FLORIDA OF CRIMINAL PROCEDURE BOOKLET

2025 Edition

Including:
Official Committee Notes
Court Commentary

Concise Legal Series™

© 2025 Big Dream Ideas LLC d/b/a Cahaba Publications ™
Birmingham, AL
spalmer@cahabapublications.com

ALL RIGHTS RESERVED. No copyright is claimed in any government work. Contents may not be reproduced, stored, or transmitted in any form or by any means, electronic or mechanical, including photocopying, recording, or by any information storage and retrieval system without permission in writing from the publisher. Copyright is not claimed as to any part of the original work prepared by any government officer or employee as part of that person's official duties.

This publication was created to provide the reader with accurate and authoritative information concerning the subject matter covered, and for general information purposes only. It is not an official source, and is not a substitute for and should not be considered legal advice. This publication was not necessarily prepared by persons licensed to practice law in a particular jurisdiction. The publisher and editor are not engaged in rendering legal or other professional advice, and this publication is not a substitute for the advice of an attorney. The publisher has endeavored to ensure the accuracy and currency of this booklet's contents, but it makes no guarantee in either regard and does not assume liability for inadvertent errors or otherwise. If you require legal or other expert advice, you should seek the services of a competent attorney or other professional.

Rules in this booklet are current through at least January 1, 2025. Subsequent amendments, if any, can be found at www.floridasupremecourt.org/decisions/rules.shtml.

ISBN: 9798410392921

Published by
Cahaba Publications ™
Birmingham, Alabama

This book contains:

Fla. R. Crim. P. 3.010-3.996

Rules/statutes in this book are current through at least December 31, 2024.

TABLE OF CONTENTS
Florida Rules of Criminal Procedure 1
I. Scope, Purpose, and Construction 1
Rule 3.010. Scope. 1
Rule 3.020. Purpose and Construction. 2
Rule 3.025. State and Prosecuting Attorney Defined. 2
II. General Provisions 3
Rule 3.030. Service and Filing of Pleadings and Documents. 3
Rule 3.040. Computation of Time. 3
Rule 3.050. Enlargement of Time. 4
Rule 3.060. Time for Service of Motions and Notice of Hearing. 4
Rule 3.070. Additional Time After Service by Mail, When Permitted, or E-Mail [Repealed]. 5
Rule 3.080. Nonverification of Pleadings. 5
Rule 3.090. Pleading Captions. 5
Rule 3.111. Providing Counsel to Indigents. 5
Rule 3.112. Minimum Standards for Attorneys in Capital Cases. 12
Rule 3.113. Minimum Standards for Attorneys in Felony Cases. 18
Rule 3.115. Duties of State Attorney; Criminal Intake. 19
Rule 3.116. Use of communication technology. 19
III. Preliminary Proceedings 22
Rule 3.120. Committing Judge. 22
Rule 3.121. Arrest Warrant. 22
Rule 3.125. Notice to Appear. 23
Rule 3.130. First Appearance. 30
Rule 3.131. Pretrial Release. 33
Rule 3.132. Pretrial Detention. 39
Rule 3.133. Pretrial Probable Cause Determinations and Adversary Preliminary Hearings. 42
Rule 3.134. Time for Filing Formal Charges. 46
Rule 3.140. Indictments; Informations. 47
Rule 3.150. Joinder of Offenses and Defendants. 60
Rule 3.151. Consolidation of Related Offenses. 62

i

Rule 3.152. Severance of Offenses and Defendants. 63
Rule 3.153. Timeliness of Defendant's Motion; Waiver. ... 65

IV. ARRAIGNMENT AND PLEAS 66
Rule 3.160. Arraignment 66
Rule 3.170. Pleas. 68
Rule 3.171. Plea Discussions And Agreements. 72
Rule 3.172. Acceptance of Guilty or Nolo Contendere Plea. 75
Rule 3.180. Presence of Defendant. 79
Rule 3.181. Notice to Seek Death Penalty. 81

V. PRETRIAL MOTIONS AND DEFENSES 81
Rule 3.190. Pretrial Motions. 81
Rule 3.191. Speedy Trial. 88
Rule 3.192. Motions for Rehearing. 97
Rule 3.200. Notice of Alibi. 97
Rule 3.201. Battered-Spouse Syndrome Defense. 99
Rule 3.202. Expert Testimony of Mental Mitigation During Penalty Phase of Capital Trial; Notice and Examination by State Expert. 100
Rule 3.203. Defendant's Intellectual Disability as a Bar to Imposition of the Death Penalty. 101
Rule 3.210. Incompetence to Proceed: Procedure for Raising the Issue. 103
Rule 3.211. Competence to Proceed: Scope of Examination and Report. 110
Rule 3.212. Competence to Proceed: Hearing and Disposition. 116
Rule 3.213. Continuing Incompetency to Proceed, Except Incompetency to Proceed with Sentencing; Disposition. 123
Rule 3.214. Incompetency to Proceed to Sentencing: Disposition. 125
Rule 3.215. Effect of Adjudication of Incompetency to Proceed: Psychotropic Medication. 125
Rule 3.216. Insanity At Time of Offense or Probation or Community Control Violation: Notice and Appointment of Experts. 127
Rule 3.217. Judgment of Not Guilty by Reason of Insanity; Disposition of Defendant. 130

Table of Contents

Rule 3.218. Commitment of a Defendant Found Not Guilty by Reason of Insanity. 131
Rule 3.219. Conditional Release. 133

VI. DISCOVERY 134
Rule 3.220. Discovery. 134

VII. SUBSTITUTION OF JUDGE 158
Rule 3.231. Substitution of Judge. 158

VIII. CHANGE OF VENUE 159
Rule 3.240. Change of Venue. 159

IX. THE TRIAL 160
Rule 3.250. Accused as Witness. 160
Rule 3.251. Right to Trial by Jury. 161
Rule 3.260. Waiver of Jury Trial. 161
Rule 3.270. Number of Jurors. 161
Rule 3.280. Alternate Jurors. 162
Rule 3.281. List of Prospective Jurors. 163
Rule 3.290. Challenge to Panel. 163
Rule 3.300. Voir Dire Examination, Oath, and Excusing of Member. 163
Rule 3.310. Time for Challenge. 164
Rule 3.315. Exercise of Challenges. 165
Rule 3.320. Manner of Challenge. 165
Rule 3.330. Determination of Challenge for Cause. 165
Rule 3.340. Effect of Sustaining Challenge. 166
Rule 3.350. Peremptory Challenges. 166
Rule 3.360. Oath of Trial Jurors. 168
Rule 3.361. Witness Attendance and Subpoenas. 168

X. CONDUCT TO TRIAL; JURY INSTRUCTIONS 169
Rule 3.370. Regulation and Separation of Jurors. 169
Rule 3.371. Juror Questions of Witnesses. 170
Rule 3.372. Juror Notebooks. 170
Rule 3.380. Motion for Judgment of Acquittal 170
Rule 3.381. Final Arguments. 171
Rule 3.390. Jury Instructions. 172
Rule 3.391. Selection of Foreperson of Jury. 173
Rule 3.400. Materials to the Jury Room. 173

Rule 3.410. Jury Request to Review Evidence or for Additional Instructions. 174
Rule 3.420. Recall of Jury for Additional Instructions. ... 175
Rule 3.430. Jury Not Recallable to Hear Additional Evidence. 175

XI. THE VERDICT 175
Rule 3.440. Rendition of Verdict; Reception and Recording. 175
Rule 3.450. Polling the Jury. 176
Rule 3.451. Judicial Comment on Verdict. 176
Rule 3.470. Proceedings on Sealed Verdict 177
Rule 3.490. Determination of Degree of Offense. 177
Rule 3.500. Verdict of Guilty Where More Than One Count. 177
Rule 3.505. Inconsistent Verdicts. 178
Rule 3.510. Determination of Attempts and Lesser Included Offenses. 178
Rule 3.520. Verdict in Case of Joint Defendants. 179
Rule 3.530. Reconsideration of Ambiguous or Defective Verdict. 179
Rule 3.540. When Verdict May Be Rendered. 179
Rule 3.550. Disposition of Defendant. 180
Rule 3.560. Discharge of Jurors. 180
Rule 3.570. Irregularity in Rendition, Reception, and Recording of Verdict. 180
Rule 3.575. Motion to Interview Juror. 181

XII. POST-TRIAL-MOTIONS 181
Rule 3.580. Court May Grant New Trial. 181
Rule 3.590. Time for and Method of Making Motions; Procedure; Custody Pending Hearing. 182
Rule 3.600. Grounds for New Trial. 184
Rule 3.610. Motion for Arrest of Judgment; Grounds. ... 185
Rule 3.620. When Evidence Sustains Only Conviction of Lesser Offense. 186
Rule 3.630. Sentence Before or After Motion Filed. 186
Rule 3.640. Effect of Granting New Trial. 186

XIII. JUDGMENT 187
Rule 3.650. Judgment Defined. 187
Rule 3.670. Rendition of Judgment. 187
Rule 3.680. Judgment on Informal Verdict. 188
Rule 3.690. Judgment of Not Guilty; Defendant Discharged and Sureties Exonerated. 189
Rule 3.691. Post-Trial Release. 189
Rule 3.692. Petition to Seal or Expunge. 190
Rule 3.693. Petition to Seal or Expunge; Human Trafficking. 192
Rule 3.694. Petition to Seal or Expunge; Lawful Self-Defense Expunction. 194

XIV. SENTENCE 196
Rule 3.700. Sentence Defined; Pronouncement and Entry; Sentencing Judge. 196
Rule 3.701. Sentencing Guidelines. 197
Rule 3.702. Sentencing Guidelines (1994). 201
Rule 3.703. Sentencing Guidelines (1994 as amended). 208
Rule 3.704. The Criminal Punishment Code. 219
Rule 3.710. Presentence Report. 229
Rule 3.711. Presentence Report: When Prepared. 230
Rule 3.712. Presentence Report: Disclosure. 231
Rule 3.713. Presentence Investigation Disclosure: Parties. 231
Rule 3.720. Sentencing Hearing. 232
Rule 3.721. Record of the Proceedings. 233
Rule 3.730. Issuance of Capias When Necessary to Bring Defendant Before Court. 234
Rule 3.750. Procedure When Pardon Is Alleged as Cause for Not Pronouncing Sentence. 234
Rule 3.760. Procedure When Nonidentity Is Alleged as Cause for Not Pronouncing Sentence. 235
Rule 3.770. Procedure When Pregnancy Is Alleged as Cause for Not Pronouncing Death Sentence. 235
Rule 3.780. Sentencing Hearing for Capital Cases. 236
Rule 3.781. Sentencing Hearing to Consider the Imposition of a Life Sentence for Juvenile Offenders. 236
Rule 3.790. Probation and Community Control. 238

Rule 3.800. Correction, Reduction, and Modification of Sentences..242
Rule 3.801. Correction of Jail Credit. 247
Rule 3.802. Review of Sentences for Juvenile Offenders. 248

XV. EXECUTION OF SENTENCE..........................251
Rule 3.810. Commitment of Defendant; Duty of Sheriff.251
Rule 3.811. Insanity At Time of Execution: Capital Cases. 251
Rule 3.812. Hearing on Insanity At Time of Execution: Capital Cases...253
Rule 3.820. Habeas Corpus. 254

XVI. CRIMINAL CONTEMPT..........................254
Rule 3.830. Direct Criminal Contempt. 254
Rule 3.840. Indirect Criminal Contempt. 255

XVII. POSTCONVICTION RELIEF..............................261
Rule 3.850. Motion To Vacate; Set Aside; Or Correct Sentence. 261
Rule 3.851. Collateral Relief After Death Sentence Has Been Imposed and Affirmed on Direct Appeal. 272
Rule 3.852. Capital Postconviction Public Records Production. 290
Rule 3.853. Motion for Postconviction DNA Testing......299

XVIII. FORMS 301

Florida Rules of Criminal Procedure

I. Scope, Purpose, and Construction

Rule 3.010. Scope.

These rules shall govern the procedure in all criminal proceedings in state courts including proceedings involving direct and indirect criminal contempt, proceedings under rule 3.850, and criminal traffic offenses as provided by section III, Florida Rules of Traffic Court. These rules shall not apply to direct or indirect criminal contempt of a court acting in any appellate capacity. These rules shall not apply to rules 3.811 and 3.812. These rules shall be known as the Florida Rules of Criminal Procedure and may be cited as Fla. R. Crim. P.

Committee Notes

1968 Adoption. These rules are not intended to apply to municipal courts, but are intended to apply to all state courts where "crimes" are charged.

1972 Amendment. Amended to provide for applicability of rules to vehicular traffic offenses, when made so by the traffic court rules.

1992 Amendment. The rule is amended to refer to "Florida Rules of Criminal Procedure" and "Fla. R. Crim. P." rather than to "Rules of Criminal Procedure" and "R. Crim. P." Although the Florida Bar Rules of Criminal Procedure already contains this language, the West publications, Florida Rules of Court (1991) and Florida Criminal Law and Rules (1991), do not. The published version of rule 3.010, In re Florida Rules of Criminal Procedure, 272 So.2d 65 (Fla. 1973), and the single published amendment to the rule, In re Amendments to the Florida Rules of Criminal Procedure, 518 So.2d 256 (Fla. 1987), also do not contain these additions. The Florida Bar publication, Florida Criminal Rules and Practice, in a commentary to rule 3.010, indicates that the Florida Supreme Court changed the citation form in an order effective January 1, 1977. The commentary indicates that the order stated in pertinent part:

In order to provide the clarity of citations in briefs filed in this court and other legal writings, the following amendments to the procedural rules adopted by this court pursuant to Article V, Section 2(a), of the Florida Constitution are hereby adopted.

* * *

The last sentence of Rule 3.010 of the Florida Rules of Criminal Procedure is amended as follows: "These Rules shall be known as the Florida Rules of Criminal Procedure and may be cited as Fla. R. Crim. P."

However, these changes were apparently inadvertently omitted when the 1987 amendments were published. The proposed 1992 amendments again incorporate into the rule the language set out in the court's 1977 order.

The amendments would enable clearer identification of the rules and achieve consistency of style with other sets of court rules, in particular, rule 9.800(i), Fla. R. App. P., which provides that the proper citation to the Florida Rules of Criminal Procedure is Fla. R. Crim. P.

Rule 3.020. Purpose and Construction.

These rules are intended to provide for the just determination of every criminal proceeding. They shall be construed to secure simplicity in procedure and fairness in administration.

Committee Notes

1968 Adoption. Substantially the same as Federal Rule 2.

1972 Amendment. Same as prior rule.

Rule 3.025. State and Prosecuting Attorney Defined.

Whenever the terms "state," "state attorney," "prosecutor," "prosecution," "prosecuting officer," or "prosecuting attorney" are used in these rules, they shall be construed to mean the prosecuting authority representing the State of Florida.

Committee Notes

2000 Adoption. This provision is new. Its purpose is to include the Office of Statewide Prosecution as a prosecuting authority under these rules. No substantive changes are intended by the adoption of this rule.

Rule 3.030. Service and Filing of Pleadings and Documents.

II. General Provisions

Rule 3.030. Service and Filing of Pleadings and Documents.

(a) Service. Every pleading subsequent to the initial indictment or information on which a defendant is to be tried unless the court otherwise orders, and every order not entered in open court, every written motion unless it is one about which a hearing ex parte is authorized, and every written notice, demand, and similar document must be served on each party in conformity with Florida Rule of General Practice and Judicial Administration 2.516. Nothing in these rules requires a plea of not guilty be in writing.

(b) Filing. Filings of all pleadings and documents must comply with Florida Rules of General Practice and Judicial Administration 2.505, 2.515, and 2.525.

(c) Deposit with the Clerk. Any paper document that is a judgment and sentence or required by statute or rule to be sworn to or notarized must be filed and deposited with the clerk immediately after it is filed. This requirement does not apply to the documents filed under rules 3.111(b)(5)(C), 3.121, 3.125, 3.133(a)(3), 3.140(g), 3.160, 3.190, 3.240, 3.692, 3.693, 3.694, 3.811, 3.840, and 3.984. This requirement also does not apply to the documents filed by attorneys under rules 3.600, 3.801(c), 3.850(c), or 3.853(b).

(d) Maintenance of Deposited Documents. The clerk must maintain deposited original paper documents in accordance with Florida Rule of General Practice and Judicial Administration 2.430, unless otherwise ordered by the court.

Committee Notes

1968 Adoption. Taken from the Florida Rules of Civil Procedure.

1972 Amendment. Same as prior rule; (a) amended by deleting reference to trial on affidavit.

2000 Amendment. Fraudulent manipulation of electronically transmitted service should be considered contemptuous and dealt with by appropriate sanctions by the court.

Rule 3.040. Computation of Time.

Computation of time shall be governed by Florida Rule of General Practice and Judicial Administration 2.514, except for the periods

3

of time of less than 7 days contained in rules 3.130, 3.132(a) and (c), and 3.133(a).

Committee Notes
1968 Adoption. Taken from the Florida Rules of Civil Procedure.
1972 Amendment. Same as prior rule.
1988 Amendment. The 1983 amendments resulted in the reallocation of the time periods in rule 3.131 to rule 3.133, and also added an important 5-day period in the new rule regarding pretrial detention in rule 3.132.
Court Commentary
1975 Amendment. Underlined portion is the only change. The effect is to remove the 72-hour provision of proposed rule 3.131 from the Saturday, Sunday, and legal holiday exception.

Rule 3.050. Enlargement of Time.

When by these rules or by a notice given thereunder or by order of court an act is required or allowed to be done at or within a specified time, the court for good cause shown may, at any time, in its discretion (1) with or without notice, order the period enlarged if a request therefor is made before the expiration of the period originally prescribed or extended by a previous order or (2) upon motion made and notice after the expiration of the specified period, permit the act to be done when the failure to act was the result of excusable neglect; but it may not, except as provided by statute or elsewhere in these rules, extend the time for making a motion for new trial, for taking an appeal, or for making a motion for a judgment of acquittal.

Committee Notes
1968 Adoption. Taken from the Florida Rules of Civil Procedure.
1972 Amendment. Same as prior rule.

Rule 3.060. Time for Service of Motions and Notice of Hearing.

A copy of any written motion which may not be heard ex parte and a copy of the notice of the hearing thereof, shall be served on the adverse party a reasonable time before the time specified for the hearing.

Rule 3.070. Additional Time After Service by Mail, When Permitted, or E-Mail [Repealed].

Committee Notes

1968 Adoption. Taken from the Florida Rules of Civil Procedure.

1972 Amendment. Same as prior rule.

Rule 3.070. Additional Time After Service by Mail, When Permitted, or E-Mail [Repealed].

Rule 3.080. Nonverification of Pleadings.

Except when otherwise specifically provided by these rules or an applicable statute, every written pleading or other document of a party represented by an attorney need not be verified or accompanied by an affidavit.

Committee Notes

1968 Adoption. Taken from rules of civil procedure.

1972 Amendment. Same as prior rule.

Rule 3.090. Pleading Captions.

Every pleading, motion, order, judgment, or other document shall have a caption containing the name of the court, the file number, the name of the first party on each side with an appropriate indication of other parties, and a designation identifying the party filing it and its nature, to include if the pleading or document is sworn or the nature of the order, as the case may be. All documents filed in the action shall be styled in such a manner as to indicate clearly the subject matter of the document and the party requesting or obtaining relief.

Rule 3.111. Providing Counsel to Indigents.

(a) When Counsel Provided. A person entitled to appointment of counsel as provided herein shall have counsel appointed when the person is formally charged with an offense, or as soon as feasible after custodial restraint, or at the first appearance before a committing judge, whichever occurs earliest.

(b) Cases Applicable.

(1) Counsel shall be provided to indigent persons in all prosecutions for offenses punishable by incarceration including appeals from the conviction thereof. In the discretion of the court, counsel does not have to be provided to an indigent person

5

in a prosecution for a misdemeanor or violation of a municipal ordinance if the judge, at least 15 days prior to trial, files in the cause a written order of no incarceration certifying that the defendant will not be incarcerated in the case pending trial or probation violation hearing, or as part of a sentence after trial, guilty or nolo contendere plea, or probation revocation. This 15-day requirement may be waived by the defendant or defense counsel.

(A) If the court issues an order of no incarceration after counsel has been appointed to represent the defendant, the court may discharge appointed counsel unless the defendant is incarcerated or the defendant would be substantially disadvantaged by the discharge of appointed counsel.

(B) If the court determines that the defendant would be substantially disadvantaged by the discharge of appointed counsel, the court shall either:

(i) not discharge appointed counsel; or

(ii) discharge appointed counsel and allow the defendant a reasonable time to obtain private counsel, or if the defendant elects to represent himself or herself, a reasonable time to prepare for trial.

(C) If the court withdraws its order of no incarceration, it shall immediately appoint counsel if the defendant is otherwise eligible for the services of the public defender. The court may not withdraw its order of no incarceration once the defendant has been found guilty or pled nolo contendere.

(2) Counsel may be provided to indigent persons in all proceedings arising from the initiation of a criminal action against a defendant, including postconviction proceedings and appeals therefrom, extradition proceedings, mental competency proceedings, and other proceedings that are adversary in nature, regardless of the designation of the court in which they occur or the classification of the proceedings as civil or criminal.

(3) Counsel may be provided to a partially indigent person on request, provided that the person shall defray that portion of the cost of representation and the reasonable costs of investigation as he or she is able without substantial hardship to the person or the person's family, as directed by the court.

Rule 3.111. Providing Counsel to Indigents.

(4) "Indigent" shall mean a person who is unable to pay for the services of an attorney, including costs of investigation, without substantial hardship to the person or the person's family; "partially indigent" shall mean a person unable to pay more than a portion of the fee charged by an attorney, including costs of investigation, without substantial hardship to the person or the person's family.

(5) Before appointing a public defender the court shall:

(A) inform the accused that, if the public defender or other counsel is appointed, a lien for the services rendered by counsel may be imposed as provided by law;

(B) make inquiry into the financial status of the accused in a manner not inconsistent with the guidelines established by section 27.52, Florida Statutes. The accused shall respond to the inquiry under oath;

(C) require the accused to execute an affidavit of insolvency as required by section 27.52, Florida Statutes.

(c) Duty of Booking Officer. In addition to any other duty, the officer who commits a defendant to custody has the following duties:

(1) The officer shall immediately advise the defendant:

(A) of the right to counsel;

(B) that, if the defendant is unable to pay a lawyer, one will be provided immediately at no charge.

(2) If the defendant requests counsel or advises the officer that he or she cannot afford counsel, the officer shall immediately and effectively place the defendant in communication with the (office of) public defender of the circuit in which the arrest was made.

(3) If the defendant indicates that he or she has an attorney or is able to retain an attorney, the officer shall immediately and effectively place the defendant in communication with the attorney or the Lawyer Referral Service of the local bar association.

(4) The public defender of each judicial circuit may interview a defendant when contacted by, or on behalf of, a defendant who is, or claims to be, indigent as defined by law.

(A) If the defendant is in custody and reasonably appears to be indigent, the public defender shall tender such advice as is indicated by the facts of the case, seek the setting of a reasonable bail, and otherwise represent the defendant pending a formal judicial determination of indigency.

(B) If the defendant is at liberty on bail or otherwise not in custody, the public defender shall elicit from the defendant only the information that may be reasonably relevant to the question of indigency and shall immediately seek a formal judicial determination of indigency. If the court finds the defendant indigent, it shall immediately appoint counsel to represent the defendant.

(d) Waiver of Counsel.

(1) The failure of a defendant to request appointment of counsel or the announced intention of a defendant to plead guilty shall not, in itself, constitute a waiver of counsel at any stage of the proceedings.

(2) A defendant shall not be considered to have waived the assistance of counsel until the entire process of offering counsel has been completed and a thorough inquiry has been made into both the accused's comprehension of that offer and the accused's capacity to make a knowing and intelligent waiver. Before determining whether the waiver is knowing and intelligent, the court shall advise the defendant of the disadvantages and dangers of self-representation.

(3) Regardless of the defendant's legal skills or the complexity of the case, the court shall not deny a defendant's unequivocal request to represent himself or herself, if the court makes a determination of record that the defendant has made a knowing and intelligent waiver of the right to counsel, and does not suffer from severe mental illness to the point where the defendant is not competent to conduct trial proceedings by himself or herself.

(4) A waiver of counsel made in court shall be of record; a waiver made out of court shall be in writing with not less than 2 attesting witnesses. The witnesses shall attest the voluntary execution thereof.

(5) If a waiver is accepted at any stage of the proceedings, the offer of assistance of counsel shall be renewed by the court at each subsequent stage of the proceedings at which the defendant appears without counsel.

Rule 3.111. Providing Counsel to Indigents.

(e) Withdrawal of Defense Counsel After Judgment and Sentence. The attorney of record for a defendant in a criminal proceeding shall not be relieved of any duties, nor be permitted to withdraw as counsel of record, except with approval of the lower tribunal on good cause shown on written motion, until after:

(1) the filing of:

(A) a notice of appeal;

(B) a statement of judicial acts to be reviewed, if a transcript will require the expenditure of public funds;

(C) directions to the clerk, if necessary; and

(D) a designation of that portion of the reporter's transcript that supports the statement of judicial acts to be reviewed, if a transcript will require expenditure of public funds; or

(2) substitute counsel has been obtained or appointed, or a statement has been filed with the appellate court that the appellant has exercised the right to self-representation. In publicly funded cases, the public defender for the local circuit court shall be appointed initially until the record is transmitted to the appellate court; or

(3) the time has expired for filing of a notice of appeal, and no notice has been filed.

Orders allowing withdrawal of counsel are conditional, and counsel shall remain of record for the limited purpose of representing the defendant in the lower tribunal regarding any sentencing error that the lower tribunal is authorized to address during the pendency of the direct appeal under Rule 3.800(b)(2).

Committee Notes

1972 Adoption. Part 1 of the ABA Standard relating to providing defense services deals with the general philosophy for providing criminal defense services and while the committee felt that the philosophy should apply to the Florida Rules of Criminal Procedure, the standards were not in such form to be the subject of that particular rule. Since the standards deal with the national situation, contained in them were alternative methods of providing defense services, i.e., assigned counsel vs. defender system; but, Florida, already having a defender system, need not be concerned with the assigned counsel system.

(a) Taken from the first sentence of ABA Standard 5.1. There was considerable discussion within the committee concerning the time within which counsel should be appointed and who should notify defendant's counsel. The commentary in the ABA Standard under 5.1a, b, convinced the committee to adopt the language here contained.

(b) Standard 4.1 provides that counsel should be provided in all criminal cases punishable by loss of liberty, except those types where such punishment is not likely to be imposed. The committee determined that the philosophy of such standard should be recommended to the Florida Supreme Court. The committee determined that possible deprivation of liberty for any period makes a case serious enough that the accused should have the right to counsel.

(c) Based on the recommendation of ABA Standard 5.1b and the commentary thereunder which provides that implementation of a rule for providing the defendant with counsel should not be limited to providing a means for the accused to contact a lawyer.

(d) From standard 7.2 and the commentaries thereunder.

1980 Amendment. Modification of the existing rule (the addition of (b)(5)(A)-(C)) provides a greater degree of uniformity in appointing counsel to indigent defendants. The defendant is put on notice of the lien for public defender services and must give financial information under oath.

A survey of Florida judicial circuits by the Committee on Representation of Indigents of the Criminal Law Section (1978-79) disclosed the fact that several circuits had no procedure for determining indigency and that there were circuits in which no affidavits of insolvency were executed (and no legal basis for establishing or collecting lien monies).

1992 Amendment. In light of State v. District Court of Appeal of Florida, First District, 569 So.2d 439 (Fla. 1990), in which the supreme court pronounced that motions seeking belated direct appeal based on ineffective assistance of counsel should be filed in the trial court pursuant to rule 3.850, the committee recommends that rule 3.111(e) be amended to detail with specificity defense counsel's duties to perfect an appeal prior to withdrawing after judgment and sentence. The present provision merely notes that such withdrawal is governed by Florida Rule of Appellate Procedure 9.140(b)(3).

Rule 3.111. Providing Counsel to Indigents.

1998 Amendment. The amendments to (d)(2)-(3) were adopted to reflect State v. Bowen, 698 So.2d 248 (Fla. 1997), which implicitly overruled Cappetta v. State, 204 So.2d 913 (Fla. 4th DCA 1967), rev'd on other grounds 216 So.2d 749 (Fla. 1968). See Fitzpatrick v. Wainwright, 800 F.2d 1057 (11th Cir. 1986), for a list of factors the court may consider. See also McKaskle v. Wiggins, 465 U.S. 168, 104 S.Ct. 944, 79 L.Ed.2d 122 (1984), and Savage v. Estelle, 924 F.2d 1459 (9th Cir. 1990), cert. denied 501 U.S. 1255, 111 S.Ct. 2900, 115 L.Ed.2d 1064 (1992), which suggest that the defendant's right to self-representation is limited when the defendant is not able or willing to abide by the rules of procedure and courtroom protocol.

2000 Amendment. This rule applies only to judicial proceedings and is inapplicable to investigative proceedings and matters. See rule 3.010.

2002 Amendment. Indigent defendants are entitled to counsel if they are either currently in custody or might be incarcerated in their case. See Alabama v. Shelton, 122 S.Ct. 1764, 1767 (2002) (Sixth Amendment forbids imposition of suspended sentence that may "end up in the actual deprivation of a person's liberty" unless defendant accorded "the guiding hand of counsel"). See also Tur v. State, 797 So. 2d 4 (Fla. 3d DCA 2001) (uncounseled plea to criminal charge cannot result in jail sentence based on violation of probationary sentence for that charge); Harris v. State, 773 So.2d 627 (Fla. 4th DCA 2000).

Discharge of the public defender based on an order certifying no incarceration that is entered after the public defender has already spent considerable time and resources investigating the case and preparing a defense may leave the defendant "in a position worse than if no counsel had been appointed in the first place." State v. Ull, 642 So. 2d 721, 724 (Fla. 1994).

In determining whether a defendant's due process rights would be violated by the discharge of the public defender, the court should consider all of the relevant circumstances, including, but not limited to:

1. The stage of the proceedings at which the order of no incarceration is entered.

2. The extent of any investigation and pretrial preparation by the public defender.

3. Any prejudice that might result if the public defender is discharged.

4. The nature of the case and the complexity of the issues.

5. The relationship between the defendant and the public defender.

Counsel may be provided to indigent persons in all other proceedings in, or arising from, a criminal case and the court should resolve any doubts in favor of the appointment of counsel for the defendant. See Graham v. State, 372 So.2d 1363, 1365 (Fla. 1979). See form found at Fla.R.Crim.P. 3.994.

2005 Amendment. See Affidavit of Indigent Status as provided by In re Approval of Form for Use by Clerks of the Circuit Courts Pursuant to Rule 10-2.1(a) of the Rules Regulating the Florida Bar, 877 So. 2d 720 (Fla. 2004).

Rule 3.112. Minimum Standards for Attorneys in Capital Cases.

(a) Statement of Purpose. The purpose of these rules is to set minimum standards for attorneys in capital cases to help ensure that competent representation will be provided to capital defendants in all cases. Minimum standards that have been promulgated concerning representation for defendants in criminal cases generally and the level of adherence to such standards required for noncapital cases should not be adopted as sufficient for death penalty cases. Counsel in death penalty cases should be required to perform at the level of an attorney reasonably skilled in the specialized practice of capital representation, zealously committed to the capital case, who has had adequate time and resources for preparation. These minimum standards for capital cases are not intended to preclude any circuit from adopting or maintaining standards having greater requirements.

(b) Definitions. A capital trial is defined as any first-degree murder case in which the State has not formally waived the death penalty on the record. A capital appeal is any appeal in which the death penalty has been imposed. A capital postconviction proceeding is any postconviction proceeding where the defendant is still under a sentence of death.

(c) Applicability. This rule applies to all defense counsel handling capital trials and capital appeals, who are appointed or retained on or after July 1, 2002. Subdivision (k) of this rule applies to all lead counsel handling capital postconviction cases, who are appointed or retained on or after April 1, 2015.

Rule 3.112. Minimum Standards for Attorneys in Capital Cases.

(d) Lists of Qualified and Disqualified Conflict Counsel.

(1) Every circuit shall maintain a list of conflict counsel qualified for appointment in capital cases in each of three categories:

(A) lead trial counsel;

(B) trial co-counsel; and

(C) appellate counsel.

(2) The chief judge for each circuit shall maintain a list of qualified counsel pursuant to section 27.40(3)(a), Florida Statutes.

(3) The chief judge for each circuit shall maintain a list of counsel who are disqualified to provide capital case representation pursuant to section 27.7045, Florida Statutes, and such list and any amendments thereto shall be forwarded to the chief judge of every other circuit.

(e) Appointment of Counsel. A court must appoint lead counsel and, upon written application and a showing of need by lead counsel, should appoint co-counsel to handle every capital trial in which the defendant is not represented by retained counsel. Lead counsel shall have the right to select co-counsel from attorneys on the lead counsel or co-counsel list. Both attorneys shall be reasonably compensated for the trial and sentencing phase. Except under extraordinary circumstances, only one attorney may be compensated for other proceedings. In capital cases in which the Public Defender or Criminal Conflict and Civil Regional Counsel is appointed, the Public Defender or Criminal Conflict and Civil Regional Counsel shall designate lead and co-counsel.

(f) Lead Trial Counsel. Lead trial counsel assignments should be given to attorneys who:

(1) are members of the bar admitted to practice in the jurisdiction or admitted to practice pro hac vice; and

(2) are experienced and active trial practitioners with at least five years of litigation experience in the field of criminal law; and

(3) have prior experience as lead counsel in no fewer than nine state or federal jury trials of serious and complex cases which were tried to completion, as well as prior experience as lead defense counsel or co-counsel in at least two state or federal cases tried to completion in which the death penalty was sought. In addition, of the nine jury trials which were tried to completion, the attorney should have been lead counsel in at least three cases in which the charge was murder; or alternatively, of the nine jury trials, at least one was a murder trial and an additional five were felony jury trials; and

(4) are familiar with the practice and procedure of the criminal courts of the jurisdiction; and

(5) are familiar with and experienced in the utilization of expert witnesses and evidence, including but not limited to psychiatric and forensic evidence; and

(6) have demonstrated the necessary proficiency and commitment which exemplify the quality of representation appropriate to capital cases, including but not limited to the investigation and presentation of evidence in mitigation of the death penalty; and

(7) have attended within the last two years a continuing legal education program of at least twelve hours' duration devoted specifically to the defense of capital cases.

(g) Co-counsel. Trial co-counsel assignments should be given to attorneys who:

(1) are members of the bar admitted to practice in the jurisdiction or admitted to practice pro hac vice; and

(2) qualify as lead counsel under paragraph (f) of these standards or meet the following requirements:

(A) are experienced and active trial practitioners with at least three years of litigation experience in the field of criminal law; and

(B) have prior experience as lead counsel or co-counsel in no fewer than three state or federal jury trials of serious and complex cases which were tried to completion, at least two of which were trials in which the charge was murder; or alternatively, of the three jury trials, at least one was a murder trial and one was a felony jury trial; and

(C) are familiar with the practice and procedure of the criminal courts of the jurisdiction; and

(D) have demonstrated the necessary proficiency and commitment which exemplify the quality of representation appropriate to capital cases, and

(E) have attended within the last two years a continuing legal education program of at least twelve hours' duration devoted specifically to the defense of capital cases.

Rule 3.112. Minimum Standards for Attorneys in Capital Cases.

(h) Appellate Counsel. Appellate counsel assignments should be given to attorneys who:

(1) are members of the bar admitted to practice in the jurisdiction or admitted to practice pro hac vice; and

(2) are experienced and active trial or appellate practitioners with at least five years of experience in the field of criminal law; and

(3) have prior experience in the appeal of at least one case where a sentence of death was imposed, as well as prior experience as lead counsel in the appeal of no fewer than three felony convictions in federal or state court, at least one of which was an appeal of a murder conviction; or alternatively, have prior experience as lead counsel in the appeal of no fewer than six felony convictions in federal or state court, at least two of which were appeals of a murder conviction; and

(4) are familiar with the practice and procedure of the appellate courts of the jurisdiction; and

(5) have demonstrated the necessary proficiency and commitment which exemplify the quality of representation appropriate to capital cases; and

(6) have attended within the last two years a continuing legal education program of at least twelve hours' duration devoted specifically to the defense of capital cases.

(i) Notice of Appearance. An attorney who is retained or appointed in place of the Public Defender or Criminal Conflict and Civil Regional Counsel to represent a defendant in a capital case shall immediately file a notice of appearance certifying that he or she meets the qualifications of this rule. If the office of the Public Defender or Criminal Conflict and Civil Regional Counsel is appointed to represent the defendant, the Public Defender or Criminal Conflict and Civil Regional Counsel shall certify that the individuals or assistants assigned as lead and co-counsel meet the requirements of this rule. A notice of appearance filed under this rule shall be served on the defendant.

(j) Limitation on Caseloads.

(1) Generally. As soon as practicable, the trial court should conduct an inquiry relating to counsel's availability to provide effective assistance of counsel to the defendant. In assessing the availability of prospective counsel, the court should consider the number of capital or other cases then being handled by the attorney and any other circumstances bearing on the attorney's readiness to provide effective assistance of counsel to the defendant in a timely fashion. No appointment should be made to an attorney who may be unable to provide effective legal representation as a result of an unrealistically high caseload. Likewise, a private attorney should not undertake the representation of a defendant in a capital case if the attorney's caseload is high enough that it might impair the quality of legal representation provided to the defendant.

(2) Public Defender. If a Public Defender or Criminal Conflict and Civil Regional Counsel seeks to refuse appointment to a new capital case based on a claim of excessive caseload, the matter should be referred to the Chief Judge of the circuit or to the administrative judge as so designated by the Chief Judge. The Chief Judge or his or her designate should coordinate with the Public Defender or Criminal Conflict and Civil Regional Counsel to assess the number of attorneys involved in capital cases, evaluate the availability of prospective attorneys, and resolve any representation issues.

(k) Qualifications of Lead Counsel in Capital Postconviction Proceedings. In order to serve as lead counsel, as set forth in rule 3.851, for the defendant in a capital postconviction proceeding, an attorney shall have:

(1) been a member of any bar for at least 5 years; and

(2) at least 3 years of experience in the field of postconviction litigation; and

(3) prior participation in a combined total of 5 proceedings in any of the following areas, at least 2 of which shall be from subdivision (k)(3)(C), (k)(3)(D), or (k)(3)(E) below:

(A) capital trials;

(B) capital sentencings;

(C) capital postconviction evidentiary hearings;

(D) capital collateral postconviction appeals;

(E) capital federal habeas proceedings.

(l) Exceptional Circumstances. In the event that the trial court determines that exceptional circumstances require counsel not meeting the requirements of this rule, the trial court shall enter an order specifying, in writing, the exceptional circumstances requiring deviation from the rule and the court's explicit

Rule 3.112. Minimum Standards for Attorneys in Capital Cases.

determination that counsel chosen will provide competent representation in accord with the policy concerns of the rule.

Committee Notes

These standards are based on the general premise that the defense of a capital case requires specialized skill and expertise. The Supreme Court has not only the authority, but the constitutional responsibility to ensure that indigent defendants are provided with competent counsel, especially in capital cases where the State seeks to take the life of the indigent defendant. The Supreme Court also has exclusive jurisdiction under Article V section 15 of the Florida Constitution to "[r]egulate the admission of persons to the practice of law and the discipline of persons admitted." Implied in this grant of authority is the power to set the minimum requirements for the admission to practice law, see In re Florida Board of Bar Examiners, 353 So. 2d 98 (Fla. 1977), as well as the minimum requirements for certain kinds of specialized legal work. The Supreme Court has adopted minimum educational and experience requirements for board certification in other specialized fields of the law.

The experience and continuing educational requirements in these standards are based on existing local standards in effect throughout the state as well as comparable standards in effect in other states. Specifically, the committee considered the standards for the appointment of counsel in capital cases in the Second, Sixth, Eleventh, Fifteenth, and Seventeenth Circuits, the statewide standards for appointing counsel in capital cases in California, Indiana, Louisiana, Ohio, and New York, and the American Bar Association standards for appointment of counsel in capital cases.

These standards are not intended to establish any independent legal rights. For example, the failure to appoint co-counsel, standing alone, has not been recognized as a ground for relief from a conviction or sentence. See Ferrell v. State, 653 So. 2d 367 (Fla. 1995); Lowe v. State, 650 So. 2d 969 (Fla. 1994); Armstrong v. State, 642 So. 2d 730 (Fla. 1994). Rather, these cases stand for the proposition that a showing of inadequacy of representation in the particular case is required. See Strickland v. Washington, 466 U.S. 668, 104 S.Ct. 2052, 80 L.Ed.2d 674 (1984). These rulings are not affected by the adoption of these standards. Any claims of ineffective assistance of counsel will be controlled by Strickland.

The American Bar Association Standards and many other state standards require the appointment of two lawyers at the trial level in every prosecution that could result in the imposition of the death penalty. The committee has modified this requirement by allowing the trial court some discretion as to the number of attorneys, and by eliminating certain provisions that may be unnecessary or economically unfeasible. Paragraph (e) minimizes the potential duplication of expenses by limiting the compensable participation of co-counsel. In addition, the standard adopted herein requires an initial showing by lead counsel of the need for co-counsel and, while the standard suggests that co-counsel should ordinarily be appointed, the ultimate decision is left to the discretion of the trial court.

The committee emphasizes that the right to appointed counsel is not enlarged by the application of these standards. The court should appoint conflict counsel only if there is a conflict and the defendant otherwise qualifies for representation by the Public Defender. A defendant who is represented by retained counsel is not entitled to the appointment of a second lawyer at public expense merely because that defendant is unable to bear the cost of retaining two lawyers.

Court Commentary

2014 Amendment. The Steering Committee added minimum requirements for lead counsel in capital postconviction proceedings to ensure a requisite level of expertise in capital postconviction cases and to permit the State the opportunity to seek opt-in treatment pursuant to 28 U.S.C. §§ 2261-2266.

Rule 3.113. Minimum Standards for Attorneys in Felony Cases.

Before an attorney may participate as counsel of record in the circuit court for any adult felony case, including postconviction proceedings before the trial court, the attorney must complete a course, approved by The Florida Bar for continuing legal education credits, of at least 100 minutes and covering the legal and ethical obligations of discovery in a criminal case, including the requirements of rule 3.220, and the principles established in Brady v. Maryland, 373 U.S. 83 (1963) and Giglio v. United States, 405 U.S. 150 (1972).

Rule 3.115. Duties of State Attorney; Criminal Intake.

Court Commentary

2014 Adoption. The Supreme Court has exclusive jurisdiction under Article V, section 15 of the Florida Constitution to "regulate the admission of persons to the practice of law and the discipline of persons admitted." Implied in this grant of authority is the power to set minimum requirements for the admission to practice law, see In re Florida Board of Bar Examiners, 353 So. 2d 98 (Fla. 1977), as well as minimum requirements for certain kinds of specialized legal work. The Supreme Court has adopted minimum educational and experience requirements for attorneys in capital cases, see, e.g., rule 3.112, and for board certification in other specialized fields of law.

The concept of a two-hour continuing legal education (CLE) requirement was proposed in the 2012 Final Report of the Florida Innocence Commission.

The CLE requirement is not intended to establish any independent legal rights. Any claim of ineffective assistance of counsel will be controlled by Strickland v. Washington, 466 U.S. 668 (1984).

It is intended that The Florida Prosecuting Attorneys Association and The Florida Public Defender Association will develop a seminar that will be approved for CLE credit by The Florida Bar. It is also intended that attorneys will be able to electronically access that seminar, at no cost, via The Florida Bar's website, the Florida Prosecuting Attorneys Association's website, and/or the Florida Public Defender Association's website.

The rule is not intended to apply to counsel of record in direct or collateral adult felony appeals.

Rule 3.115. Duties of State Attorney; Criminal Intake.

The state attorney shall provide the personnel or procedure for criminal intake in the judicial system. All sworn complaints charging the commission of a criminal offense shall be filed in the office of the clerk of the circuit court and delivered to the state attorney for further proceedings.

Rule 3.116. Use of communication technology.

(a) Definitions. The definitions for the terms "audio communication technology," "audio-video communication technology," and "communication technology" in Florida Rule of General Practice and Judicial Administration 2.530(a) apply to this

19

rule and to other rules in the Florida Rules of Criminal Procedure that use those terms.

(b) Generally. Use of communication technology in proceedings subject to the Florida Rules of Criminal Procedure is governed by this rule, except that rules 3.130(a), 3.160(a), 3.180(b), 3.220(h), and 3.851(f) govern the use of audio-video communication technology in the manner authorized by those rules.

(c) Pretrial Conferences. A judge may, upon the court's own motion or upon the written request of a party, direct that communication technology be used by one or more parties for attendance at a pretrial conference, except that, before a judge may direct that the defendant participate in the pretrial conference using communication technology, the defendant or the defendant's counsel must waive the defendant's physical attendance at the pretrial conference pursuant to rules 3.180(a)(3) and 3.220(o)(1). A judge must give notice to the parties and consider any objections they may have to the use of communication technology before directing that communication technology be used. The decision to use communication technology over the objection of parties will be in the discretion of the trial court, except as noted below.

(1) *Non-Evidentiary Pretrial Conferences.* A judge must grant a request to use communication technology for a nonevidentiary pretrial conference scheduled for 30 minutes or less unless the judge determines that good cause exists to deny the request.

(d) Testimony.

(1) *Generally.* A judge may allow testimony to be taken through communication technology if all parties consent.

(2) *Procedure.* Any party desiring to present testimony through communication technology must, prior to the hearing or trial at which the testimony is to be presented, contact all parties to determine whether each party consents to this form of testimony. The party seeking to present the testimony must move for permission to present testimony through communication technology, which motion must set forth good cause as to why the testimony should be allowed in this form.

(3) *Oath.* The oath must be administered for testimony taken through communication technology in the manner provided by Florida Rule of General Practice and Judicial Administration 2.530(b)(2)(B).

Rule 3.116. Use of communication technology.

(4) *Confrontation Rights.* The defendant must make an informed waiver of any otherwise applicable confrontation rights.

(e) Burden of Expense. The cost for the use of the communication technology is the responsibility of the requesting party unless otherwise directed by the court.

Workgroup on the Continuity of Court Operations and Proceedings During and After COVID-19 Note

2022 Adoption. This rule is created to authorize the use of communication technology for criminal proceedings while safeguarding the rights of the accused. It is based on Florida Rule of General Practice and Judicial Administration 2.530, as amended by In re Amends. to Fla. Rules of Jud. Admin., 73 So. 3d 210, 211 (Fla. 2011), but updates and revises the text of that version of the rule to: (1) use the terms "audio communication technology," "audiovideo communication technology," and "communication technology"; (2) identify other rules in the Florida Rules of Criminal Procedure that will continue to govern the use of audio-video communication technology under specified circumstances; (3) consolidate subdivisions (b) and (c) of rule 2.530, as amended in 2011, to recognize proposed amended rules 3.180(a)(3) and 3.220(o)(1) and provide that a court may, on its own motion or the written request of a party, direct the use of communication technology by one or more parties for attendance at a pretrial conference, except that, before a judge may direct that the defendant participate in the pretrial conference using communication technology, a waiver of the defendant's physical attendance must be obtained pursuant to rules 3.180(a)(3) and 3.220(o)(1); (4) substitute the term "a pretrial conference" for the phrase "a motion hearing, pretrial conference, or a status conference" used in subdivision (b) of rule 2.530, as amended in 2011, because case law has construed the term in the context of rules 3.180(a)(3) and 3.220(o)(1) as including a motion hearing and a status conference; and (5) add authority for the oath to be administered to a witness who is testifying through audio-video communication technology by an authorized person who is not physically present with the witness subject to specified requirements.

III. Preliminary Proceedings

Rule 3.120. Committing Judge.

Each state and county judge is a committing judge and may issue a summons to, or a warrant for the arrest of, a person against whom a complaint is made in writing and sworn to before a person authorized to administer oaths, when the complaint states facts that show that such person violated a criminal law of this state within the jurisdiction of the judge to whom the complaint is presented. The judge may take testimony under oath to determine if there is reasonable ground to believe the complaint is true. The judge may commit the offender to jail, may order the defendant to appear before the proper court to answer the charge in the complaint, or may discharge the defendant from custody or from any undertaking to appear. The judge may authorize the clerk to issue a summons.

Committee Notes

1968 Adoption. This is substantially the same as part of section 901.01, Florida Statutes. (The remaining part should be retained as a statute.) It differs from the statute by requiring the complaint to be in writing and by identifying the initiating instrument as a "complaint," thus adopting the federal terminology which is more meaningful and modern. Some doubt was expressed as to whether the terms of the statute incorporated in the rule are within the rulemaking power of the Supreme Court.

1972 Amendment. Substantially same as former rule. Altered to incorporate the provision for testimony under oath formerly contained in rule 3.121(a), and authorize the execution of the affidavit before a notary or other person authorized to administer oaths.

Rule 3.121. Arrest Warrant.

(a) Issuance. An arrest warrant, when issued, shall:

    (1) be in writing and in the name of the State of Florida;

    (2) set forth substantially the nature of the offense;

    (3) command that the person against whom the complaint was made be arrested and brought before a judge;

    (4) specify the name of the person to be arrested or, if the name is unknown to the judge, designate the person by any name or

description by which the person can be identified with reasonable certainty, and include a photograph if reasonably available;

(5) state the date when issued and the county where issued;

(6) be signed by the judge with the title of the office; or, may be electronically signed by the judge if the arrest warrant bears the affiant's signature, or electronic signature, is supported by an oath or affirmation administered by the judge, or other person authorized by law to administer oaths, and, if submitted electronically, is submitted by reliable electronic means; and

(7) for offenses where a right to bail exists, set the amount of bail or other conditions of release, and the return date.

(b) Amendment. No arrest warrant shall be dismissed nor shall any person in custody be discharged because of any defect as to form in the warrant; but the warrant may be amended by the judge to remedy such defect.

Committee Notes

1968 Adoption. (a) This is substantially the same as section 901.02, Florida Statutes, except that the rule requires a written complaint. Also, the rule does not incorporate that seldom used part of the statute that permits the magistrate to issue an arrest warrant upon affidavits made before the prosecuting attorney.

(b) This is the same as section 901.03, Florida Statutes.

(c) This is the same as section 901.05, Florida Statutes, except for modernizing the language.

1972 Amendment. (a) of former rule has been deleted, as its substance is now contained in rules 3.120 and 3.130; (b) has been renumbered as (a); (c) has been renumbered as (b).

Rule 3.125. Notice to Appear.

(a) Definition. Unless indicated otherwise, notice to appear means a written order issued by a law enforcement officer in lieu of physical arrest requiring a person accused of violating the law to appear in a designated court or governmental office at a specified date and time.

(b) By Arresting Officer. If a person is arrested for an offense declared to be a misdemeanor of the first or second degree or a violation, or is arrested for violation of a municipal or county ordinance triable in the county, and demand to be taken before a judge is not made, notice to appear may be issued by the arresting officer unless:

(1) the accused fails or refuses to sufficiently identify himself or herself or supply the required information;

(2) the accused refuses to sign the notice to appear;

(3) the officer has reason to believe that the continued liberty of the accused constitutes an unreasonable risk of bodily injury to the accused or others;

(4) the accused has no ties with the jurisdiction reasonably sufficient to assure the accused's appearance or there is substantial risk that the accused will refuse to respond to the notice;

(5) the officer has any suspicion that the accused may be wanted in any jurisdiction; or

(6) it appears that the accused previously has failed to respond to a notice or a summons or has violated the conditions of any pretrial release program.

(c) By Booking Officer. If the arresting officer does not issue notice to appear because of one of the exceptions listed in subdivision (b) and takes the accused to police headquarters, the booking officer may issue notice to appear if the officer determines that there is a likelihood that the accused will appear as directed, based on a reasonable investigation of the accused's:

(1) residence and length of residence in the community;

(2) family ties in the community;

(3) employment record;

(4) character and mental condition;

(5) past record of convictions; or

(6) past history of appearance at court proceedings.

(d) How and When Served. If notice to appear is issued, it shall be prepared in quadruplicate. The officer shall deliver 1 copy of the notice to appear to the arrested person and the person, to secure release, shall give a written promise to appear in court by signing the 3 remaining copies: 1 to be retained by the officer and 2 to be filed with the clerk of the court. These 2 copies shall be sworn to by the arresting officer before a notary public or a deputy clerk. If notice to appear is issued under subdivision (b), the notice shall be issued immediately upon arrest. If notice to appear is issued under subdivision (c), the notice shall be issued immediately upon completion of the investigation. The arresting officer or other duly

Rule 3.125. Notice to Appear.

authorized official then shall release from custody the person arrested.

(e) Copy to the Clerk of the Court. With the sworn notice to appear, the arresting officer shall file with the clerk a list of witnesses and their addresses and a list of tangible evidence in the cause. One copy shall be retained by the officer and 2 copies shall be filed with the clerk of the court.

(f) Copy to State Attorney. The clerk shall deliver 1 copy of the notice to appear and schedule of witnesses and evidence filed therewith to the state attorney.

(g) Contents. If notice to appear is issued, it shall contain the:

(1) name and address of the accused;

(2) date of offense;

(3) offense(s) charged—by statute and municipal ordinance if applicable;

(4) counts of each offense;

(5) time and place that the accused is to appear in court;

(6) name and address of the trial court having jurisdiction to try the offense(s) charged;

(7) name of the arresting officer;

(8) name(s) of any other person(s) charged at the same time; and

(9) signature of the accused.

(h) Failure to Appear. If a person signs a written notice to appear and fails to respond to the notice to appear, a warrant of arrest shall be issued under rule 3.121.

(i) Traffic Violations Excluded. Nothing contained herein shall prevent the operation of a traffic violations bureau, the issuance of citations for traffic violations, or any procedure under chapter 316, Florida Statutes.

(j) Rules and Regulations. Rules and regulations of procedure governing the exercise of authority to issue notices to appear shall be established by the chief judge of the circuit.

(k) Procedure by Court.

(1) When the accused appears before the court under the requirements of the notice to appear, the court shall advise the defendant as set forth in rule 3.130(b), and the provisions of that rule shall apply. The accused at such appearance may elect to waive the right to counsel and trial and enter a plea of guilty or

nolo contendere by executing the waiver form contained on the notice to appear, and the court may enter judgment and sentence in the cause.

(2) In the event the defendant enters a plea of not guilty, the court may set the cause for jury or nonjury trial on the notice to appear under the provisions of rules 3.140 and 3.160. When the court sets a trial date by the court, the clerk shall, without further praecipe, issue witness subpoenas to the law enforcement officer who executed the notice to appear and to the witnesses whose names and addresses appear on the list filed by the officer, requiring their attendance at trial.

(l) Form of Notice to Appear and Schedule of Witnesses and Evidence. The notice to appear and schedule of witnesses and evidence shall be in substantially the following form:

IN THE COUNTY COURT,
IN AND FOR _____ COUNTY, FLORIDA
NOTICE TO APPEAR

_____

Agency Case #

STATE OF FLORIDA, COUNTY OF _____

In the name of _____ County, Florida: The undersigned certifies that he or she has just and reasonable grounds to believe, and does believe, that:

On (date) _____, at _____ ( )a.m. ( )p.m.

_____	_____	_____	_____
Last Name	First	M.I.	Aliases

_____	_____
Street — City and State	Date and Place of Birth

_____	_____	_____
Phone	Race/Sex	Height

_____	_____	_____
Weight Scars/Marks	Hair	Eyes

_____	_____	_____
Occupation	Place of Employment	Employment Phone

Rule 3.125. Notice to Appear.

_____   _____   _____

Complexion   Driver's License #   Yr./St.   Social Security #

at (location) _____ in County, Florida, committed the following offense(s):

(1)_____ (2) _____ in violation of section(s): ____:_____ ( ) State Statute

_____:_____ ( ) Municipal Ord.

DID (Narrative): _____

_____

_____

_____   _____   _____

Name of Officer   ID   Agency

[ ] Mandatory appearance in court, _____ (location) on __ _____(date), at _____ ( )a.m. ( )p.m.

[ ] You need not appear in court, but must comply with instructions on back.

CO-DEFENDANTS:

1. _____

Name DOB Address   [ ] Cited   [ ] Jailed

2. _____

Name DOB Address   [ ] Cited   [ ] Jailed

If you are a person with a disability who needs any accommodation in order to participate in this proceeding, you are entitled, at no cost to you, to the provision of certain assistance. Please contact [identify applicable court personnel by name, address, and telephone number] at least 7 days before your scheduled court appearance, or immediately upon receiving this notification if the time before the scheduled appearance is less than 7 days; if you are hearing or voice impaired, call 711.

I AGREE TO APPEAR AT THE TIME AND PLACE DESIGNATED ABOVE TO ANSWER THE OFFENSE CHARGED OR TO PAY THE FINE SUBSCRIBED. I UNDERSTAND THAT SHOULD I WILLFULLY FAIL TO APPEAR BEFORE THE COURT AS REQUIRED BY THIS NOTICE TO APPEAR, I MAY BE HELD IN CONTEMPT OF COURT AND A WARRANT FOR MY ARREST SHALL BE ISSUED.

Florida Rules of Criminal Procedure Booklet: 2025 Edition

_____

Signature of Defendant

I swear the above and reverse and attached statements are true and correct to the best of my knowledge and belief.

_____

Complainant

_____

Agency or Department

Sworn to and subscribed before me on _____ (date).

_____

Notary Public, State of Florida

WAIVER INFORMATION

If you desire to plead guilty or nolo contendere (no contest) and you need not appear in court as indicated on the face of this notice, you may present this notice at the county court named on the reverse of this page.

From _____ (date), _____ (hour) to _____ (date), _____ (hour) and pay a fine of dollars in cash, money order, or certified check.

The waiver below must be completed and attached. Read carefully.

Your failure to answer this summons in the manner subscribed will result in a warrant being issued on a separate and additional charge.

"In consideration of my not appearing in court, I the undersigned, do hereby enter my appearance on the affidavit for the offense charged on the other side of this notice and waive the reading of the affidavit in the above named cause and the right to be present at the trial of said action. I hereby enter my plea of Guilty [ ] or Nolo Contendere [ ], and waive my right to prosecute appeal or error proceedings.

"I understand the nature of the charge against me; I understand my right to have counsel and waive this right and the right to a continuance. I waive my right to trial before a judge or jury. I plead Guilty [ ] or Nolo Contendere [ ] to the charge, being fully aware that my signature to this plea will have the same effect as a judgment of this court."

Total Fine and Cost _____

Rule 3.125. Notice to Appear.

Defendant Signature _____

Address _____

IN THE COUNTY COURT, IN AND FOR _____ COUNTY, FLORIDA ISCHEDULE OF WITNESSES ANDEVIDENCE FOR NOTICE TO APPEAR

_____

Agency Case #

_____

Last Name First M.I. Aliases

_____

Address

(date of notice to appear).

Offense(s):   (1)

(2)

TANGIBLE EVIDENCE: (If none, write "None")

Item: _____

Obtained from (person and/or place): _____

first received by: _____

given to: _____

WITNESSES: (If none, write "None")

#1 Name: _____

Res. Tel. No. _____ Address: _____

Bus. Tel. No. _____ Business: _____

Testimony: _____

_____

#2 Name: _____

Res. Tel. No. _____ Address: _____

Bus. Tel. No. _____ Business: _____

Testimony: _____

_____

#3 Name: _____

Res. Tel. No. _____ Address: _____

Bus. Tel. No. _____ Business: _____

Testimony: _____

I certify that the foregoing is a complete list of witnesses and evidence known to me.

_____

Investigating Officer

_____

Agency

Committee Notes

1992 Amendment. The amendment deletes subdivision (k) and reletters subdivisions (l) and (m). The elimination of subdivision (k) will entitle individuals charged with criminal violations to the same discovery, without regard to the nature of the charging instrument. As amended, persons charged by way of a notice to appear can obtain the same discovery as persons charged by way of either an information or an indictment. In this regard the committee also has proposed amendments to rule 3.220(b)(1), (b)(2), (c)(1), and (h)(1) to change the reference from "indictment or information" to "charging document."

Rule 3.130. First Appearance.

(a) Prompt First Appearance. Except when previously released in a lawful manner, every arrested person shall be taken before a judge, either in person or by electronic audiovisual device in the discretion of the court, within 24 hours of arrest. In the case of a child in the custody of juvenile authorities, against whom an information or indictment has been filed, the child shall be taken for a first appearance hearing within 24 hours of the filing of the information or indictment. The chief judge of the circuit for each county within the circuit shall designate 1 or more judges from the circuit court, or county court, to be available for the first appearance and proceedings. The state attorney or an assistant state attorney and public defender or an assistant public defender shall attend the first appearance proceeding either in person or by other electronic means. First appearance hearings shall be held with adequate notice to the public defender and state attorney. An official record of the proceedings shall be maintained. If the defendant has retained counsel or expresses a desire to and is financially able, the attendance of the public defender or assistant public defender is not required at the first appearance, and the judge shall follow the procedure outlined in subdivision (c)(2).

Rule 3.130. First Appearance.

(b) Advice to Defendant.

(1) Notice of Charges and Rights. At the defendant's first appearance the judge shall immediately inform the defendant of the charge, including an alleged violation of probation or community control, and provide the defendant with a copy of the complaint. The judge shall also adequately advise the defendant that:

(A) the defendant is not required to say anything, and that anything the defendant says may be used against him or her;

(B) if unrepresented, that the defendant has a right to counsel, and, if financially unable to afford counsel, that counsel will be appointed; and

(C) the defendant has a right to communicate with counsel, family, or friends, and if necessary, will be provided reasonable means to do so.

(2) Use of Video Recording to Provide Notice of Rights. If the defendant was advised of the rights listed in subdivisions (b)(1)(A)—(b)(1)(C) by pre-recorded video, the judge shall confirm separately with each individual defendant that such defendant had an opportunity to view and understands the rights explained in the video recording.

(c) Counsel for Defendant.

(1) Appointed Counsel. If practicable, the judge should determine prior to the first appearance whether the defendant is financially able to afford counsel and whether the defendant desires representation. When the judge determines that the defendant is entitled to court-appointed counsel and desires counsel, the judge shall immediately appoint counsel. This determination must be made and, if required, counsel appointed no later than the time of the first appearance and before any other proceedings at the first appearance. If necessary, counsel may be appointed for the limited purpose of representing the defendant only at first appearance or at subsequent proceedings before the judge.

(2) Retained Counsel. When the defendant has employed counsel or is financially able and desires to employ counsel to represent him or her at first appearance, the judge shall allow the defendant a reasonable time to send for counsel and shall, if necessary, postpone the first appearance hearing for that purpose. The judge shall also, on request of the defendant, require an officer to communicate a message to such counsel as the defendant may name. The officer shall, with diligence and without cost to the defendant if the counsel is within the county, perform the duty. If the postponement will likely result in the continued incarceration of the defendant beyond a 24-hour period, at the request of the defendant the judge may appoint counsel to represent the defendant for the first appearance hearing.

(3) Opportunity to Confer. No further steps in the proceedings should be taken until the defendant and counsel have had an adequate opportunity to confer, unless the defendant has intelligently waived the right to be represented by counsel.

(4) Waiver of Counsel. The defendant may waive the right to counsel at first appearance. The waiver, containing an explanation of the right to counsel, shall be in writing and signed and dated by the defendant. This written waiver of counsel shall, in addition, contain a statement that it is limited to first appearance only and shall in no way be construed to be a waiver of counsel for subsequent proceedings.

(d) Pretrial Release. The judge shall proceed to determine conditions of release pursuant to rule 3.131. For a defendant who has been arrested for violation of his or her probation or community control by committing a new violation of law, the judge:

(1) may order the offender to be taken before the court that granted the probation or community control if the offender admits the violation; or

(2) if the offender does not admit the violation at first appearance hearing, the judge may commit and order the offender to be brought before the court that granted probation or community control, or may release the offender with or without bail to await further hearing, notwithstanding section 907.041, Florida Statutes, relating to pretrial detention and release. In determining whether to require or set the amount of bail, the judge may consider whether the offender is more likely than not to receive a prison sanction for the violation.

Committee Notes

1972 Amendment. Same as prior rule except (b), which is new.

Rule 3.131. Pretrial Release.

(a) Right to Pretrial Release. Unless charged with a capital offense or an offense punishable by life imprisonment and the proof of guilt is evident or the presumption is great, every person charged with a crime or violation of municipal or county ordinance shall be entitled to pretrial release on reasonable conditions. As a condition of pretrial release, whether such release is by surety bail bond or recognizance bond or in some other form, the defendant shall refrain from any contact of any type with the victim, except through pretrial discovery pursuant to the Florida Rules of Criminal Procedure and shall comply with all conditions of pretrial release as ordered by the court. Upon motion by the defendant when bail is set, or upon later motion properly noticed pursuant to law, the court may modify the condition precluding victim contact if good cause is shown and the interests of justice so require. The victim shall be permitted to be heard at any proceeding in which such modification is considered, and the state attorney shall notify the victim of the provisions of this subdivision and of the pendency of any such proceeding. If no conditions of release can reasonably protect the community from risk of physical harm to persons, assure the presence of the accused at trial, or assure the integrity of the judicial process, the accused may be detained.

(b) Hearing at First Appearance — Conditions of Release.

(1) Unless the state has filed a motion for pretrial detention pursuant to rule 3.132, the court shall conduct a hearing to determine pretrial release. For the purpose of this rule, bail is defined as any of the forms of release stated below. Except as otherwise provided by this rule, there is a presumption in favor of release on nonmonetary conditions for any person who is granted pretrial release. The judicial officer shall impose the first of the following conditions of release that will reasonably protect the community from risk of physical harm to persons, assure the presence of the accused at trial, or assure the integrity of the judicial process; or, if no single condition gives that assurance, shall impose any combination of the following conditions:

(A) personal recognizance of the defendant;

(B) execution of an unsecured appearance bond in an amount specified by the judge;

(C) placement of restrictions on the travel, association, or place of abode of the defendant during the period of release;

(D) placement of the defendant in the custody of a designated person or organization agreeing to supervise the defendant;

(E) execution of a bail bond with sufficient solvent sureties, or the deposit of cash in lieu thereof; provided, however, that any criminal defendant who is required to meet monetary bail or bail with any monetary component may satisfy the bail by providing an appearance bond; or

(F) any other condition deemed reasonably necessary to assure appearance as required, including a condition requiring that the person return to custody after specified hours.

(2) The judge shall at the defendant's first appearance consider all available relevant factors to determine what form of release is necessary to assure the defendant's appearance. If a monetary bail is required, the judge shall determine the amount. Any judge setting or granting monetary bond shall set a separate and specific bail amount for each charge or offense. When bail is posted each charge or offense requires a separate bond.

(3) In determining whether to release a defendant on bail or other conditions, and what that bail or those conditions may be, the court may consider the nature and circumstances of the offense charged and the penalty provided by law; the weight of the evidence against the defendant; the defendant's family ties, length of residence in the community, employment history, financial resources, need for substance abuse evaluation and/or treatment, and mental condition; the defendant's past and present conduct, including any record of convictions, previous flight to avoid prosecution, or failure to appear at court proceedings; the nature and probability of danger that the defendant's release poses to the community; the source of funds used to post bail; whether the defendant is already on release pending resolution of another criminal proceeding or is on probation, community control, parole, or other release pending completion of sentence; and any other facts the court considers relevant.

(4) No person charged with a dangerous crime, as defined in section 907.041(4)(a), Florida Statutes, shall be released on nonmonetary conditions under the supervision of a pretrial release service, unless the service certifies to the court that it has investigated or otherwise verified the conditions set forth in section 907.041(3)(b), Florida Statutes.

(5) All information provided by a defendant in connection with any application for or attempt to secure bail, to any court, court personnel, or individual soliciting or recording such information for the purpose of evaluating eligibility for or securing bail for the defendant, under circumstances such that the defendant knew or should have known that the information was to be used in connection with an application for bail, shall be accurate, truthful, and complete, without omissions, to the best knowledge of the defendant. Failure to comply with the provisions of this subdivision may result in the revocation or modification of bail. However, no defendant shall be compelled to provide information regarding his or her criminal record.

(6) Information stated in, or offered in connection with, any order entered pursuant to this rule need not strictly conform to the rules of evidence.

(c) Consequences of Failure to Appear.

(1) Any defendant who willfully and knowingly fails to appear and breaches a bond as specified in section 903.26, Florida Statutes, and who voluntarily appears or surrenders shall not be eligible for a recognizance bond.

(2) Any defendant who willfully and knowingly fails to appear and breaches a bond as specified in section 903.26, Florida Statutes, and who is arrested at any time following forfeiture shall not be eligible for a recognizance bond or any form of bond that does not require a monetary undertaking or commitment equal to or greater than $2,000 or twice the value of the monetary commitment or undertaking of the original bond, whichever is greater.

(d) Subsequent Application for Setting or Modification of Bail.

(1) When a judicial officer not possessing trial jurisdiction orders a defendant held to answer before a court having jurisdiction to try the defendant, and bail has been denied or sought to be modified, application by motion may be made to the court having jurisdiction to try the defendant or, in the absence of the judge of the trial court, to the circuit court. The motion shall be determined promptly. No judge of a court of equal or inferior jurisdiction may remove a condition of bail or reduce the amount of bond required, unless the judge:

> **(A)** imposed the conditions of bail or set the amount of bond required;

(B) is the chief judge of the circuit in which the defendant is to be tried;

(C) has been assigned to preside over the criminal trial of the defendant; or

(D) is the first appearance judge and was authorized by the judge initially setting or denying bail to modify or set conditions of release.

(2) Applications by the defendant for modification of bail on any felony charge must be heard by a court in person at a hearing, with the defendant present and with at least 3 hours' notice to the state attorney and county attorney, if bond forfeiture proceedings are handled by the county attorney. The state may apply for modification of bail by showing good cause and with at least 3 hours' notice to the attorney for the defendant.

(3) If any trial court fixes bail and refuses its reduction before trial, the defendant may institute habeas corpus proceedings seeking reduction of bail. If application is made to the supreme court or district court of appeal, notice and a copy of such application shall be given to the attorney general and the state attorney. Such proceedings shall be determined promptly.

(e) Bail Before Conviction; Condition of Undertaking.

(1) If a person is admitted to bail for appearance for a preliminary hearing or on a charge that a judge is empowered to try, the condition of the undertaking shall be that the person will appear for the hearing or to answer the charge and will submit to the orders and process of the judge trying the same and will not depart without leave.

(2) If the person is admitted to bail after being held to answer by a judge, or after an indictment or information on which the person is to be tried has been filed, the condition of undertaking shall be that the person will appear to answer the charges before the court in which he or she may be prosecuted and submit to the orders and process of the court and will not depart without leave.

(f) Revocation of Pretrial Release.

(1) Any judge presiding at a first appearance hearing may revoke a defendant's pretrial release status pursuant to s. 903.0471 on a case not assigned to the first appearance judge but that is pending in the same judicial circuit as the first appearance hearing.

Rule 3.131. Pretrial Release.

(2) The court in its discretion for good cause, any time after a defendant who is at large on bail appears for trial, may commit the defendant to the custody of the proper official to abide by the judgment, sentence, and any further order of the court.

(g) Arrest and Commitment by Court. The court in which the cause is pending may direct the arrest and commitment of the defendant who is at large on bail when:

(1) there has been a breach of the undertaking;

(2) it appears that the defendant's sureties or any of them are dead or cannot be found or are insufficient or have ceased to be residents of the state; or

(3) the court is satisfied that the bail should be increased or new or additional security required.

The order for the commitment of the defendant shall recite generally the facts on which it is based and shall direct that the defendant be arrested by any official authorized to make arrests and that the defendant be committed to the official in whose custody he or she would be if he or she had not been given bail, to be detained by such official until legally discharged. The defendant shall be arrested pursuant to such order on a certified copy thereof, in any county, in the same manner as on a warrant of arrest. If the order provided for is made because of the failure of the defendant to appear for judgment, the defendant shall be committed. If the order is made for any other cause, the court may determine the conditions of release, if any.

(h) Bail after Recommitment. If the defendant applies to be admitted to bail after recommitment, the court that recommitted the defendant or the court under (d)(1) shall determine conditions of release, if any, subject to the limitations of subdivision (b).

(i) Qualifications of Surety after Order of Recommitment. If the defendant offers bail after recommitment, each surety shall possess the qualifications and sufficiency and the bail shall be furnished in all respects in the manner prescribed for admission to bail before recommitment.

(j) Issuance of Capias; Bail Specified. On the filing of either an indictment or information charging the commission of a crime, if the person named therein is not in custody or at large on bail for the offense charged, the judge shall issue or shall direct the clerk to issue, either immediately or when so directed by the prosecuting attorney, a capias for the arrest of the person. If the person named in the indictment or information is a child and the child has been served with a promise to appear under the Florida Rules of Juvenile

Procedure, capias need not be issued. Upon the filing of the indictment or information, the judge shall endorse the amount of bail, if any, and may authorize the setting or modification of bail by the judge presiding over the defendant's first appearance hearing. This endorsement shall be made on the capias and signed by the judge.

(k) Summons on Misdemeanor Charge. When a complaint is filed charging the commission of a misdemeanor only and the judge deems that process should issue as a result, or when an indictment or information on which the defendant is to be tried charging the commission of a misdemeanor only, and the person named in it is not in custody or at large on bail for the offense charged, the judge shall direct the clerk to issue a summons instead of a capias unless the judge has reasonable ground to believe that the person will not appear in response to a summons, in which event an arrest warrant or a capias shall be issued with the amount of bail endorsed on it. The summons shall state substantially the nature of the offense, the title of the hearing to be conducted, and shall command the person against whom the complaint was made to appear before the judge issuing the summons or the judge having jurisdiction of the offense at a time and place stated in it.

(l) **Summons When Defendant Is Corporation.** On the filing of an indictment or information or complaint charging a corporation with the commission of a crime, whether felony or misdemeanor, the judge shall direct the clerk to issue or shall issue a summons to secure its appearance to answer the charge. If, after being summoned, the corporation does not appear, a plea of not guilty shall be entered and trial and judgment shall follow without further process.

Committee Notes

1977 Amendment. Subdivision (a) was repealed by Chapter 76-138, § 2, Laws of Florida, insofar as it was inconsistent with the provision of that statute. Subdivision (a) has been amended so as to comply with the legislative act.

1968 Adoption. (a) Same as section 903.01, Florida Statutes.

(b) Same as section 903.04, Florida Statutes.

(c) Same as section 903.02, Florida Statutes.

(d) Same as section 903.12, Florida Statutes.

(e) Substantially same as section 903.13, Florida Statutes.

(f) Same as section 903.19, Florida Statutes.

(g) Same as section 918.01, Florida Statutes.

(h) Substantially same as section 903.23, Florida Statutes.

(i) Same as section 903.24, Florida Statutes.

(j) Same as section 903.25, Florida Statutes.

(k) and (l) Formerly rule 3.150(c). These proposals contain the essentials of present sections 907.01, 907.02, and 901.09(3), Florida Statutes, a change of some of the terminology being warranted for purpose of clarity.

(m) Formerly rule 3.150(c). This proposal contains all of the essentials of section 907.03, Florida Statutes, and that part of section 901.14, Florida Statutes, pertaining to post indictment or postinformation procedure. A charge by affidavit is provided.

Although subdivision (g) is the same as section 918.01, Florida Statutes, its constitutionality was questioned by the subcommittee, constitutional right to bail and presumption of innocence.

1972 Amendment. Same as prior rule except (b), which is new. (k), (l), and (m) are taken from prior rule 3.150.

1977 Amendment. This proposal amends subdivision (b)(4) of the present rule [formerly rule 3.130(b)(4)] to expand the forms of pretrial release available to the judge. The options are the same as those available under the federal rules without the presumption in favor of release on personal recognizance or unsecured appearance.

This proposal leaves it to the sound discretion of the judge to determine the least onerous form of release which will still insure the defendant's appearance.

It also sets forth the specific factors the judge should take into account in making this determination.

1983 Amendment. Rule 3.131(d) is intended to replace former rule 3.130(f) and therefore contemplates all subsequent modifications of bail including all increases or reductions of monetary bail or any other changes sought by the state or by the defendant.

Rule 3.132. Pretrial Detention.

(a) Motion Filed at First Appearance. A person arrested for an offense for which detention may be ordered under section 907.041, Florida Statutes, shall be taken before a judicial officer for a first appearance within 24 hours of arrest. The state may file with the judicial officer at first appearance a motion seeking pretrial detention, signed by the state attorney or an assistant, setting forth with particularity the grounds and the essential facts on which pretrial detention is sought and certifying that the state attorney has received testimony under oath supporting the grounds and the essential facts alleged in the motion. If no such motion is filed, the judicial officer may inquire whether the state intends to file a motion for pretrial detention, and if so, grant the state no more than three days to file a motion under this subdivision. Upon a showing by the state of probable cause that the defendant committed the offense and exigent circumstances, the defendant shall be detained in custody pending the filing of the motion. If, after inquiry, the State indicates it does not intend to file a motion for pretrial detention, or fails to establish exigent circumstances for holding defendant in custody pending the filing of the motion, or files a motion that is facially insufficient, the judicial officer shall proceed to determine the conditions of release pursuant to the provisions of rule 3.131(b). If the motion for pretrial detention is facially sufficient, the judicial officer shall proceed to determine whether there is probable cause that the person committed the offense. If probable cause is found, the person may be detained in custody pending a final hearing on pretrial detention. If probable cause is established after first appearance pursuant to the provisions of rule 3.133 and the person has been released from custody, the person may be recommitted to custody pending a final hearing on pretrial detention.

(b) Motion Filed after First Appearance. A motion for pretrial detention may be filed at any time prior to trial. The motion shall be made to the court with trial jurisdiction. On receipt of a facially sufficient motion and a determination of probable cause, unless otherwise previously established, that an offense eligible for pretrial detention has been committed, the following shall occur:

(1) In the event of exigent circumstances, the court shall issue a warrant for the arrest of the named person, if the person has been released from custody. The person may be detained in custody pending a final hearing on pretrial detention.

(2) In the absence of exigent circumstances, the court shall order a hearing on the motion as provided in (c) below.

(c) Final Order.

(1) Hearing Required. A final order of pretrial detention shall be entered only after a hearing in the court of trial jurisdiction. The hearing shall be held within 5 days of the filing of the motion or the date of taking the person in custody pursuant to a motion for pretrial detention, whichever is later. The state attorney has the burden of showing beyond a reasonable doubt the need for pretrial detention pursuant to the criteria in section 907.041, Florida Statutes. The defendant may request a continuance. The state shall be entitled to 1 continuance for good cause. No continuance shall exceed 5 days unless there are extenuating circumstances. The defendant may be detained pending the hearing, but in no case shall the defendant be detained in excess of 10 days, unless the delay is sought by the defendant. The person sought to be detained is entitled to representation by counsel, to present witnesses and evidence, and to cross-examine witnesses. The court may admit relevant evidence and testimony under oath without complying with the rules of evidence, but evidence secured in violation of the United States Constitution or the Constitution of the State of Florida shall not be admissible. A final order of pretrial detention shall not be based exclusively on hearsay evidence. No testimony by the defendant shall be admissible to prove the guilt of the defendant at any other judicial proceeding, but may be admitted in an action for perjury based on the defendant's statements made at the pretrial detention hearing or for impeachment.

(2) Findings and Conclusions to Be Recorded. The court's pretrial detention order shall be based solely on evidence produced at the hearing and shall contain findings of fact and conclusions of law to support it. The order shall be made either in writing or orally on the record. The court shall render its findings within 24 hours of the pretrial detention hearing.

(3) Dissolution of Order. The defendant shall be entitled to dissolution of the pretrial detention order whenever the court finds that a subsequent event has eliminated the basis for detention.

(4) Further Proceedings on Order. If any trial court enters a final order of pretrial detention, the defendant may obtain review by motion to the appropriate appellate court. If motion for review is taken to the supreme court or the district court of appeal, notice and a copy of the motion shall be served on the attorney general and the state attorney; if review is taken to the circuit court, service shall be on the state attorney.

Rule 3.133. Pretrial Probable Cause Determinations and Adversary Preliminary Hearings.

(a) Nonadversary Probable Cause Determination.

(1) Defendant in Custody. In all cases in which the defendant is in custody, a nonadversary probable cause determination shall be held before a judge within 48 hours from the time of the defendant's arrest; provided, however, that this proceeding shall not be required when a probable cause determination has been previously made by a judge and an arrest warrant issued for the specific offense for which the defendant is charged. The judge after a showing of extraordinary circumstance may continue the proceeding for not more than 24 hours beyond the 48-hour period. The judge, after a showing that an extraordinary circumstance still exists, may continue the proceeding for not more than 24 additional hours following the expiration of the initial 24-hour continuance. This determination shall be made if the necessary proof is available at the time of the first appearance as required under rule 3.130, but the holding of this determination at that time shall not affect the fact that it is a nonadversary proceeding.

(2) Defendant on Pretrial Release. A defendant who has been released from custody before a probable cause determination is made and who is able to establish that the pretrial release conditions are a significant restraint on his or her liberty may file a written motion for a nonadversary probable cause determination setting forth with specificity the items of significant restraint that a finding of no probable cause would eliminate. The motion shall be filed within 21 days from the date of arrest, and notice shall be given to the state. A judge who finds significant restraints on the defendant's liberty shall make a probable cause determination within 7 days from the filing of the motion.

(3) Standard of Proof. Upon presentation of proof, the judge shall determine whether there is probable cause for detaining the arrested person pending further proceedings. The defendant need not be present. In determining probable cause to detain the defendant, the judge shall apply the standard for issuance of an arrest warrant, and the finding may be based on sworn

Rule 3.133. Pretrial Probable Cause Determinations and Adversary Preliminary Hearings.

complaint, affidavit, deposition under oath, or, if necessary, on testimony under oath properly recorded.

(4) Action on Determination. If probable cause is found, the defendant shall be held to answer the charges. If probable cause is not found or the specified time periods are not complied with, the defendant shall be released from custody unless an information or indictment has been filed, in which event the defendant shall be released on recognizance subject to the condition that he or she appear at all court proceedings or shall be released under a summons to appear before the appropriate court at a time certain. Any release occasioned by a failure to comply with the specified time periods shall be by order of the judge on a written application filed by the defendant with notice sent to the state or by a judge without a written application but with notice to the state. The judge shall order the release of the defendant after it is determined that the defendant is entitled to release and after the state has a reasonable period of time, not to exceed 24 hours, in which to establish probable cause. A release required by this rule does not void further prosecution by information or indictment but does prohibit any restraint on liberty other than appearing for trial. A finding that probable cause does or does not exist shall be made in writing, signed by the judge, and filed, together with the evidence of such probable cause, with the clerk of the court having jurisdiction of the offense for which the defendant is charged.

(b) Adversary Preliminary Hearing.

(1) When Applicable. A defendant who is not charged in an information or indictment within 21 days from the date of arrest or service of the capias on him or her shall have a right to an adversary preliminary hearing on any felony charge then pending against the defendant. The subsequent filing of an information or indictment shall not eliminate a defendant's entitlement to this proceeding.

(2) Process. The judge shall issue such process as may be necessary to secure attendance of witnesses within the state for the state or the defendant.

(3) Witnesses. All witnesses shall be examined in the presence of the defendant and may be cross-examined. Either party may request that the witnesses be sequestered. At the conclusion of the testimony for the prosecution, the defendant who so elects shall be sworn and testify in his or her own behalf, and in such cases the defendant shall be warned in advance of testifying that anything he or she may say can be used against him or her at a subsequent trial. The defendant may be cross-examined in the same manner as other witnesses, and any witnesses offered by the defendant shall be sworn and examined.

(4) Record. At the request of either party, the entire preliminary hearing, including all testimony, shall be recorded verbatim stenographically or by mechanical means and at the request of either party shall be transcribed. If the record of the proceedings, or any part thereof, is transcribed at the request of the prosecuting attorney, a copy of this transcript shall be furnished free of cost to the defendant or the defendant's counsel.

(5) Action on Hearing. If from the evidence it appears to the judge that there is probable cause to believe that an offense has been committed and that the defendant has committed it, the judge shall cause the defendant to be held to answer to the circuit court; otherwise, the judge shall release the defendant from custody unless an information or indictment has been filed, in which event the defendant shall be released on recognizance subject to the condition that he or she appear at all court proceedings or shall be released under a summons to appear before the appropriate court at a time certain. Such release does not, however, void further prosecution by information or indictment but does prohibit any restraint on liberty other than appearing for trial. A finding that probable cause does or does not exist shall be made in writing, signed by the judge, and, together with the evidence received in the cause, shall be filed with the clerk of the circuit court.

(c) Additional Nonadversary Probable Cause Determinations and Preliminary Hearings. If there has been a finding of no probable cause at a nonadversary determination or adversary preliminary hearing, or if the specified time periods for holding a nonadversary probable cause determination have not been complied with, a judge may thereafter make a determination of probable cause at a nonadversary probable cause determination, in which event the defendant shall be retained in custody or returned to custody upon appropriate process issued by the judge. A defendant who has been retained in custody or returned to custody by such a determination shall be allowed an adversary

Rule 3.133. Pretrial Probable Cause Determinations and Adversary Preliminary Hearings.

preliminary hearing in all instances in which a felony offense is charged.

Committee Notes

1975 Amendment. This is a complete rewrite of the preliminary hearing rule.

1968 Adoption. (Notes are to former rule 1.122.)

(a) Substantially the same as section 902.01, Florida Statutes; the word "examination" is changed to "hearing" to conform to modern terminology.

(b) through (j) Substantially the same as sections 902.02 through 902.10, 902.13, and 902.14, Florida Statutes, except for exchange of "hearing" for "examination."

(k) Parts of section 902.11, Florida Statutes, and all of section 902.12, Florida Statutes, were omitted because of conflict with case law: Escobedo v. Illinois, 378 U.S. 478, 84 S.Ct. 1758, 12 L.Ed.2d 977 (1964); White v. Maryland, 373 U.S. 59, 83 S.Ct. 1050, 10 L.Ed.2d 193 (1963).

(l) Taken from Federal Rule of Criminal Procedure 5(c). Previously Florida had no statute or rule defining what the magistrate should do at the conclusion of the preliminary hearing.

(m) Substantially the same as section 902.18, Florida Statutes, except "without delay" changed to "within 7 days." Some specific time limit was felt necessary because of frequent delay by magistrates while defendants remain in jail.

1972 Amendment. The ABA Standards on Pre-Trial Release provide for a person arrested to be taken before a committing magistrate without unreasonable delay for immediate judicial consideration of the release decision. The committee determined that, since a determination of probable cause at this immediate hearing presents difficult logistical problems for the state and defense counsel, the question of probable cause should be decided at a later preliminary hearing. For this reason, subdivisions (c), (d), and (e) of the former rule have been deleted in favor of the hearing provision now contained in rule 3.130.

(a) A revised version of former rule 3.122(a).

(b) New. Establishes the time period in which the preliminary hearing must take place.

(c)(1) Substantially the same as former rule 3.122(b). Amended to provide for advice of counsel relative to waiver and for written waiver.

(c)(2) Amended to delete provisions relating to recording of proceedings as same are now contained in subdivision (h).

(d) Same as prior rule 3.122(g).

(e) Same as prior rule 3.122(h).

(f) Substantially the same as prior rule 3.122(i); language modernized by slight changes.

(g) Same as prior rule 3.122(j).

(h) New rule to provide for record of proceedings.

(i) Same as prior rule 3.122(l).

(j) Substantially the same as prior rule 3.122(m). Time period for transmission of papers is reduced. (2) provides for transmission of any transcript of proceedings.

1977 Amendment. The rule corrects several deficiencies in the prior rule:

(1) In the prior rule no specific mechanism was provided to effect the release which is allowed. This revision provides such a mechanism and coordinates the mechanism with the additional procedures created by subdivision (c).

(2) Once a determination of no probable cause was made and the defendant was released, no method was provided for reversing the process in those instances in which the determination is palpably in error or in instances in which it is later possible to establish probable cause.

(3) The prior rule allowed the unconditioned release of a defendant without the possibility of recapture simply because of a technical failure to abide by the rather arbitrary time limits established for the conduct of a nonadversary probable cause determination and regardless of the ability to establish probable cause. The new rule allows a determination or redetermination of probable cause to be made in instances in which to do so is sensible. The defendant is protected by the provision allowing an adversary preliminary hearing as a check against any possible abuse.

Rule 3.134. Time for Filing Formal Charges.

The state shall file formal charges on defendants in custody by information, or indictment, or in the case of alleged misdemeanors by whatever documents constitute a formal charge, within 30 days from the date on which the defendants are arrested or from the date of the service of capiases upon them. If the defendants remain uncharged, the court on the 30th day and with notice to the state shall:

(1) Order that the defendants automatically be released on their own recognizance on the 33rd day unless the state files formal charges by that date; or

(2) If good cause is shown by the state, order that the defendants automatically be released on their own recognizance on the 40th day unless the state files formal charges by that date.

In no event shall any defendants remain in custody beyond 40 days unless they have been formally charged with a crime.

Rule 3.140. Indictments; Informations.

(a) Methods of Prosecution.

(1) Capital Crimes. An offense that may be punished by death shall be prosecuted by indictment.

(2) Other Crimes. The prosecution of all other criminal offenses shall be as follows:

In circuit courts and county courts, prosecution shall be solely by indictment or information, except that prosecution in county courts for violations of municipal ordinances and metropolitan county ordinances may be by affidavit or docket entries and prosecutions for misdemeanors, municipal ordinances, and county ordinances may be by notice to appear issued and served pursuant to rule 3.125. A grand jury may indict for any offense. When a grand jury returns an indictment for an offense not triable in the circuit court, the circuit judge shall either issue a summons returnable in the county court or shall bail the accused for trial in the county court, and the judge, or at the judge's direction, the clerk of the circuit court, shall certify the indictment and file it in the records of the county court.

(b) Nature of Indictment or Information. The indictment or information on which the defendant is to be tried shall be a plain, concise, and definite written statement of the essential facts constituting the offense charged.

(c) Caption, Commencement, Date, and Personal Statistics.

(1) Caption. No formal caption is essential to the validity of an indictment or information on which the defendant is to be tried.

Upon objection made as to its absence a caption shall be prefixed in substantially the following manner:

In the (name of court)

State of Florida versus (name of defendant)

or, in the case of municipal ordinance cases in county court,

City of / County versus (name of defendant).

Any defect, error, or omission in a caption may be amended as of course, at any stage of the proceeding, whether before or after a plea to the merits, by court order.

(2) Commencement. All indictments or informations on which the defendant is to be tried shall expressly state that the prosecution is brought in the name and by the authority of the State of Florida. Indictments shall state that the defendant is charged by the grand jury of the county. Informations shall state that the appropriate prosecuting attorney makes the charge.

(3) Date. Every indictment or information on which the defendant is to be tried shall bear the date (day, month, year) that it is filed in each court in which it is so filed.

(4) Personal Statistics. Every indictment or information shall include the defendant's race, gender, and date of birth when any of these facts are known. Failure to include these facts shall not invalidate an otherwise sufficient indictment or information.

(d) The Charge.

(1) Allegation of Facts; Citation of Law Violated. Each count of an indictment or information on which the defendant is to be tried shall allege the essential facts constituting the offense charged. In addition, each count shall recite the official or customary citation of the statute, rule, regulation, or other provision of law that the defendant is alleged to have violated. Error in or omission of the citation shall not be ground for dismissing the count or for a reversal of a conviction based thereon if the error or omission did not mislead the defendant to the defendant's prejudice.

(2) Name of Accused. The name of the accused person shall be stated, if known, and if not known, the person may be described by any name or description by which the person can be identified with reasonable certainty. If the grand jury, prosecuting attorney, or affiant making the charge does not know either the name of the accused or any name or description by which the accused can be identified with reasonable certainty, the indictment or information, as the case may be, shall so allege and the accused may be charged by a fictitious name.

(3) Time and Place. Each count of an indictment or information on which the defendant is to be tried shall contain allegations stating as definitely as possible the time and place of the commission of the offense charged in the act or transaction or on 2 or more acts or transactions connected together, provided the court in which the indictment or information is filed has jurisdiction to try all of the offenses charged.

(4) Allegation of Intent to Defraud. If an intent to defraud is required as an element of the offense to be charged, it shall be sufficient to allege an intent to defraud, without naming therein the particular person or body corporate intended to be defrauded.

(e) Incorporation by Reference. Allegations made in 1 count shall not be incorporated by reference in another count.

(f) Endorsement and Signature; Indictment. An indictment shall be signed by the foreperson or the acting foreperson of the grand jury returning it. The state attorney or acting state attorney or an assistant state attorney shall make and sign a statement on the indictment to the effect that he or she has advised the grand jury returning the indictment as authorized and required by law. No objection to the indictment on the ground that the statement has not been made shall be entertained after the defendant pleads to the merits.

(g) Signature, Oath, and Certification; Information. An information charging the commission of a felony shall be signed by the state attorney, or a designated assistant state attorney, under oath stating his or her good faith in instituting the prosecution and certifying that he or she has received testimony under oath from the material witness or witnesses for the offense. An information charging the commission of a misdemeanor shall be signed by the state attorney, or a designated assistant state attorney, under oath stating his or her good faith in instituting the prosecution. No objection to an information on the ground that it was not signed or verified, as herein provided, shall be entertained after the defendant pleads to the merits.

(h) Conclusion. An indictment or information on which the defendant is to be tried need contain no formal conclusion.

(i) Surplusage. An unnecessary allegation may be disregarded as surplusage and, on motion of the defendant, may be stricken from the pleading by the court.

(j) Amendment of Information. An information on which the defendant is to be tried that charges an offense may be amended on the motion of the prosecuting attorney or defendant at any time prior to trial because of formal defects.

(k) Form of Certain Allegations. Allegations concerning the following items may be alleged as indicated below:

(1) Description of Written Instruments. Instruments consisting wholly or in part of writing or figures, pictures, or designs may be described by any term by which they are usually known or may be identified, without setting forth a copy or facsimile thereof.

(2) Words; Pictures. Necessary averments relative to spoken or written words or pictures may be made by the general purport of such words or pictures without setting forth a copy or facsimile thereof.

(3) Judgments; Determinations; Proceedings. A judgment, determination, or proceeding of any court or official, civil or military, may be alleged generally in such a manner as to identify the judgment, determination, or proceeding, without alleging facts conferring jurisdiction on the court or official.

(4) Exceptions; Excuses; Provisos. Statutory exceptions, excuses, or provisos relative to offenses created or defined by statute need not be negatived by allegation.

(5) Alternative or Disjunctive Allegations. For an offense that may be committed by doing 1 or more of several acts, or by 1 or more of several means, or with 1 or more of several intents or results, it is permissible to allege in the disjunctive or alternative such acts, means, intents, or results.

(6) Offenses Divided into Degrees. For an offense divided into degrees it is sufficient to charge the commission of the offense without specifying the degree.

(7) Felonies. It shall not be necessary to allege that the offense charged is a felony or was done feloniously.

(l) Custody of Indictment or Information. Unless the defendant named therein has been previously released on a citation, order to appear, personal recognizance, or bail, or has been summoned to appear, or unless otherwise ordered by the court having jurisdiction, all indictments or informations and the records thereof shall be in the custody of the clerk of the court to which they are presented and shall not be inspected by any person other than the judge, clerk, attorney general, and prosecuting attorney until the defendant is in custody or until 1 year has elapsed between the return of an indictment or the filing of an information, after which time they shall be opened for public inspection.

(m) Defendant's Right to Copy of Indictment or Information. Each person who has been indicted or informed against for an offense shall, on application to the clerk, be furnished a copy of the indictment or information and the endorsements thereon, at least 24 hours before being required to plead to the indictment or information if a copy has not been so furnished. A failure to furnish a copy shall not affect the validity of any subsequent proceeding against the defendant if he or she pleads to the indictment or information.

(n) Statement of Particulars. The court, on motion, shall order the prosecuting attorney to furnish a statement of particulars when the indictment or information on which the defendant is to be tried fails to inform the defendant of the particulars of the offense sufficiently to enable the defendant to prepare a defense. The statement of particulars shall specify as definitely as possible the place, date, and all other material facts of the crime charged that are specifically requested and are known to the prosecuting attorney, including the names of persons intended to be defrauded. Reasonable doubts concerning the construction of this rule shall be resolved in favor of the defendant.

(o) Defects and Variances. No indictment or information, or any count thereof, shall be dismissed or judgment arrested, or new trial granted on account of any defect in the form of the indictment or information or of misjoinder of offenses or for any cause whatsoever, unless the court shall be of the opinion that the indictment or information is so vague, indistinct, and indefinite as to mislead the accused and embarrass him or her in the preparation of a defense or expose the accused after conviction or acquittal to substantial danger of a new prosecution for the same offense.

Committee Notes

1968 Adoption. Introductory Statement: The contention may be made that the authority of the Supreme Court of Florida to govern practice and procedure in all courts by court rule does not include the power to vary in any way from present statutory law governing the work product of the grand jury, viz., the indictment. Such a contention must, of necessity, be based in part, at least, upon the assumption that the grand jury is not an integral part of the judicial system of Florida but is a distinct entity which serves that system. The Supreme Court of Florida, in State v. Clemons, 150 So.2d 231 (Fla. 1963), seems to have taken a position contrary to such an assumption.

Regardless of whether such a contention is valid, it seems beyond controversy that the essentials of the indictment, as in the case of an information, are so intimately associated with practice and procedure in the courts that the individual or group having the responsibility of determining its makeup and use is thus empowered to govern a substantial segment of such practice and procedure. The conclusion seems to be inescapable, therefore, that, since the constitution grants to the supreme court authority over this phase of the judicial scheme, the following material is appropriate for consideration as a part of the proposed rules:

(a)(1) Capital Crimes. This recommendation is consistent with present Florida law. See § 10 DR, Fla. Const. (1885, as amended) (now Art. I, § 15, Fla. Const. (1968 as amended)); § 904.01, Fla. Stat. (1963). The terminology "which may be punished by death" is deemed preferable to the terminology "capital crime" of the constitution and "capital offenses" of the statute because of its definitive nature. The recommended terminology is utilized in Federal Rule of Criminal Procedure 7(a) and in the American Law Institute's Code of Criminal Procedure, section 115. The terminology used in the 1963 Code of Criminal Procedure of Illinois is "when death is a possible punishment." See § 110-4.

Section 10, DR, Florida Constitution, provides: "No person shall be tried for a capital crime unless on presentment or indictment by a grand jury." No provision is made in the recommendation for prosecution by presentment. This omission is consistent with the apparent legislative construction placed on this section. Section 904.01, Florida Statutes, provides "All capital offenses shall be tried by indictment by a grand jury." Since presentments traditionally have not been used as trial accusatorial writs in Florida, there

Rule 3.140. Indictments; Informations.

seems little reason, at this date, to question that the constitution authorizes the implementing authority, be it the legislature or the supreme court, to use one of the specified methods of prosecution to the exclusion of the other.

(a)(2) Other Crimes. In criminal courts of record and the Court of Record of Escambia County, the constitution of Florida requires that prosecutions be by information. (§§ 9(5) & 10, Art. V). In county judges' courts having elective prosecuting attorneys, present statutory law permits prosecutions by indictment (§ 904.02) and affidavit (Ch. 937). The additional method of prosecution by information is provided as a step toward attaining uniformity with other courts in the prosecution of noncapital offenses, at least to the extent that a prosecutor desires to use an information. This addition involved consideration of whether a nonelected prosecutor serving in a county judge's court, which often is the case, has the authority to use an information as an accusatorial writ. Since this question has not been definitely resolved under present law, caution dictated the specification that the prosecuting attorney be elected as a prerequisite to the use of an information.

In all courts not hereinabove mentioned that have elective prosecuting attorneys, trial by indictment or information is consistent with present Florida constitutional law and most of the statutory law. (See § 10, DR, Fla. Const., §§ 904.01 & 904.02, Fla. Stat.; cf. § 932.56, where an affidavit may be used in cases appealed from a justice of the peace court and which is tried de novo in a circuit court.) In specially created courts having elective prosecutors and which are not otherwise provided for in foregoing provisions of this rule, it was felt that prosecution by indictment or information should be allowed, even though present statutory authority may limit prosecutions in such courts to the use of an information, e.g., the Court of Record of Alachua County.

In courts not having elective prosecutors, prosecution by information is not recommended because of the aforementioned doubt as to the authority of a nonelected prosecutor to use an information as an accusatorial writ. With reference to the present court structure of Florida this part of the proposal applies only to county judges' courts and justice of the peace courts. The only variation from present procedure contemplated by this part of the proposal is the use of an indictment as a basis for prosecution in a justice of the peace court.

Under this proposal a grand jury may indict for any criminal offense. This recommendation is based on the premise that a grand jury's power to indict should not be limited by virtue of levels in a state court structure. A grand jury should be considered as a guardian of the public peace against all criminal activity and should be in a position to act directly with reference thereto. While practicalities dictate that most non-capital felonies and misdemeanors will be tried by information or affidavit, if appropriate, even if an indictment is permissible as an alternative procedure, it is well to retain the grand jury's check on prosecutors in this area of otherwise practically unrestricted discretion.

The procedure proposed for the circuit judge to follow if a grand jury returns an indictment for an offense not triable in the circuit court applies, with appropriate variations, much of the procedure presently used when a grand jury returns an indictment triable in a criminal court of record. See §32.18, Fla. Stat.

(b) Nature of Indictment or Information. This provision appears in rule 7(c) of the Rules of Criminal Procedure for the United States District Court (hereafter referred to as the federal rules for purposes of brevity). It may be deemed appropriate for incorporation into the recommendations since it preserves to the defendant expressly the right to a formal written accusation and at the same time permits the simplification of the form of the accusation and the elimination of unnecessary phraseology.

(c) Caption, Commencement, and Date.

(1) Caption. Section 906.02, Florida Statutes, contains the essentials of this proposal. It is well settled at common law that the caption is no part of the indictment and that it may be amended. The caption may be considered as serving the purpose of convenience by making more readily identifiable a particular accusatorial writ. The proposal makes it possible for this convenience to be served if either party wishes it, yet does not provide that the caption be a matter of substance. The essentials of this recommendation also appear in section 149 of the American Law Institute's Code of Criminal Procedure.

(2) Commencement. This proposal apparently is directly contrary to section 906.02(1), Florida Statutes, which treats the caption and the commencement in the same manner, i.e., that neither is necessary to the validity of the indictment or information but may be present as mere matters of convenience. This legislative assumption may not be a correct one and caution dictates that a meaningful commencement be included. Section 20, article V, of the Constitution of Florida provides that the style of all process shall be: " 'The State of Florida' and all prosecutions shall be conducted in the name and by the authority of the State." As contemplated in the proposal, the commencement expressly states the sovereign authority by which the accusatorial writ is issued and the agent of that authority. Section 906.02(2), Florida Statutes, seems to contemplate that there will be included in the indictment an express provision concerning the agency of the state responsible for its presentation, viz., the grand jury, by stating, "It is unnecessary to allege that the grand jurors were empaneled, sworn or charged, or that they present the indictment upon their oaths or affirmations." The American Law Institute's commentary on the commencement (A.L.I. Code of Criminal Procedure, p. 529 et seq.) indicates that there is much confusion between what information should be in the commencement as distinguished from the caption.

(3) Date. Since in many cases the beginning of the prosecution is co-existent with the issuance of the indictment or information, the date the writ bears may be of great significance, particularly with reference to the tolling of a statute of limitations. If the date of a grand jury's vote of a true bill or a prosecutor's making oath to an information differs from the date of filing of the indictment or information with the appropriate clerk, it seems the date of filing is the preferable date for a writ to bear since until the filing transpires there is no absolute certainty that the prosecution actually will leave the province of the grand jury or prosecutor.

(d) The Charge.

(1) Allegation of Facts; Citation of Law Violated. This proposal is consistent with various sections of chapter 906, Florida Statutes, in that the charge is adequately alleged when based on the essentials of the offense; surplusage should be guarded against. The citation of the law allegedly violated contributes to defining the charge and conserves time in ascertaining the exact nature of the charge. The 1963 Illinois Criminal Code, section 111-3(a)(2), and Federal Rule of Criminal Procedure 7(c) contain similar provisions.

(2) Name of Accused. The provision concerning the method of stating the name of the accused is consistent with the very elaborate section 906.08, Florida Statutes, which seems unnecessarily long. It is deemed desirable that when a fictitious name is used the necessity therefor should be indicated by allegation.

(3) Time and Place. This provision is consistent with present Florida law. (See Morgan v. State, 51 Fla. 76, 40 So. 828 (1906), as to "time"; see Rimes v. State, 101 Fla. 1322, 133 So. 550 (1931), as to "place".) The provision is patterned after section 111-3(4) of the 1963 Illinois Code of Criminal Procedure.

(4) Joinder of Offenses. The essence of this proposal is presently found in section 906.25, Florida Statutes, federal rule 8(a), and section 111-4(a) of the 1963 Illinois Code of Criminal Procedure.

(5) Joinder of Defendants. This proposal is taken from federal rule 8(b). Its substance also appears in section 111-4(b) of the Illinois Code of Criminal Procedure. Although section 906.25, Florida Statutes, does not expressly contain this provision, there is little doubt that its broad language includes it.

(6) Allegation of Intent to Defraud. The language of this proposal presently appears in section 906.18, Florida Statutes, except for the provision concerning affidavit. Its continuation seems advisable as an aid to drawing allegations in charging instruments, although such information if known to the prosecutor may be required to be given in a bill of particulars upon motion of the defendant. (See subdivision (n) of this rule.) At times such information may be unknown to the prosecutor. A part of the statute is purposely not included in the proposal. The excluded part states "and on the trial it shall be sufficient, and shall not be deemed a variance, if there appear to be an intent to defraud the United States or any state, county, city, town or parish, or any body corporate, or any public officer in his official capacity, or any copartnership or members thereof, or any particular person." It seems that this part of the statute is stated in terms of the law of evidence rather than practice and procedure and should not be included in the rules, although apparently being a logical conclusion from the part included in the proposal.

(e) Incorporation by Reference. Although provision for incorporation by reference appears in federal rule 7(c), the prohibition of such incorporation is recommended with the thought that even though repetition may be minimized by incorporation, confusion, vagueness, and misunderstanding may be fostered by such procedure.

(f) Endorsement and Signature; Indictment. The requirement that the indictment be endorsed "A true bill" and be signed by the foreman or acting foreman of the grand jury presently appears in section 905.23, Florida Statutes. There apparently is no valid

Rule 3.140. Indictments; Informations.

reason for changing this requirement since it serves the useful purpose of lending authenticity to the indictment as a legal product of the grand jury. The requirement of the foreman's signature also appears in federal rule 6(c), 1963, Illinois CCP section 111-3(b), and A.L.I. Model Code of Criminal Procedure section 125.

The provision pertaining to the statement and signature of the prosecuting attorney varies from present Florida law and is offered in alternative form. Florida statutes presently provide that an indictment shall be signed by a state attorney (§§ 27.21 & 27.22). Federal rule 7(c) also provides for the signature of the attorney for the government.

No requirement presently is made in Florida necessitating an express explanatory statement preceding such signature. Presumably the justification for the signature appears in the Florida statutes that require the aforementioned officers to wait upon the grand jury as advisors, as examiners of witnesses, and to draw indictments. (See §§ 905.16, 905.17, 905.19, 905.22, 27.02, 27.16, 27.21, & 27.22, Fla. Stat.)

Vagueness remains concerning the significance of the signature, however. Since the prosecuting attorney cannot be present while the grand jury is deliberating or voting (see section 905.17, Florida Statutes) and has no voice in the decision of whether an indictment is found (see section 905.26, Florida Statutes), a logical question arises concerning the necessity for the prosecuting attorney's signature on the indictment. The provision for the statement is made for the purpose of clarifying the reason for the signature.

(g) Signature, Oath, and Certification; Information. Section 10, DR, Florida Constitution, requires that informations be under oath of the prosecuting attorney of the court in which the information is filed. Article V, section 9(5), Florida Constitution, contains the same requirement concerning informations filed by the prosecuting attorney in a criminal court of record. This proposal also does not deviate from present Florida statutory law as found in section 906.04, Florida Statutes. This statute has received judicial approval. (See Champlin v. State, 122 So.2d 412 (Fla. 2d DCA 1960).) It should be noted here that the prosecutor's statement under oath is defined as to the purpose served by the signature.

(h) Conclusion. A similar provision currently appears in section 906.03, Florida Statutes, and should be included in the rules because of its tendency to minimize unnecessary statements in accusatorial writs. Provision is added for the affidavit as an accusatorial writ.

(i) Surplusage. The first part of the proposal, providing for the disregarding of unnecessary allegations as surplusage, is similar to section 906.24, Florida Statutes. The part concerned with striking such material is patterned after federal rule 7(d). The parts are properly complementary.

(j) Amendment of Information. This proposal contains no provision for an amendment of an indictment since, presumably, a grand jury may not amend an indictment which it has returned and which is pending, although it may return another indictment and the first indictment may be disposed of by a nolle prosequi. (See 17 Fla. Jur. Indictments and Informations, 9 (1958).) A federal indictment cannot be amended without reassembling the grand jury (see Ex parte Bain, 121 U.S. 1 (1887)); consequently the federal rules contain no provision for the amendment of an indictment. (It may be that the Supreme Court of Florida will feel inclined to include in the rules an express statement concerning amendments of an indictment. None is included here, however.)

The proposal is patterned after section 111-5 of the 1963 Illinois Code of Criminal Procedure, with one exception. The exception arises due to the fact that the Illinois Code provision applies to indictments as well as informations, the position in Illinois apparently being assumed that an indictment may be amended, at least with reference to specified items listed in the statute, as well as other formalities.

(k) Form of Certain Allegations. Several statutes in chapter 906, Florida Statutes, are concerned with the manner of making allegations in indictments and informations. Some of these sections are of such general application that it seems advisable to include their substance in the rules; others are so restricted that it may be deemed appropriate to recommend other disposition of them.

The proposals made in (1) through (7) here are based on the substance of the designated Florida statutes:

Proposal (1): section 906.09.

Proposal (2): section 906.10.

Proposal (3): section 906.11.

Proposal (4): section 906.12.

Proposal (5): section 906.13.

Rule 3.140. Indictments; Informations.

Proposal (6): section 906.23.

Proposal (7): section 906.17.

(l) Custody and Inspection. The proposal is taken verbatim from section 906.27, Florida Statutes. The necessity for specific provision for the custody and inspection of accusatorial writs seems to be proper to include here.

(m) Defendant's Right to Copy of Indictment or Information. The procedure contained in this proposal is presently required under section 906.28, Florida Statutes, and seems to be unobjectionable.

(n) Statement of Particulars. The phrase, "bill of particulars," has been modernized by changing "bill" to "statement." Historically, a "bill" is a written statement. The first sentence of this proposal is taken from section 906.27, Florida Statutes, the only change being the narrowing of the scope of the judicial discretion now granted by the statute. The latter part of the proposal is recommended in order to clarify the requirements of the rule. Provision for the accusatorial affidavit has been added.

(o) Defects and Variances. This proposal presently appears in Florida law in the form of section 906.25, Florida Statutes. The statute has been the object of much judicial construction and it seems inadvisable to divide it into parts merely for convenience in placing these parts under more appropriate titles, such as "Pre-Trial Motions," "Motion for New Trial," etc.

The intimate relation the statute has with indictments and informations justifies its inclusion here. The useful purposes served by the court constructions dictate the use of the statutory language without change.

1972 Amendment. Substantially the same as prior rule. References to trial by affidavit have been deleted throughout this rule and all Florida Rules of Criminal Procedure because of the passage of the 1972 amendment to article V of the Florida Constitution.

(a)(2) Amended to refer only to circuit courts and county courts. Reference to trial of vehicular traffic offenses transferred to rule 3.010 and made applicable to all rules of criminal procedure.

Former rule (d)(4) and (d)(5) transferred to new rule 3.150. Former rule (d)(6) renumbered as (d)(4).

1973 Amendment. The purpose of the amendment is to provide the same method for prosecution of violations of metropolitan county ordinances as for violations of municipal ordinances.

Rule 3.150. Joinder of Offenses and Defendants.

(a) Joinder of Offenses. Two or more offenses that are triable in the same court may be charged in the same indictment or information in a separate count for each offense, when the offenses, whether felonies or misdemeanors, or both, are based on the same act or transaction or on 2 or more connected acts or transactions.

(b) Joinder of Defendants. Two or more defendants may be charged in the same indictment or information on which they are to be tried when:

(1) each defendant is charged with accountability for each offense charged;

(2) each defendant is charged with conspiracy and some of the defendants are also charged with 1 or more offenses alleged to have been committed in furtherance of the conspiracy; or

(3) even if conspiracy is not charged and all defendants are not charged in each count, it is alleged that the several offenses charged were part of a common scheme or plan.

Such defendants may be charged in 1 or more counts together or separately, and all of the defendants need not be charged in each count.

(c) Joint Representation. When 2 or more defendants have been jointly charged under rule 3.150(b) or have been joined for trial and are represented by the same attorney or by attorneys who are associated in the practice of law, the court shall, as soon as practicable, inquire into such joint representation and shall personally advise each defendant of the right to effective assistance of counsel, including separate representation. The court shall take such measures as are necessary to protect each defendant's right to counsel.

Committee Notes

1968 Adoption. (Notes are to rule 1.140(d)(4) and (5).)

(4) Joinder of Offenses. The essence of this proposal is presently found in section 906.25, Florida Statutes, federal rule 8(a), and section 111-4(a) of the 1963 Illinois Code of Criminal Procedure.

Rule 3.150. Joinder of Offenses and Defendants.

(5) Joinder of Defendants. This proposal is taken from federal rule 8(b). Its substance also appears in section 111-4(b) of the Illinois Code of Criminal Procedure. While section 906.25, Florida Statutes, does not expressly contain this provision, there is little doubt that its broad language includes it.

1972 Amendment. Provisions of former rule 3.150 are transferred to and incorporated in rule 3.130, Pretrial Release.

(a) Substantially the same as former rule 3.140(d)(4) except that it omits proviso that the court have jurisdiction to try all offenses charged. The proviso seems redundant.

(b) Substantially the same as ABA Standard 1.2 of ABA Standards Relating to Joinder and Severance but omits sub-paragraph (c)(2) which would permit joinder of charges "so closely connected in respect to time, place, and occasion that it would be difficult to separate proof of one charge from proof of the others." The ABA commentary on this standard concedes that in such cases the chances are considerable that defendants would have a right to severance. Difficulty of separating proof is a good reason for denying a right to join charges. The committee is of the opinion that defendants not connected in the commission of an act and not connected by conspiracy or by common scheme or plan should not, under any circumstances, be joined. The suggested rule omits the provision of former rule 3.140(d)(4) permitting joinder of 2 or more defendants in a single indictment or information, if they are alleged to have participated in the same series of acts or transactions constituting more than 1 offense. If all defendants participated in a series of connected acts or transactions constituting 2 or more offenses, the offenses can be joined under rule 3.150(a).

The last sentence of the suggested rule is the last sentence of former rule 3.140(d)(5).

2004 Amendment. This rule is intended to provide a uniform procedure for judges to follow when codefendants are represented by the same attorney, by the same law firm, or by attorneys who are associated in the practice of law. This provision is substantially derived from Rule 44, Fed. R. Crim. P. See also Larzelere v. State, 676 So. 2d 394 (Fla. 1996).

Court Commentary

2004 Amendment. Like Federal Rule of Criminal Procedure 44(c), new subdivision (c) does not specify the particular measures that the court must take to protect a defendant's right to counsel. Because the measures that will best protect a defendant's right to counsel can vary from case to case, this determination is left within the court's discretion. One possible course of action is to advise the defendant of the possible conflict of interest that could arise from dual representation and to obtain a voluntary, knowing, and intelligent waiver of the right to obtain separate representation. See Larzelere v. State, 676 So. 2d 394 (Fla. 1996). Another option is to require separate representation. See Fed. R. Crim. P. 44(c) advisory committee notes 1979 amendment.

Rule 3.151. Consolidation of Related Offenses.

(a) Related Offenses. For purposes of these rules, 2 or more offenses are related offenses if they are triable in the same court and are based on the same act or transaction or on 2 or more connected acts or transactions.

(b) Consolidation of Indictments or Informations. Two or more indictments or informations charging related offenses shall be consolidated for trial on a timely motion by a defendant or by the state. The procedure thereafter shall be the same as if the prosecution were under a single indictment or information. Failure to timely move for consolidation constitutes a waiver of the right to consolidation.

(c) Dismissal of Related Offenses after Trial. When a defendant has been tried on a charge of 1 of 2 or more related offenses, the charge of every other related offense shall be dismissed on the defendant's motion unless a motion by the defendant for consolidation of the charges has been previously denied, or unless the defendant has waived the right to consolidation, or unless the prosecution has been unable, by due diligence, to obtain sufficient evidence to warrant charging the other offense or offenses.

(d) Plea. A defendant may plead guilty or nolo contendere to a charge of 1 offense on the condition that other charges or related offenses be dismissed or that no charges of other related offenses be instituted. Should the court find that the condition cannot be fulfilled, the plea shall be considered withdrawn.

Committee Notes

1968 Adoption. This rule is almost the same as federal rule 13, with provisions added for trial by affidavit.

1972 Amendment. (a) To same general effect as ABA Standard with changes to conform to rules 3.150(a) and 3.190(k).

Rule 3.152. Severance of Offenses and Defendants.

(b) Limits motion for consolidation to defendant and provides that defendant waives his or her right to consolidation by failing to file a timely motion. Under standards relating to joinder of offenses and defendants, the prosecution may avoid the necessity for consolidation by charging offenses and defendants in a single indictment or information where consolidation is permissible. Omits provision of ABA Standard authorizing denial of consolidation if prosecuting attorney does not have "sufficient evidence to warrant trying" 1 of the "offenses" or if the court finds that the ends of justice would be defeated by consolidation. The lack of "sufficient evidence to warrant" trial of 1 of several charges of "related offenses" would be quite rare. In the rare case in which there is such a lack of evidence, the appropriate remedy would be a motion for continuance of all pending charges of related offenses, showing that the lack of evidence could probably be cured by a reasonable delay. The committee does not favor separate trials of charges of related offenses over the defendant's objection.

(c) Florida has no similar rule. Omits exception in ABA Standard in case "the prosecuting attorney did not have sufficient evidence to warrant trying (the) offense" or upon a finding that "the ends of justice would be defeated if the motion was granted." See comment on (b). The rule is not intended to restrict defendant's substantive rights.

(d) Florida has no similar rule. The first sentence of ABA Standard is considered by the committee to state a rule of substantive law and is omitted as unnecessary.

1977 Amendment. The changes from the prior rule are intended to provide equal treatment for both the state and the defendant.

Rule 3.152. Severance of Offenses and Defendants.
(a) Severance of Offenses.

(1) In case 2 or more offenses are improperly charged in a single indictment or information, the defendant shall have a right to a severance of the charges on timely motion.

(2) In case 2 or more charges of related offenses are joined in a single indictment or information, the court nevertheless shall grant a severance of charges on motion of the state or of a defendant:

(A) before trial on a showing that the severance is appropriate to promote a fair determination of the defendant's guilt or innocence of each offense; or

(B) during trial, only with defendant's consent, on a showing that the severance is necessary to achieve a fair determination of the defendant's guilt or innocence of each offense.

(b) Severance of Defendants.

(1) On motion of the state or a defendant, the court shall order a severance of defendants and separate trials:

(A) before trial, on a showing that the order is necessary to protect a defendant's right to a speedy trial, or is appropriate to promote a fair determination of the guilt or innocence of 1 or more defendants; or

(B) during trial, only with defendant's consent and on a showing that the order is necessary to achieve a fair determination of the guilt or innocence of 1 or more defendants.

(2) If a defendant moves for a severance of defendants on the ground that an oral or written statement of a codefendant makes reference to him or her but is not admissible against him or her, the court shall determine whether the state will offer evidence of the statement at the trial. If the state intends to offer the statement in evidence, the court shall order the state to submit its evidence of the statement for consideration by the court and counsel for defendants and if the court determines that the statement is not admissible against the moving defendant, it shall require the state to elect 1 of the following courses:

(A) a joint trial at which evidence of the statement will not be admitted;

(B) a joint trial at which evidence of the statement will be admitted after all references to the moving defendant have been deleted, provided the court determines that admission of the evidence with deletions will not prejudice the moving defendant; or

(C) severance of the moving defendant.

(3) In cases in which, at the close of the state's case or at the close of all of the evidence, the evidence is not sufficient to support a finding that allegations on which the joinder of a defendant is based have been proved, the court shall, on motion of that defendant, grant a severance unless the court finds that severance is unnecessary to achieve a fair determination of that defendant's guilt or innocence.

Committee Notes

1968 Adoption. This subdivision rewords and adds to federal rule 14. It covers subject matter of section 918.02, Florida Statutes.

1972 Amendment. (a)(1) Severance on timely motion by defendant is mandatory if multiple offenses are improperly joined.

(a)(2) Provides for severance of offenses before trial on showing that severance will promote a fair determination of guilt or innocence substantially as provided by former rule 3.190(j)(2) and, unlike any Florida rule, distinguishes motion during trial.

(b)(1) Based on ABA Standard 2.3(b). Expands rule 3.190(j) to include defendant's right to speedy trial as ground for severance and, unlike any Florida rule, distinguishes between motion before and motion during trial.

(b)(2) Based on ABA Standard 2.3, subparagraphs (a) and (c). Requires court to determine whether the statement will be offered as distinguished from asking the state its intention. Requires production of evidence of the statement in the event it will be offered so that the court and counsel can intelligently deal with the problem. Florida has no similar rule.

(b)(3) Substantially the same as ABA Standard, except that the proposed rule requires severance unless the court affirmatively finds that severance is unnecessary. Florida has no similar rule.

Rule 3.153. Timeliness of Defendant's Motion; Waiver.

(a) Timeliness; Waiver. A defendant's motion for severance of multiple offenses or defendants charged in a single indictment or information shall be made before trial unless opportunity therefor did not exist or the defendant was not aware of the grounds for such a motion, but the court in its discretion may entertain such a motion at the trial. The right to file such a motion is waived if it is not timely made.

(b) Renewal of Motion. If a defendant's pretrial motion for severance is overruled, the defendant may renew the motion on the same grounds at or before the close of all the evidence at the trial.

Committee Notes

1972 Adoption. (a) Relates solely to defendant's motion for severance. Florida has no similar rule.

(b) Florida has no similar rule.

IV. Arraignment and Pleas

Rule 3.160. Arraignment.

(a) Nature of Arraignment. The arraignment shall be conducted in open court or by audiovisual device in the discretion of the court and shall consist of the judge or clerk or prosecuting attorney reading the indictment or information on which the defendant will be tried to the defendant or stating orally to the defendant the substance of the charge or charges and calling on the defendant to plead thereto. The reading or statement as to the charge or charges may be waived by the defendant. If the defendant is represented by counsel, counsel may file a written plea of not guilty at or before arraignment and thereupon arraignment shall be deemed waived.

(b) Effect of Failure to Arraign or Irregularity of Arraignment. Neither a failure to arraign nor an irregularity in the arraignment shall affect the validity of any proceeding in the cause if the defendant pleads to the indictment or information on which the defendant is to be tried or proceeds to trial without objection to such failure or irregularity.

(c) Plea of Guilty after Indictment or Information Filed. If a person who has been indicted or informed against for an offense, but who has not been arraigned, desires to plead guilty thereto, the person may so inform the court having jurisdiction of the offense, and the court shall, as soon as convenient, arraign the defendant and permit the defendant to plead guilty to the indictment or information.

(d) Time to Prepare for Trial. After a plea of not guilty the defendant is entitled to a reasonable time in which to prepare for trial.

(e) Defendant Not Represented by Counsel. Prior to arraignment of any person charged with the commission of a crime, if he or she is not represented by counsel, the court shall advise the person of the right to counsel and, if he or she is financially unable to obtain counsel, of the right to be assigned court-appointed counsel to represent him or her at the arraignment and at all subsequent proceedings. The person shall execute an affidavit that he or she is unable financially or otherwise to obtain counsel, and if the court shall determine the reason to be true, the court shall appoint counsel to represent the person.

If the defendant, however, understandingly waives representation by counsel, he or she shall execute a written waiver of such representation, which shall be filed in the case. If counsel is appointed, a reasonable time shall be accorded to counsel before the defendant shall be required to plead to the indictment or information on which he or she is to be arraigned or tried, or otherwise to proceed further.

Committee Notes

1968 Adoption. (a) A combination of section 908.01, Florida Statutes, and Federal Rule of Criminal Procedure 10.

(b) Same as section 908.02, Florida Statutes.

(c) Same as section 909.15, Florida Statutes, except provision is made for trial by affidavit.

(d) Same as section 909.20, Florida Statutes.

(e) Federal rule 44 provides:

"If the defendant appears in court without counsel the court shall advise him of his right to counsel and assign counsel to represent him at every stage of the proceeding unless he elects to proceed without counsel or is able to obtain counsel."

A presently proposed amendment to such rule provides:

"(a) Right to Assigned Counsel. Every defendant who is unable to obtain counsel shall be entitled to have counsel assigned to represent him at every stage of the proceedings from his initial appearance before the commissioner or the court through appeal, unless he waives such appointment.

"(b) Assignment Procedure. The procedures for implementing the right set out in subdivision (a) shall be those provided by law or by local rules of district courts of appeal."

In lieu of such latter, blanket provision, it is suggested that the rule provide, as stated, for inquiry of the defendant and determination by the court as to the defendant's desire for and inability to obtain counsel, after being advised of entitlement thereto. Many defendants, of course, will waive counsel.

In view of Harvey v. Mississippi, 340 F.2d 263 (5th Cir. 1965), and White v. Maryland, 373 U.S. 59, 83 S.Ct. 1050, 10 L.Ed.2d 193

(1963), holding that entitlement to counsel does not depend upon whether the offense charged is a felony or misdemeanor, it is suggested that the word "crime" be used instead of "felony" only in the first sentence of the proposed rule.

In Hamilton v. Alabama, 368 U.S. 52, 82 S.Ct. 157, 7 L.Ed.2d 114 (1961), involving breaking and entering with intent to commit rape, the Supreme Court held the defendant was entitled to counsel at the arraignment, if the arraignment be deemed a part of the trial, as apparently it is under Alabama law. In Ex parte Jeffcoat, 109 Fla. 207, 146 So. 827 (1933), the Supreme Court of Florida held the arraignment to be a mere formal preliminary step to an answer or plea. However, in Sardinia v. State, 168 So.2d 674 (Fla. 1964), the court recognized the accused's right to counsel upon arraignment. Section 909.21, Florida Statutes, provides for appointment of counsel in capital cases.

1972 Amendment. Substantially the same as prior rule. The committee considered changes recommended by The Florida Bar and incorporated the proposed change relating to written plea of not guilty and waiver of arraignment.

1992 Amendment. The amendment allows the judge to participate in the arraignment process by including the judge as one of the designated individuals who may advise the defendant of the pending charges. Apparently, the 1988 amendment to rule 3.160(a) inadvertently eliminated the judge from the arraignment procedure. In re Rule 3.160(a), Florida Rules of Criminal Procedure, 528 So.2d 1179, 1180 (Fla. 1988). The prior amendment did include the judge. The Florida Bar Re: Amendment to Rules - Criminal Procedure, 462 So.2d 386 (Fla. 1984). While the language of rule 3.160(a) as presently set out in the Florida Bar pamphlet, Florida Rules of Criminal Procedure, is identical to the language of this proposed amendment (that is, it includes the judge in the arraignment process), the West publications, Florida Criminal Laws and Rules (1991) and Florida Rules of Court (1991), nevertheless follow the language set out in 528 So.2d at 1180.

Rule 3.170. Pleas.

(a) Types of Plea; Court's Discretion. A defendant may plead not guilty, guilty, or, with the consent of the court, nolo contendere. Except as otherwise provided by these rules, all pleas to a charge shall be in open court and shall be entered by the defendant. If the sworn complaint charges the commission of a misdemeanor, the

Rule 3.170. Pleas.

defendant may plead guilty to the charge at the first appearance under rule 3.130, and the judge may thereupon enter judgment and sentence without the necessity of any further formal charges being filed. A plea of not guilty may be entered in writing by counsel. Every plea shall be entered of record, but a failure to enter it shall not affect the validity of any proceeding in the cause.

(b) Pleading to Other Charges. Having entered a plea in accordance with this rule, the defendant may, with the court's permission, enter a plea of guilty or nolo contendere to any and all charges pending against him or her in the State of Florida over which the court would have jurisdiction and, when authorized by law, to charges pending in a court of lesser jurisdiction, if the prosecutor in the other case or cases gives written consent thereto. The court accepting such a plea shall make a disposition of all such charges by judgment, sentence, or otherwise. The record of the plea and its disposition shall be filed in the court of original jurisdiction of the offense. If a defendant secures permission to plead to other pending charges and does so plead, the entry of such a plea shall constitute a waiver by the defendant of venue and all nonjurisdictional defects relating to such charges.

(c) Standing Mute or Pleading Evasively. If a defendant stands mute, or pleads evasively, a plea of not guilty shall be entered.

(d) Failure of Corporation to Appear. If the defendant is a corporation and fails to appear, a plea of not guilty shall be entered of record.

(e) Plea of Not Guilty; Operation in Denial. A plea of not guilty is a denial of every material allegation in the indictment or information on which the defendant is to be tried.

(f) Withdrawal of Plea of Guilty or No Contest. The court may in its discretion, and shall on good cause, at any time before a sentence, permit a plea of guilty or no contest to be withdrawn and, if judgment of conviction has been entered thereon, set aside the judgment and allow a plea of not guilty, or, with the consent of the prosecuting attorney, allow a plea of guilty or no contest of a lesser included offense, or of a lesser degree of the offense charged, to be substituted for the plea of guilty or no contest. The fact that a defendant may have entered a plea of guilty or no contest and later withdrawn the plea may not be used against the defendant in a trial of that cause.

(g) Vacation of Plea and Sentence Due to Defendant's Noncompliance.

(1) Whenever a plea agreement requires the defendant to comply with some specific terms, those terms shall be expressly made a part of the plea entered into in open court.

(2) Unless otherwise stated at the time the plea is entered:

(A) The state may move to vacate a plea and sentence within 60 days of the defendant's noncompliance with the specific terms of a plea agreement.

(B) When a motion is filed pursuant to subdivision (g)(2)(A) of this rule, the court shall hold an evidentiary hearing on the issue unless the defendant admits noncompliance with the specific terms of the plea agreement.

(C) No plea or sentence shall be vacated unless the court finds that there has been substantial noncompliance with the express plea agreement.

(D) When a plea and sentence is vacated pursuant to this rule, the cause shall be set for trial within 90 days of the order vacating the plea and sentence.

(h) Plea of Guilty to Lesser Included Offense or Lesser Degree. The defendant, with the consent of the court and of the prosecuting attorney, may plead guilty to any lesser offense than that charged that is included in the offense charged in the indictment or information or to any lesser degree of the offense charged.

(i) Plea of Guilty to an Offense Divided into Degrees; Determination of the Degree. When an indictment or information charges an offense that is divided into degrees without specifying the degree, if the defendant pleads guilty, generally the court shall, before accepting the plea, examine witnesses to determine the degree of the offense of which the defendant is guilty.

(j) Time and Circumstances of Plea. No defendant, whether represented by counsel or otherwise, shall be called on to plead unless and until he or she has had a reasonable time within which to deliberate thereon.

(k) Responsibility of Court on Pleas. No plea of guilty or nolo contendere shall be accepted by a court without the court first determining, in open court, with means of recording the proceedings stenographically or mechanically, that the circumstances surrounding the plea reflect a full understanding of the significance

Rule 3.170. Pleas.

of the plea and its voluntariness and that there is a factual basis for the plea of guilty. A complete record of the proceedings at which a defendant pleads shall be kept by the court.

(l) Motion to Withdraw the Plea after Sentencing. A defendant who pleads guilty or nolo contendere without expressly reserving the right to appeal a legally dispositive issue may file a motion to withdraw the plea within thirty days after rendition of the sentence, but only upon the grounds specified in Florida Rule of Appellate Procedure 9.140(b)(2)(A)(ii)(a)-(e) except as provided by law.

(m) Motion to Withdraw the Plea after Drug Court Transfer. A defendant who pleads guilty or nolo contendere to a charge for the purpose of transferring the case, pursuant to section 910.035, Florida Statutes, may file a motion to withdraw the plea upon successful completion of the drug court treatment program.

Committee Notes

1968 Adoption. (a) Patterned after the major portion of Federal Rule of Criminal Procedure 11.

(b) Same as section 909.07, Florida Statutes, except the word "made" is substituted for "pleaded."

(c) Taken from a part of section 908.03, Florida Statutes.

(d) Taken from a part of section 908.03, Florida Statutes.

(e) Same as section 909.16, Florida Statutes, except that provision is added for trial by affidavit.

(f) Essentially the same as section 909.13, Florida Statutes.

(g) Essentially the same as section 909.09, Florida Statutes, except for the addition of the charge by affidavit.

(h) Same as section 909.11, Florida Statutes, except provision is made for a charge by affidavit.

1972 Amendment. This general topic is found in ABA Standard relating to pleas of guilty. The Standards are divided into 3 parts: receiving and acting upon a plea; withdrawal of the plea; and plea discussions and plea agreements. The first and second parts are considered under this rule.

(a) Same as first part of existing rule; substance of second sentence of existing rule transferred to new subdivision (j); new provision permits, with court approval, plea of not guilty to be made in writing.

(b) From ABA Standard 1.2; the purpose of this rule is to permit a defendant to plead guilty or nolo contendere to all cases pending against the defendant, thus avoiding multiple judicial and prosecutorial labors. New concept of permitting this procedure even though the other cases are pending in other counties is taken from Federal Rule of Criminal Procedure 20 which has successfully met the purpose explained above.

(c) Same as prior rule.

(d) Same as prior rule.

(e) Same as prior rule.

(f) Last sentence added from ABA Standard 2.2.

(g) Same as prior rule.

(h) Same as prior rule.

(i) This should be done in accordance with Boykin v. Alabama, 395 U.S. 238, 89 S.Ct. 1709, 23 L.Ed.2d 274 (1969), and Garcia v. State, 228 So.2d 300 (Fla. 1969). This should also include advising a defendant so pleading of the possibility of an action or charge against him or her as a multiple felon if the circumstances so warrant.

(j) From first sentence of present rule 3.170(a) with addition of requirement of determination of factual basis for a plea of guilty as provided by last sentence of federal rule 11. While requiring the presence of a court reporter, the proposed rule does not require that the reporter transcribe and file a transcript of the proceedings on a plea of guilty or nolo contendere, although the committee considers that such a requirement by the trial judge is desirable.

1973 Amendment. The purpose of this amendment is to provide a method whereby a defendant may plead guilty to a misdemeanor at first appearance without the necessity of the state attorney subsequently filing an information.

Rule 3.171. Plea Discussions And Agreements.

(a) In General. Ultimate responsibility for sentence determination rests with the trial judge. However, the prosecuting attorney and the defense attorney, or the defendant when representing himself or herself, are encouraged to discuss and to agree on pleas that may be entered by a defendant. The discussion and agreement must be conducted with the defendant's counsel. If the defendant represents himself or herself, all discussions between the defendant and the prosecuting attorney shall be of record.

Rule 3.171. Plea Discussions And Agreements.

(b) Responsibilities of the Prosecuting Attorney.

(1) A prosecuting attorney may:

(A) engage in discussions with defense counsel or a defendant who is without counsel with a view toward reaching an agreement that, upon the defendant's entering a plea of guilty or nolo contendere to a charged offense or to a lesser or related offense, the prosecuting attorney will do any of the following:

(i) abandon other charges; or

(ii) make a recommendation, or agree not to oppose the defendant's request for a particular sentence, with the understanding that such recommendation or request shall not be binding on the trial judge; or

(iii) agree to a specific sentence; and

(B) consult with the victim, investigating officer, or other interested persons and advise the trial judge of their views during the course of plea discussions.

(2) The prosecuting attorney shall:

(A) apprise the trial judge of all material facts known to the attorney regarding the offense and the defendant's background prior to acceptance of a plea by the trial judge; and

(B) maintain the record of direct discussions with a defendant who represents himself or herself and make the record available to the trial judge upon the entry of a plea arising from these discussions.

(c) Responsibilities of Defense Counsel.

(1) Defense counsel shall not conclude any plea agreement on behalf of a defendant-client without the client's full and complete consent thereto, being certain that any decision to plead guilty or nolo contendere is made by the defendant.

(2) Defense counsel shall advise defendant of:

(A) all plea offers; and

(B) all pertinent matters bearing on the choice of which plea to enter and the particulars attendant upon each plea and the likely results thereof, as well as any possible alternatives that may be open to the defendant.

(d) Responsibilities of the Trial Judge. After an agreement on a plea has been reached, the trial judge may have made known to him or her the agreement and reasons therefor prior to the acceptance of the plea. Thereafter, the judge shall advise the parties whether other factors (unknown at the time) may make his or her concurrence impossible.

Committee Notes

1972 Amendment. New in Florida. Most criminal cases are disposed of by pleas of guilty arrived at by negotiations between prosecutor and defense counsel, but there was no record of the "plea negotiations," "plea bargaining," or "compromise." The result has been a flood of postconviction claims which require evidentiary hearings and frequently conflicting testimony concerning the plea negotiations. There has also been criticism of the practice of requiring a defendant, upon a negotiated guilty plea, to give a negative reply to the court's inquiry concerning any "promise" made to the defendant. This is designed to avoid the foregoing pitfalls and criticisms by having the negotiations made of record and permitting some control of them. See Commentary to Standard 3.1 ABA Standards relating to pleas of guilty.

(a) From Standard 3.1a.

(b) From Standard 3.2.

(c) From Standard 3.3 except for omission of that part of standard which prohibits trial judge from participating in plea discussions.

(d) From Standard 3.4.

1977 Amendment. This is a rewording of the prior rule in order to set out the responsibilities of the participants. The rule recognizes the ultimate responsibility of the trial judge, but it encourages prosecution and defense counsel to assist the trial judge in this regard. When the circumstances of the case so merit, it is the responsibility of each respective party to discuss a fair disposition in lieu of trial. For protection of the prosecutor and the defendant, plea discussions between the state and a pro se defendant should be recorded, in writing or electronically.

(b) New in Florida.

(1)(i) Restatement of policy followed by extensive revision in the form of Federal Rule of Criminal Procedure 11(e)(1).

(1)(ii) The rule sets out discretionary minimum professional prosecutorial procedure where either victim or law enforcement officers are involved to better guide the trial judge.

Rule 3.172. Acceptance of Guilty or Nolo Contendere Plea.

(2)(i) Mandatory responsibility of prosecutor contemplates disposition with no presentence investigation.

(2)(ii) Mandatory record protects both the prosecutor and the pro se defendant.

(c)(1) Renumbering subdivision (b) of prior rule.

(2)(i) New in Florida. This proposed language makes it mandatory for defense counsel to advise fully defendant of all plea offers by the state. Defense counsel should also discuss and explain to the defendant those matters which trial judge will inquire about before accepting a plea.

(2)(ii) Same as prior rule 3.171(b), paragraph 2.

(d) Now embraces and renumbers former rule 3.171(c). The content of former rule 3.171(d) now appears as part of new rule 3.172.

Rule 3.172. Acceptance of Guilty or Nolo Contendere Plea.

(a) Voluntariness; Factual Basis. Before accepting a plea of guilty or nolo contendere, the trial judge shall determine that the plea is voluntarily entered and that a factual basis for the plea exists. Counsel for the prosecution and the defense shall assist the trial judge in this function.

(b) Open Court. All pleas shall be taken in open court, except that when good cause is shown a plea may be taken in camera.

(c) Determination of Voluntariness. Except when a defendant is not present for a plea pursuant to the provisions of rule 3.180(d), the trial judge must, when determining voluntariness, place the defendant under oath, address the defendant personally, and determine on the record that he or she understands:

> **(1) Nature of the Charge.** The nature of the charge to which the plea is offered, the maximum possible penalty, and any mandatory minimum penalty provided by law.
>
> **(2) Right to Representation.** If not represented by an attorney, that the defendant has the right to be represented by an attorney at every stage of the proceeding and, if necessary, an attorney will be appointed to represent him or her.
>
> **(3) Right to Trial By Jury and Attendant Rights.** The right to plead not guilty or to persist in that plea if it has already been made, the right to be tried by a jury, and at that trial a defendant has the right to the assistance of counsel, the right to compel attendance of witnesses on his or her behalf, the right to

confront and cross-examine witnesses against him or her, and the right not to testify or be compelled to incriminate himself or herself.

(4) Effect of Plea. Upon a plea of guilty, or nolo contendere without express reservation of the right to appeal, he or she gives up the right to appeal all matters relating to the judgment, including the issue of guilt or innocence, but does not impair the right to review by appropriate collateral attack.

(5) Waiving Right to Trial. If the defendant pleads guilty or is adjudged guilty after a plea of nolo contendere there will not be a further trial of any kind, so that by pleading guilty or nolo contendere he or she waives the right to a trial.

(6) Questioning by Judge. If the defendant pleads guilty or nolo contendere, the trial judge may ask the defendant questions about the offense to which he or she has pleaded, and if the defendant answers these questions under oath, on the record, and in the presence of counsel, the answers may later be used against him or her in a prosecution for perjury.

(7) Terms of Plea Agreement. The complete terms of any plea agreement, including specifically all obligations the defendant will incur as a result.

(8) Deportation Consequences.

(A) If the defendant is not a citizen of the United States, a finding of guilt by the court, and the court's acceptance of the defendant's plea of guilty or no contest, regardless of whether adjudication of guilt has been withheld, may have the additional consequence of changing his or her immigration status, including deportation or removal from the United States.

(B) The court should advise the defendant to consult with counsel if he or she needs additional information concerning the potential deportation consequences of the plea.

(C) If the defendant has not discussed the potential deportation consequences with his or her counsel, prior to accepting the defendant's plea, the court is required, upon request, to allow a reasonable amount of time to permit the defendant to consider the appropriateness of the plea in light of the advisement described in this section.

(D) This admonition should be given to all defendants in all cases, and the trial court must not require at the time of entering a plea that the defendant disclose his or her legal status in the United States.

(9) Sexually Violent or Sexually Motivated Offenses. If the defendant pleads guilty or nolo contendere, and the offense to which the defendant is pleading is a sexually violent offense or a sexually motivated offense, or if the defendant has been previously convicted of such an offense, the plea may subject the defendant to involuntary civil commitment as a sexually violent predator upon completion of his or her sentence. It shall not be necessary for the trial judge to determine whether the present or prior offenses were sexually motivated, as this admonition shall be given to all defendants in all cases.

(10) Driver License Suspension or Revocation. If the defendant pleads guilty or nolo contendere and the offense to which the defendant is pleading is one for which automatic, mandatory driver license suspension or revocation is required by law to be imposed, either by the court or by a separate agency, the plea will provide the basis for the suspension or revocation of the defendant's driver license.

(d) DNA Evidence Inquiry. Before accepting a defendant's plea of guilty or nolo contendere to a felony, the judge must inquire whether counsel for the defense has reviewed the discovery disclosed by the state, whether such discovery included a listing or description of physical items of evidence, and whether counsel has reviewed the nature of the evidence with the defendant. The judge must then inquire of the defendant and counsel for the defendant and the state whether physical evidence containing DNA is known to exist that could exonerate the defendant. If no such physical evidence is known to exist, the court may accept the defendant's plea and impose sentence. If such physical evidence is known to exist, upon defendant's motion specifying the physical evidence to be tested, the court may postpone the proceeding and order DNA testing.

(e) Acknowledgment by Defendant. Before the trial judge accepts a guilty or nolo contendere plea, the judge must determine that the defendant either:

(1) acknowledges his or her guilt; or

(2) acknowledges that he or she feels the plea to be in his or her best interest, while maintaining his or her innocence.

(f) Proceedings of Record. The proceedings at which a defendant pleads guilty or nolo contendere shall be of record.

(g) Withdrawal of Plea Offer or Negotiation. No plea offer or negotiation is binding until it is accepted by the trial judge formally after making all the inquiries, advisements, and determinations required by this rule. Until that time, it may be withdrawn by either party without any necessary justification.

(h) Withdrawal of Plea When Judge Does Not Concur. If the trial judge does not concur in a tendered plea of guilty or nolo contendere arising from negotiations, the plea may be withdrawn.

(i) Evidence. Except as otherwise provided in this rule, evidence of an offer or a plea of guilty or nolo contendere, later withdrawn, or of statements made in connection therewith, is not admissible in any civil or criminal proceeding against the person who made the plea or offer.

(j) Prejudice. Failure to follow any of the procedures in this rule shall not render a plea void absent a showing of prejudice.

Committee Notes

1977 Adoption. New in Florida. In view of the supreme court's emphasis on the importance of this procedure as set forth in Williams v. State, 316 So.2d 267 (Fla. 1975), the committee felt it appropriate to expand the language of former rule 3.170(j) (deleted) and establish a separate rule. Incorporates Federal Rule of Criminal Procedure 11(c) and allows for pleas of convenience as provided in North Carolina v. Alford, 400 U.S. 25, 91 S.Ct. 160, 27 L.Ed.2d 162 (1970).

(a), (b) Mandatory record of voluntariness and factual predicate is proper responsibility of counsel as well as the court.

(c)(iv) This waiver of right to appeal is a change from the proposed amendments to the rules of criminal procedure now pending. A sentence if lawful is not subject to appellate review; a judgment, however, is. The committee was of the opinion that the proposed rule should be expanded to include a waiver of appeal from the judgment as well as the sentence. Waivers of appeal have been approved. United States ex rel. Amuso v. LaValle, 291 F.Supp. 383 (E.D.N.Y. 1968), aff'd 427 F.2d 328 (2d Cir. 1970); State v. Gibson, 68 N.J. 499, 348 A.2d 769 (1975); People v. Williams, 36 N.Y.2d 829, 370 N.Y.S.2d 904, 331 N.E.2d 684 (1975).

(vii) Requires the court to explain the plea agreement to the defendant, including conditions subsequent such as conditions of probation.

(e) Provides a readily available record (either oral or by use of standard forms) in all cases where a felony is charged.

(h) Rewording of federal rule 11(e)(6).

2005 Amendment. Rule 3.172(c)(9) added. See section 394.910, et seq., Fla. Stat.; and State v. Harris, 881 So.2d 1079 (Fla. 2004).

2015 Amendment. In view of the holdings in Padilla v. Kentucky, 559 U.S. 356, 130 S. Ct. 1473 (2010), and Hernandez v. State, 124 So. 3d 757 (Fla. 2012), the Committee felt it appropriate to expand the requirements in subdivision (c)(8).

Rule 3.180. Presence of Defendant.

(a) Presence of Defendant. In all prosecutions for crime the defendant shall be present:

(1) at first appearance;

(2) when a plea is made, unless a written plea of not guilty shall be made in writing under the provisions of rule 3.170(a);

(3) at any pretrial conference, unless waived by the defendant in writing;

(4) at the beginning of the trial during the examination, challenging, impaneling, and swearing of the jury;

(5) at all proceedings before the court when the jury is present;

(6) when evidence is addressed to the court out of the presence of the jury for the purpose of laying the foundation for the introduction of evidence before the jury;

(7) at any view by the jury;

(8) at the rendition of the verdict; and

(9) at the pronouncement of judgment and the imposition of sentence.

(b) Presence; Definition. Except as permitted by rule 3.130 relating to first appearance hearings, a defendant is present for purposes of this rule if the defendant is physically in attendance for the courtroom proceeding, and has a meaningful opportunity to be heard through counsel on the issues being discussed.

(c) Defendant Absenting Self.

(1) **Trial.** If the defendant is present at the beginning of the trial and thereafter, during the progress of the trial or before the verdict of the jury has been returned into court, voluntarily absents himself or herself from the presence of the court without leave of court, or is removed from the presence of the

court because of his or her disruptive conduct during the trial, the trial of the cause or the return of the verdict of the jury in the case shall not thereby be postponed or delayed, but the trial, the submission of the case to the jury for verdict, and the return of the verdict thereon shall proceed in all respects as though the defendant were present in court at all times.

(2) Sentencing. If the defendant is present at the beginning of the trial and thereafter absents himself or herself as described in subdivision (1), or if the defendant enters a plea of guilty or no contest and thereafter absents himself or herself from sentencing, the sentencing may proceed in all respects as though the defendant were present at all times.

(d) Defendant May be Tried in Absentia for Misdemeanors. Persons prosecuted for misdemeanors may, at their own request, by leave of court, be excused from attendance at any or all of the proceedings aforesaid.

(e) Presence of Corporation. A corporation may appear by counsel at all times and for all purposes.

Committee Notes

1968 Adoption. (a) The suggested rule is in great part a recopying of section 914.01, Florida Statutes:

In (3) the words "at the beginning of the trial" are recommended for inclusion to avoid questions arising as to the necessity for the defendant's presence at times other than upon trial, such as when the jury venire is ordered, etc.

Subdivision (a)(8) is not in the present statute. However, it is deemed advisable to include it, as the several sections of chapter 921, Florida Statutes, particularly section 921.07, appear to impliedly or expressly require the defendant's presence at such times.

(c) The statute and the suggested rule make no distinction between capital and other cases. In all probability, however, were a person on trial for a capital case to escape during trial, a mistrial should be ordered if such person were not captured within a reasonable time.

(d) It is suggested that this language be used rather than the all inclusive general language of the present statute as to misdemeanor cases.

(e) This provision does not appear in section 914.01, Florida Statutes, but it is a part of Federal Rule of Criminal Procedure 43. It is deemed useful to include it.

1972 Amendment. Same as prior rule except (3) added to conform to rule 3.220(k); other subdivisions renumbered.

Rule 3.181. Notice to Seek Death Penalty.

In a prosecution for a capital offense, if the prosecutor intends to seek the death penalty, the prosecutor must give notice to the defendant of the state's intent to seek the death penalty. The notice must be filed with the court within 45 days of arraignment. The notice must contain a list of the aggravating factors the state intends to prove and has reason to believe it can prove beyond a reasonable doubt. The court may allow the prosecutor to amend the notice upon a showing of good cause.

Committee Notes

2016 Amendment. This is a new rule, in response to legislation, and intended to complement Florida Rules of Criminal Procedure 3.202 (Expert Testimony of Mental Mitigation During Penalty Phase of Capital Trial; Notice and Examination by State Expert) and 3.780 (Sentencing Hearing for Capital Cases).

V. Pretrial Motions and Defenses

Rule 3.190. Pretrial Motions.

(a) In General. Every pretrial motion and pleading in response to a motion shall be in writing and signed by the party making the motion or the attorney for the party. This requirement may be waived by the court for good cause shown. Each motion or other pleading shall state the ground or grounds on which it is based. A copy shall be served on the adverse party. A certificate of service must accompany the filing of any pleading.

(b) Motion to Dismiss; Grounds. All defenses available to a defendant by plea, other than not guilty, shall be made only by motion to dismiss the indictment or information, whether the same shall relate to matters of form, substance, former acquittal, former jeopardy, or any other defense.

(c) Time for Moving to Dismiss. Unless the court grants further time, the defendant shall move to dismiss the indictment or information either before or at arraignment. The court in its discretion may permit the defendant to plead and thereafter to file a motion to dismiss at a time to be set by the court. Except for objections based on fundamental grounds, every ground for a motion to dismiss that is not presented by a motion to dismiss within the time provided herein, shall be considered waived. However, the court may at any time entertain a motion to dismiss on any of the following grounds:

(1) The defendant is charged with an offense for which the defendant has been pardoned.

(2) The defendant is charged with an offense for which the defendant previously has been placed in jeopardy.

(3) The defendant is charged with an offense for which the defendant previously has been granted immunity.

(4) There are no material disputed facts and the undisputed facts do not establish a prima facie case of guilt against the defendant.

The facts on which the motion is based should be alleged specifically and the motion sworn to.

(d) Traverse or Demurrer. The state may traverse or demur to a motion to dismiss that alleges factual matters. Factual matters alleged in a motion to dismiss under subdivision (c)(4) of this rule shall be considered admitted unless specifically denied by the state in the traverse. The court may receive evidence on any issue of fact necessary to the decision on the motion. A motion to dismiss under subdivision (c)(4) of this rule shall be denied if the state files a traverse that, with specificity, denies under oath the material fact or facts alleged in the motion to dismiss. The demurrer or traverse shall be filed a reasonable time before the hearing on the motion to dismiss.

(e) Effect of Sustaining a Motion to Dismiss. If the motion to dismiss is sustained, the court may order that the defendant be held in custody or admitted to bail for a reasonable specified time pending the filing of a new indictment or information. If a new indictment or information is not filed within the time specified in the order, or within such additional time as the court may allow for good cause shown, the defendant, if in custody, shall be discharged, unless some other charge justifies a continuation in custody. If the defendant has been released on bail, the defendant and the sureties

Rule 3.190. Pretrial Motions.

shall be exonerated; if money or bonds have been deposited as bail, the money or bonds shall be refunded.

(f) Motion for Continuance.

(1) **Definition.** A continuance within the meaning of this rule is the postponement of a cause for any period of time.

(2) **Cause.** On motion of the state or a defendant or on its own motion, the court may grant a continuance, in its discretion for good cause shown.

(3) **Time for Filing.** A motion for continuance may be made only before or at the time the case is set for trial, unless good cause for failure to so apply is shown or the ground for the motion arose after the cause was set for trial.

(4) **Certificate of Good Faith.** A motion for continuance shall be accompanied by a certificate of the movant's counsel that the motion is made in good faith.

(5) **Affidavits.** The party applying for a continuance may file affidavits in support of the motion, and the adverse party may file counter-affidavits in opposition to the motion.

(g) Motion to Suppress Evidence in Unlawful Search.

(1) **Grounds.** A defendant aggrieved by an unlawful search and seizure may move to suppress anything so obtained for use as evidence because:

(A) the property was illegally seized without a warrant;

(B) the warrant is insufficient on its face;

(C) the property seized is not the property described in the warrant;

(D) there was no probable cause for believing the existence of the grounds on which the warrant was issued; or

(E) the warrant was illegally executed.

(2) **Contents of Motion.** Every motion to suppress evidence shall state clearly the particular evidence sought to be suppressed, the reasons for suppression, and a general statement of the facts on which the motion is based.

(3) **Hearing.** Before hearing evidence, the court shall determine if the motion is legally sufficient. If it is not, the motion shall be denied. If the court hears the motion on its merits, the defendant shall present evidence supporting the defendant's position and the state may offer rebuttal evidence.

(4) Time for Filing. The motion to suppress shall be made before trial unless opportunity therefor did not exist or the defendant was not aware of the grounds for the motion, but the court may entertain the motion or an appropriate objection at the trial.

(h) Motion to Suppress a Confession or Admission Illegally Obtained.

(1) Grounds. On motion of the defendant or on its own motion, the court shall suppress any confession or admission obtained illegally from the defendant.

(2) Contents of Motion. Every motion made by a defendant to suppress a confession or admission shall identify with particularity any statement sought to be suppressed, the reasons for suppression, and a general statement of the facts on which the motion is based.

(3) Time for Filing. The motion to suppress shall be made before trial unless opportunity therefor did not exist or the defendant was not aware of the grounds for the motion, but the court in its discretion may entertain the motion or an appropriate objection at the trial.

(4) Hearing. The court shall receive evidence on any issue of fact necessary to be decided to rule on the motion.

(i) Motion to Take Deposition to Perpetuate Testimony.

(1) After the filing of an indictment or information on which a defendant is to be tried, the defendant or the state may apply for an order to perpetuate testimony. The application shall be verified or supported by the affidavits of credible persons that a prospective witness resides beyond the territorial jurisdiction of the court or may be unable to attend or be prevented from attending a trial or hearing, that the witness's testimony is material, and that it is necessary to take the deposition to prevent a failure of justice. The court shall order a commission to be issued to take the deposition of the witnesses to be used in the trial and that any nonprivileged designated books, papers, documents, or tangible objects be produced at the same time and place. If the application is made within 10 days before the trial date, the court may deny the application.

(2) If the defendant or the state desires to perpetuate the testimony of a witness living in or out of the state whose testimony is material and necessary to the case, the same

Rule 3.190. Pretrial Motions.

proceedings shall be followed as provided in subdivision (i)(1), but the testimony of the witness may be taken before an official court reporter, transcribed by the reporter, and filed in the trial court.

(3) If the deposition is taken on the application of the state, the defendant and the defendant's attorney shall be given reasonable notice of the time and place set for the deposition. The officer having custody of the defendant shall be notified of the time and place and shall produce the defendant at the examination and keep the defendant in the presence of the witness during the examination. A defendant not in custody may be present at the examination, but the failure to appear after notice and tender of expenses shall constitute a waiver of the right to be present. The state shall pay to the defendant's attorney and to a defendant not in custody the expenses of travel and subsistence for attendance at the examination. The state shall make available to the defendant for examination and use at the deposition any statement of the witness being deposed that is in the possession of the state and that the state would be required to make available to the defendant if the witness were testifying at trial.

(4) The application and order to issue the commission may be made either in term time or in vacation. The commission shall be issued at a time to be fixed by the court.

(5) Except as otherwise provided, the rules governing the taking and filing of oral depositions, the objections thereto, the issuing, execution, and return of the commission, and the opening of the depositions in civil actions shall apply in criminal cases.

(6) No deposition shall be used or read into evidence when the attendance of the witness can be procured. If the court determines that any person whose deposition has been taken is absent because of procurement, inducement, or threats of any person on behalf of the state or of the defendant or of any person on the defendant's behalf, the deposition shall not be read in evidence on behalf of the defendant.

(j) Motion to Expedite. On motion by the state, the court, in the exercise of its discretion, shall take into consideration the dictates of sections 825.106 and 918.0155, Florida Statutes (1995).

Committee Notes

1968 Adoption. (a) New; devised by committee.

(b) Substantially the same as section 909.02, Florida Statutes, except changes name of "motion to quash" to "motion to dismiss." This conforms to the terminology of the Federal Rules of Criminal Procedure. The statute authorizing the state to appeal from certain orders, section 924.07, Florida Statutes, should be amended by substituting the words "motion to dismiss" for "motion to quash."

(c) Combines the substance of sections 909.01 and 909.06, Florida Statutes. Subdivision (4) affords a new remedy to an accused. Although there is now a conclusive presumption of probable cause once an indictment or information is filed (see Sullivan v. State, 49 So.2d 794 (Fla. 1951)), it is felt that this rule is necessary. Primarily, this procedure will permit a pretrial determination of the law of the case when the facts are not in dispute. In a sense, this is somewhat similar to summary judgment proceedings in civil cases, but a dismissal under this rule is not a bar to a subsequent prosecution.

(d) New; based on Marks v. State, 115 Fla. 497, 155 So. 727 (1934), and what is generally regarded as the better practice. Hearing provision based on federal rule 41(e).

(e) Combines federal rule 12(b)(5) and section 909.05, Florida Statutes. With reference to the maximum time that a defendant will be held in custody or on bail pending the filing of a new indictment or information, the trial court is given discretion in setting such time as to both the indictment and information. This proposal differs from section 909.05, Florida Statutes, with reference to the filing of a new indictment in that the statute requires that the new indictment be found by the same grand jury or the next grand jury having the authority to inquire into the offense. If the supreme court has the authority to deviate from this statutory provision by court rule, it seems that the trial court should be granted the same discretion with reference to the indictment that it is granted concerning the information. The statute is harsh in that under its provisions a person can be in custody or on bail for what may be an unreasonable length of time before a grand jury is required to return an indictment in order that the custody or bail be continued.

(g)(1) This subdivision is almost the same as section 916.02(1), Florida Statutes.

(g)(2) This subdivision is almost the same as section 916.02(2), Florida Statutes.

Rule 3.190. Pretrial Motions.

(g)(3) This subdivision is almost the same as section 916.03, Florida Statutes.

(g)(4) This subdivision rewords a portion of section 916.04, Florida Statutes.

(g)(5) This subdivision rewords section 916.07, Florida Statutes.

(h) Same as federal rule 41(e) as to the points covered.

(i) This rule is based on 38-144-11 of the Illinois Code of Criminal Procedure and federal rule 41(e).

(j) This subdivision rewords and adds to federal rule 14. It covers the subject matter of section 918.02, Florida Statutes.

(k) This rule is almost the same as federal rule 13, with provision added for trial by affidavit.

(l) Substantially same as section 916.06, Florida Statutes, with these exceptions: application cannot be made until indictment, information, or trial affidavit is filed; application must be made at least 10 days before trial; oral deposition in addition to written interrogatories is permissible.

1972 Amendment. Subdivision (h) is amended to require the defendant to specify the factual basis behind the grounds for a motion to suppress evidence. Subdivision (l) is amended to permit the state to take depositions under the same conditions that the defendant can take them. Former subdivisions (j) and (k) transferred to rules 3.150, 3.151, and 3.152. Subdivisions (l) and (m) renumbered (j) and (k) respectively. Otherwise, same as prior rule.

1977 Amendment. This amendment resolves any ambiguity in the rule as to whether the state must file a general or a specific traverse to defeat a motion to dismiss filed under the authority of rule 3.190(c)(4).

See State v. Kemp, 305 So.2d 833 (Fla. 3d DCA 1974).

The amendment clearly now requires a specific traverse to specific material fact or facts.

1992 Amendment. The amendments, in addition to gender neutralizing the wording of the rule, make a minor grammatical change by substituting the word "upon" for "on" in several places. The amendments also delete language from subdivision (a) to eliminate from the rule any reference as to when pretrial motions are to be served on the adverse party. Because rule 3.030 addresses the service of pleadings and papers, such language was removed to avoid confusion and reduce redundancy in the rules.

2002 Amendment. If the trial court exercises its discretion to consider the motion to suppress during trial, the court may withhold ruling on the merits of the motion, and motion for a judgment of acquittal, and allow the case to be submitted to the jury. If the defendant is acquitted, no further proceedings regarding the motion to suppress or motion for a judgment of acquittal would be necessary. However, if the jury finds the defendant guilty of the crime charged, the trial court could then consider the motion to suppress post-trial in conjunction with the defendant's renewed motion for a judgment of acquittal or motion for new trial.

Rule 3.191. Speedy Trial.

(a) Speedy Trial without Demand. Except as otherwise provided by this rule, and subject to the limitations imposed under subdivisions (e) and (f), every person charged with a crime shall be brought to trial within 90 days of arrest if the crime charged is a misdemeanor, or within 175 days of arrest if the crime charged is a felony. If trial is not commenced within these time periods, the defendant shall be entitled to the appropriate remedy as set forth in subdivision (p). The time periods established by this subdivision shall commence when the person is taken into custody as defined under subdivision (d). A person charged with a crime is entitled to the benefits of this rule whether the person is in custody in a jail or correctional institution of this state or a political subdivision thereof or is at liberty on bail or recognizance or other pretrial release condition. This subdivision shall cease to apply whenever a person files a valid demand for speedy trial under subdivision (b).

(b) Speedy Trial upon Demand. Except as otherwise provided by this rule, and subject to the limitations imposed under subdivisions (e) and (g), every person charged with a crime by indictment or information shall have the right to demand a trial within 60 days, by filing with the court a separate pleading entitled "Demand for Speedy Trial," and serving a copy on the prosecuting authority.

(1) No later than 5 days from the filing of a demand for speedy trial, the court shall hold a calendar call, with notice to all parties, for the express purposes of announcing in open court receipt of the demand and of setting the case for trial.

(2) At the calendar call the court shall set the case for trial to commence at a date no less than 5 days nor more than 45 days from the date of the calendar call.

Rule 3.191. Speedy Trial.

(3) The failure of the court to hold a calendar call on a demand that has been properly filed and served shall not interrupt the running of any time periods under this subdivision.

(4) If the defendant has not been brought to trial within 50 days of the filing of the demand, the defendant shall have the right to the appropriate remedy as set forth in subdivision (p).

(c) Commencement of Trial. A person shall be considered to have been brought to trial if the trial commences within the time herein provided. The trial is considered to have commenced when the trial jury panel for that specific trial is sworn for voir dire examination or, on waiver of a jury trial, when the trial proceedings begin before the judge.

(d) Custody. For purposes of this rule, a person is taken into custody:

(1) when the person is arrested as a result of the conduct or criminal episode that gave rise to the crime charged; or

(2) when the person is served with a notice to appear in lieu of physical arrest.

(e) Prisoners outside Jurisdiction. A person who is in federal custody or incarcerated in a jail or correctional institution outside the jurisdiction of this state or a subdivision thereof, and who is charged with a crime by indictment or information issued or filed under the laws of this state, is not entitled to the benefit of this rule until that person returns or is returned to the jurisdiction of the court within which the Florida charge is pending and until written notice of the person's return is filed with the court and served on the prosecutor. For these persons, the time period under subdivision (a) commences on the date the last act required under this subdivision occurs. For these persons the time period under subdivision (b) commences when the demand is filed so long as the acts required under this subdivision occur before the filing of the demand. If the acts required under this subdivision do not precede the filing of the demand, the demand is invalid and shall be stricken upon motion of the prosecuting attorney. Nothing in this rule shall affect a prisoner's right to speedy trial under law.

(f) Consolidation of Felony and Misdemeanor. When a felony and a misdemeanor are consolidated for disposition in circuit court, the misdemeanor shall be governed by the same time period applicable to the felony.

(g) Demand for Speedy Trial; Accused Is Bound. A demand for speedy trial binds the accused and the state. No demand for speedy trial shall be filed or served unless the accused has a bona fide desire to obtain a trial sooner than otherwise might be provided. A demand for speedy trial shall be considered a pleading that the accused is available for trial, has diligently investigated the case, and is prepared or will be prepared for trial within 5 days. A demand filed by an accused who has not diligently investigated the case or who is not timely prepared for trial shall be stricken as invalid on motion of the prosecuting attorney. A demand may not be withdrawn by the accused except on order of the court, with consent of the state or on good cause shown. Good cause for continuances or delay on behalf of the accused thereafter shall not include nonreadiness for trial, except as to matters that may arise after the demand for trial is filed and that reasonably could not have been anticipated by the accused or counsel for the accused. A person who has demanded speedy trial, who thereafter is not prepared for trial, is not entitled to continuance or delay except as provided in this rule.

(h) Notice of Expiration of Time for Speedy Trial; When Timely. A notice of expiration of speedy trial time shall be timely if filed and served after the expiration of the periods of time for trial provided in this rule. However, a notice of expiration of speedy trial time filed before expiration of the period of time for trial is invalid and shall be stricken on motion of the prosecuting attorney.

(i) When Time May Be Extended. The periods of time established by this rule may be extended, provided the period of time sought to be extended has not expired at the time the extension was procured. An extension may be procured by:

(1) stipulation, announced to the court or signed in proper person or by counsel, by the party against whom the stipulation is sought to be enforced;

(2) written or recorded order of the court on the court's own motion or motion by either party in exceptional circumstances as hereafter defined in sub-division (l);

(3) written or recorded order of the court with good cause shown by the accused;

(4) written or recorded order of the court for a period of reasonable and necessary delay resulting from proceedings including but not limited to an examination and hearing to determine the mental competency or physical ability of the

Rule 3.191. Speedy Trial.

defendant to stand trial, for hearings on pretrial motions, for appeals by the state, for DNA testing ordered on the defendant's behalf upon defendant's motion specifying the physical evidence to be tested pursuant to section 925.12(2), Florida Statutes, and for trial of other pending criminal charges against the accused; or

(5) administrative order issued by the chief justice, under Florida Rule of General Practice and Judicial Administration 2.205(a)(2)(B)(iv), suspending the speedy trial procedures as stated therein.

(j) Delay and Continuances; Effect on Motion. If trial of the accused does not commence within the periods of time established by this rule, a pending motion for discharge shall be granted by the court unless it is shown that:

(1) a time extension has been ordered under subdivision (i) and that extension has not expired;

(2) the failure to hold trial is attributable to the accused, a codefendant in the same trial, or their counsel;

(3) the accused was unavailable for trial under subdivision (k); or

(4) the demand referred to in subdivision (g) is invalid.

If the court finds that discharge is not appropriate for reasons under subdivisions (j)(2), (j)(3), or (j)(4), the pending motion for discharge shall be denied, provided, however, that trial shall be scheduled and commence within 90 days of a written or recorded order of denial.

(k) Availability for Trial. A person is unavailable for trial if the person or the person's counsel fails to attend a proceeding at which either's presence is required by these rules, or the person or counsel is not ready for trial on the date trial is scheduled. A person who has not been available for trial during the term provided for in this rule is not entitled to be discharged. No presumption of nonavailability, attaches, but if the state objects to discharge and presents any evidence tending to show nonavailability, the accused must establish, by competent proof, availability during the term.

(l) Exceptional Circumstances. As permitted by subdivision (i) of this rule, the court may order an extension of the time periods provided under this rule when exceptional circumstances are shown to exist. Exceptional circumstances shall not include general congestion of the court's docket, lack of diligent preparation, failure to obtain available witnesses, or other avoidable or foreseeable delays. Exceptional circumstances are those that, as a matter of substantial justice to the accused or the state or both, require an order by the court. These circumstances include:

(1) unexpected illness, unexpected incapacity, or unforeseeable and unavoidable absence of a person whose presence or testimony is uniquely necessary for a full and adequate trial;

(2) a showing by the state that the case is so unusual and so complex, because the number of defendants or the nature of the prosecution or otherwise, that it is unreasonable to expect adequate investigation or preparation within the periods of time established by this rule;

(3) a showing by the state that specific evidence or testimony is not available despite diligent efforts to secure it, but will become available at a later time;

(4) a showing by the accused or the state of necessity for delay grounded on developments that could not have been anticipated and that materially will affect the trial;

(5) a showing that a delay is necessary to accommodate a codefendant, when there is reason not to sever the cases to proceed promptly with trial of the defendant; or

(6) a showing by the state that the accused has caused major delay or disruption of preparation of proceedings, as by preventing the attendance of witnesses or otherwise.

(m) Effect of Mistrial; Appeal; Order of New Trial. A person who is to be tried again or whose trial has been delayed by an appeal by the state or the defendant shall be brought to trial within 90 days from the date of declaration of a mistrial by the trial court, the date of an order by the trial court granting a new trial, the date of an order by the trial court granting a motion in arrest of judgment, or the date of receipt by the trial court of a mandate, order, or notice of whatever form from a reviewing court that makes possible a new trial for the defendant, whichever is last in time. If a defendant is not brought to trial within the prescribed time periods, the defendant shall be entitled to the appropriate remedy as set forth in subdivision (p).

(n) Discharge from Crime; Effect. Discharge from a crime under this rule shall operate to bar prosecution of the crime charged and of all other crimes on which trial has not commenced nor conviction obtained nor adjudication withheld and that were or might have been charged as a result of the same conduct or criminal episode as a lesser degree or lesser included offense.

(o) Nolle Prosequi; Effect. The intent and effect of this rule shall not be avoided by the state by entering a nolle prosequi to a crime charged and by prosecuting a new crime grounded on the same conduct or criminal episode or otherwise by prosecuting new and different charges based on the same conduct or criminal episode, whether or not the pending charge is suspended, continued, or is the subject of entry of a nolle prosequi.

(p) Remedy for Failure to Try Defendant within the Specified Time.

(1) No remedy shall be granted to any defendant under this rule until the court has made the required inquiry under subdivision (j).

(2) At any time after the expiration of the prescribed time period, the defendant may file a separate pleading entitled "Notice of Expiration of Speedy Trial Time," and serve a copy on the prosecuting authority.

(3) No later than 5 days from the date of the filing of a notice of expiration of speedy trial time, the court shall hold a hearing on the notice and, unless the court finds that one of the reasons set forth in subdivision (j) exists, shall order that the defendant be brought to trial within 10 days. A defendant not brought to trial within the 10-day period through no fault of the defendant, on motion of the defendant or the court, shall be forever discharged from the crime.

Committee Notes

1972 Amendment. Same as prior rule. The schedule is omitted as being unnecessary.

1977 Amendment. An appeal by the state from an order dismissing the case constitutes an interlocutory appeal and should be treated as such. The additional phrase removes any ambiguities in the existing rule.

1980 Amendment.

(a)(1). Speedy Trial without Demand.

1. Prisoners in Florida institutions are now treated like any other defendant [formerly (b)(1)].

2. Federal prisoners and prisoners outside Florida may claim the benefit of this subdivision once special prerequisites are satisfied under (b)(1).

3. Before a court can discharge a defendant, the court must make complete inquiry to ensure that discharge is appropriate.

(a)(2). Speedy Trial upon Demand.

1. Trial cannot be scheduled within 5 days of the filing of the demand without the consent of both the state and the defendant.

2. Before a court can discharge a defendant, the court must make complete inquiry to ensure that discharge is appropriate.

3. Prisoners in Florida are now treated like any other defendant [formerly (b)(2)].

4. Federal prisoners and prisoners outside Florida may claim the benefit of this subdivision once special prerequisites are satisfied under (b)(1).

(a)(3). Commencement of Trial.

1. Minor change in language to reflect case law.

(a)(4). Custody. [NEW]

1. Custody is defined in terms tantamount to arrest. This definition was formerly contained in (a)(1).

2. Where a notice to appear is served in lieu of arrest, custody results on the date the notice is served.

(b)(1). Prisoners outside Jurisdiction. [NEW]

1. Prisoners outside the jurisdiction of Florida may claim benefit under (a)(1) and (a)(2) after the prisoner returns to the jurisdiction of the court where the charge is pending and after the prisoner files and serves a notice of this fact.

2. As an alternative, certain prisoners may claim the benefit of sections 941.45-941.50, Florida Statutes (1979).

3. Former (b)(1) is repealed.

(b)(2) [NEW]

1. Where a misdemeanor and felony are consolidated for purposes of trial in circuit court, the misdemeanor is governed by the same time period applicable to the felony. To claim benefit under this provision, the crimes must be consolidated before the normal time period applicable to misdemeanors has expired.

2. Former (b)(2) is repealed.

(b)(3) Repealed and superseded by (b)(1).

(c). Demand for Speedy Trial.

Rule 3.191. Speedy Trial.

1. The subdivision recognizes that an invalid (spurious) demand must be stricken.

2. The subdivision now puts a 5-day limit on the time when a defendant must be prepared.

(d)(1) Motion for Discharge.

1. Under the amended provision, a prematurely filed motion is invalid and may be stricken.

(d)(2) When Time May Be Extended.

1. The terms "waiver," "tolling," or "suspension" have no meaning within the context of the subdivision as amended. The subdivision addresses extensions for a specified period of time.

2. Except for stipulations, all extensions require an order of the court.

3. The term "recorded order" refers to stenographic recording and not recording of a written order by the clerk.

(d)(3) Delay and Continuances.

1. Even though the normal time limit has expired under (a)(1) or (a)(2), a trial court may not properly discharge a defendant without making a complete inquiry of possible reasons to deny discharge. If the court finds that the time period has been properly extended and the extension has not expired, the court must simply deny the motion. If the court finds that the delay is attributable to the accused, that the accused was unavailable for trial, or that the demand was invalid, the court must deny the motion and schedule trial within 90 days. If the court has before it a valid motion for discharge and none of the above circumstances are present, the court must grant the motion.

(e) Availability for Trial.

1. Availability for trial is now defined solely in terms of required attendance and readiness for trial.

(f). Exceptional Circumstances.

1. The 2 extension limit for unavailable evidence has been discarded.

2. The new trial date paragraph was eliminated because it simply was unnecessary.

(g) Effect of Mistrial; Appeal; Order of New Trial.

1. Makes uniform a 90-day period within which a defendant must be brought to trial after a mistrial, order of new trial, or appeal by the state or defendant.

(h)(1) Discharge from Crime.

1. No change.

(h)(2) Nolle Prosequi.

1984 Amendment.

(a)(1) Repeals the remedy of automatic discharge from the crime and refers instead to the new subdivision on remedies.

(a)(2) Establishes the calendar call for the demand for speedy trial when filed. This provision, especially sought by prosecutors, brings the matter to the attention of both the court and the prosecution. The subdivision again repeals the automatic discharge for failure to meet the mandated time limit, referring to the new subdivision on remedies for the appropriate remedy.

(i) The intent of (i)(4) is to provide the state attorney with 15 days within which to bring a defendant to trial from the date of the filing of the motion for discharge. This time begins with the filing of the motion and continues regardless of whether the judge hears the motion.

This subdivision provides that, upon failure of the prosecution to meet the mandated time periods, the defendant shall file a motion for discharge, which will then be heard by the court within 5 days. The court sets trial of the defendant within 10 additional days. The total 15-day period was chosen carefully by the committee, the consensus being that the period was long enough that the system could, in fact, bring to trial a defendant not yet tried, but short enough that the pressure to try defendants within the prescribed time period would remain. In other words, it gives the system a chance to remedy a mistake; it does not permit the system to forget about the time constraints. It was felt that a period of 10 days was too short, giving the system insufficient time in which to bring a defendant to trial; the period of 30 days was too long, removing incentive to maintain strict docket control in order to remain within the prescribed time periods.

The committee further felt that it was not appropriate to extend the new remedy provisions to misdemeanors, but only to more serious offenses.

1992 Amendment. The purpose of the amendments is to gender neutralize the wording of the rule. In addition, the committee recommends the rule be amended to differentiate between 2 separate and distinct pleadings now referred to as "motion for discharge." The initial "motion for discharge" has been renamed "notice of expiration of speedy trial time."

2018 Amendment. In light of the ruling in Smart v. State, 179 So. 3d 477 (Fla. 4th DCA 2015), as well as the precedent cited therein, the committee notes that the reference to the swearing in of trial jury panel for voir dire examination contained in the Florida Rule of Criminal Procedure 3.191(c) relates to the giving of the oath contained in Florida Rule of Criminal Procedure 3.300(a). The oath is not required to be given in any particular location or by any particular official.

Rule 3.192. Motions for Rehearing.

When an appeal by the state is authorized by Florida Rule of Appellate Procedure 9.140, or sections 924.07 or 924.071, Florida Statutes, the state may file a motion for rehearing within 10 days of an order subject to appellate review. A motion for rehearing shall state with particularity the points of law or fact that, in the opinion of the state, the court has overlooked or misapprehended in its decision, and shall not present issues not previously raised in the proceeding. A response may be filed within 10 days of service of the motion. The trial court's order disposing of the motion for rehearing shall be filed within 15 days of the response but not later than 40 days from the date of the order of which rehearing is sought. A timely filed motion for rehearing shall toll rendition of the order subject to appellate review and the order shall be deemed rendered upon the filing of a signed, written order denying the motion for rehearing. This rule shall not apply to postconviction proceedings pursuant to rule 3.800(a), 3.801, 3.850, 3.851, or 3.853. Nothing in this rule precludes the trial court from exercising its inherent authority to reconsider a ruling while the court has jurisdiction of the case.

Rule 3.200. Notice of Alibi.

On the written demand of the prosecuting attorney, specifying as particularly as is known to the prosecuting attorney the place, date, and time of the commission of the crime charged, a defendant in a criminal case who intends to offer evidence of an alibi in defense shall, not less than 10 days before trial or such other time as the court may direct, file and serve on the prosecuting attorney a notice in writing of an intention to claim an alibi, which notice shall contain specific information as to the place at which the defendant claims to have been at the time of the alleged offense and, as particularly as is known to the defendant or the defendant's attorney, the names and addresses of the witnesses by whom the defendant proposes to establish the alibi. Not more than 5 days after receipt of defendant's witness list, or any other time as the court may direct, the prosecuting attorney shall file and serve on the defendant the names and addresses (as particularly as are known to the prosecuting attorney) of the witnesses the state proposes to offer in rebuttal to discredit the defendant's alibi at the trial of the cause. Both the defendant and the prosecuting attorney shall be under a continuing duty to promptly disclose the names and addresses of additional witnesses who come to the attention of either party subsequent to filing their respective witness lists as provided in this rule. If a defendant fails to file and serve a copy of the notice as herein required, the court may exclude evidence offered by the defendant for the purpose of providing an alibi, except the defendant's own testimony. If the notice is given by a defendant, the court may exclude the testimony of any witness offered by the defendant for the purpose of proving an alibi if the name and address of the witness as particularly as is known to the defendant or the defendant's attorney is not stated in the notice. If the prosecuting attorney fails to file and serve a copy on the defendant of a list of witnesses as herein provided, the court may exclude evidence offered by the state in rebuttal to the defendant's alibi evidence. If notice is given by the prosecuting attorney, the court may exclude the testimony of any witness offered by the prosecuting attorney for the purpose of rebutting the defense of alibi if the name and address of the witness as particularly as is known to the prosecuting attorney is not stated in the notice. For good cause shown the court may waive the requirements of this rule.

Committee Notes

1968 Adoption. The rule is completely new in Florida. Fourteen states have adopted notice of alibi statutes or rules: Arizona Supreme Court Rules of Criminal Procedure 192 (enacted in 1940); Ind. Ann. Stat. 91631, 91632, 91633 (1956) (enacted in 1935); Iowa Code Ann. 777 18 (1958) (enacted in 1941); Kan. Gen. Stat. Ann. 621341 (1949) (enacted in 1935); Mich. Stat. Ann. 630.14 (1947) (enacted in 1935); N.J. Superior and County Court Criminal Practice Rule 3:59 (1948) (enacted in 1934); N.Y. Code of Crim. Proc. 295L (1935) (enacted in 1935); Ohio Rev. Code Ann. 2945.58

(1953) (enacted in 1929); Okla. Stat. Ann. 22585 (1937) (enacted in 1935); S.D. Code 34.2801 (1939) (enacted in 1935); Utah Code Ann. 772217 (1953) (enacted in 1935); Vt. Stat. Ann. 136561, 6562 (1958) (enacted in 1935); Wis. Stat. Ann. 955.07 (1958) (enacted in 1935).

The rule is modeled after the Ohio, New York, and New Jersey statutes:

(1) The requirement of notice in writing is taken from the Ohio statute.

(2) The requirement of an initial demand by the prosecuting attorney is based on the New York and New Jersey statutes.

(3) The requirement of a mutual exchange of witness lists is based on those statutes which require the defendant to disclose alibi witnesses. In the interest of mutuality, the requirement of a reciprocal exchange of witness lists has been added. The enforcement provision is based on the Ohio and New York statutes. In New York, a defendant who fails to give advance notice of alibi may still give alibi testimony himself. People v. Rakiec, 23 N.Y.S.2d 607, aff'd 45 N.E.2d 812 (1942).

For an excellent article on notice of alibi statutes, court decisions thereunder, and some empirical data on the practical effect of the rules, see David M. Epstein, "Advance Notice of Alibi," 55 J. Crim. L. & Criminology 29 (1964).

1972 Amendment. Same as prior rule.

1992 Amendment. The purpose of the amendments is to gender neutralize the wording of the rule.

Rule 3.201. Battered-Spouse Syndrome Defense.

(a) Notice of Battered-Spouse Syndrome Defense. When in any criminal case it shall be intention of the defendant to rely on the defense of battered-spouse syndrome at trial, no evidence offered by the defendant for the purpose of establishing that defense shall be admitted in the case unless advance notice in writing of the defense shall have been given by the defendant as hereinafter provided.

(b) Time for Filing Notice. The defendant shall give notice of intent to rely on the defense of battered-spouse syndrome no later than 30 days prior to trial. The notice shall contain a statement of particulars showing the nature of the defense the defendant expects to prove and the names and addresses of the witnesses by whom the defendant expects to show battered-spouse syndrome, insofar as possible.

Rule 3.202. Expert Testimony of Mental Mitigation During Penalty Phase of Capital Trial; Notice and Examination by State Expert.

(a) Notice of Intent to Seek Death Penalty. The provisions of this rule apply only in those capital cases in which the state gives timely written notice of its intent to seek the death penalty.

(b) Notice of Intent to Present Expert Testimony of Mental Mitigation. When in any capital case, in which the state has given notice of intent to seek the death penalty under subdivision (a) of this rule, it shall be the intention of the defendant to present, during the penalty phase of the trial, expert testimony of a mental health professional, who has tested, evaluated, or examined the defendant, in order to establish statutory or nonstatutory mental mitigating circumstances, the defendant shall give written notice of intent to present such testimony.

(c) Time for Filing Notice; Contents. The defendant shall give notice of intent to present expert testimony of mental mitigation not less than 20 days before trial. The notice shall contain a statement of particulars listing the statutory and nonstatutory mental mitigating circumstances the defendant expects to establish through expert testimony and the names and addresses of the mental health experts by whom the defendant expects to establish mental mitigation, insofar as is possible.

(d) Appointment of State Expert; Time of Examination. After the filing of such notice and on the motion of the state indicating its desire to seek the death penalty, the court shall order that, within 48 hours after the defendant is convicted of capital murder, the defendant be examined by a mental health expert chosen by the state. Attorneys for the state and defendant may be present at the examination. The examination shall be limited to those mitigating circumstances the defendant expects to establish through expert testimony.

(e) Defendant's Refusal to Cooperate. If the defendant refuses to be examined by or fully cooperate with the state's mental health expert, the court may, in its discretion:

(1) order the defense to allow the state's expert to review all mental health reports, tests, and evaluations by the defendant's mental health expert; or

(2) prohibit defense mental health experts from testifying concerning mental health tests, evaluations, or examinations of the defendant.

Committee Notes

2016 Amendment. This is a new rule, in response to legislation, and intended to complement Florida Rules of Criminal Procedure 3.181 (Notice to Seek Death Penalty) and 3.780 (Sentencing Hearing for Capital Cases).

Rule 3.203. Defendant's Intellectual Disability as a Bar to Imposition of the Death Penalty.

(a) Scope. This rule applies in all first-degree murder cases in which the state attorney has not waived the death penalty on the record and the defendant's intellectual disability becomes an issue.

(b) Definition of Intellectual Disability. As used in this rule, the term "intellectual disability" means significantly subaverage general intellectual functioning existing concurrently with deficits in adaptive behavior and manifested during the period from conception to age 18. The term "significantly subaverage general intellectual functioning," for the purpose of this rule, means performance that is 2 or more standard deviations from the mean score on a standardized intelligence test authorized by the Department of Children and Families in rule 65G-4.011 of the Florida Administrative Code. The term "adaptive behavior," for the purpose of this rule, means the effectiveness or degree with which an individual meets the standards of personal independence and social responsibility expected of his or her age, cultural group, and community.

(c) Motion for Determination of Intellectual Disability as a Bar to Execution; Contents; Procedures.

(1) A defendant who intends to raise intellectual disability as a bar to execution shall file a written motion to establish intellectual disability as a bar to execution with the court.

(2) The motion shall state that the defendant is intellectually disabled and, if the defendant has been tested, evaluated, or examined by 1 or more experts, the names and addresses of the experts. Copies of reports containing the opinions of any experts named in the motion shall be attached to the motion. The court shall appoint an expert chosen by the state attorney if the state attorney so requests. The expert shall promptly test, evaluate, or examine the defendant and shall submit a written report of any findings to the parties and the court.

(3) If the defendant has not been tested, evaluated, or examined by 1 or more experts, the motion shall state that fact and the court shall appoint 2 experts who shall promptly test, evaluate, or examine the defendant and shall submit a written report of any findings to the parties and the court.

(4) Attorneys for the state and defendant may be present at the examinations conducted by court-appointed experts.

(5) If the defendant refuses to be examined or fully cooperate with the court appointed experts or the state's expert, the court may, in the court's discretion:

(A) order the defense to allow the court-appointed experts to review all mental health reports, tests, and evaluations by the defendant's expert;

(B) prohibit the defense experts from testifying concerning any tests, evaluations, or examinations of the defendant regarding the defendant's intellectual disability; or

(C) order such relief as the court determines to be appropriate.

(d) Time for filing Motion for Determination of Intellectual Disability as a Bar to Execution. The motion for a determination of intellectual disability as a bar to execution shall be filed not later than 90 days prior to trial, or at such time as is ordered by the court.

(e) Hearing on Motion to Determine Intellectual Disability. The circuit court shall conduct an evidentiary hearing on the motion for a determination of intellectual disability. At the hearing, the court shall consider the findings of the experts and all other evidence on the issue of whether the defendant is intellectually disabled. The court shall enter a written order prohibiting the imposition of the death penalty and setting forth the court's specific findings in support of the court's determination if the court finds that the defendant is intellectually disabled as defined in subdivision (b) of this rule. The court shall stay the proceedings for

30 days from the date of rendition of the order prohibiting the death penalty or, if a motion for rehearing is filed, for 30 days following the rendition of the order denying rehearing, to allow the state the opportunity to appeal the order. If the court determines that the defendant has not established intellectual disability, the court shall enter a written order setting forth the court's specific findings in support of the court's determination.

(f) Waiver. A claim authorized under this rule is waived if not filed in accord with the time requirements for filing set out in this rule, unless good cause is shown for the failure to comply with the time requirements.

(g) Finding of Intellectual Disability; Order to Proceed. If, after the evidence presented, the court is of the opinion that the defendant is intellectually disabled, the court shall order the case to proceed without the death penalty as an issue.

(h) Appeal. An appeal may be taken by the state if the court enters an order finding that the defendant is intellectually disabled, which will stay further proceedings in the trial court until a decision on appeal is rendered. Appeals are to proceed according to Florida Rule of Appellate Procedure 9.140(c).

(i) Motion to Establish Intellectual Disability as a Bar to Execution; Stay of Execution. The filing of a motion to establish intellectual disability as a bar to execution shall not stay further proceedings without a separate order staying execution.

Rule 3.210. Incompetence to Proceed: Procedure for Raising the Issue.

(a) Proceedings Barred during Incompetency. A person accused of an offense or a violation of probation or community control who is mentally incompetent to proceed at any material stage of a criminal proceeding must not be proceeded against while incompetent.

(1) A "material stage of a criminal proceeding" includes the trial of the case, pretrial hearings involving questions of fact on which the defendant might be expected to testify, entry of a plea, violation of probation or violation of community control proceedings, sentencing, hearings on issues regarding a defendant's failure to comply with court orders or conditions, or other matters where the mental competence of the defendant is necessary for a just resolution of the issues being

considered. The terms "competent," "competence," "incompetent," and "incompetence," as used in rules 3.210–3.219, refer to mental competence or incompetence to proceed at a material stage of a criminal proceeding.

(2) The incompetence of the defendant does not preclude such judicial action, hearings on motions of the parties, discovery proceedings, or other procedures that do not require the personal participation of the defendant.

(b) Motion for Evaluation. If at or in anticipation of any material stage(s) of a criminal proceeding the court, on its own motion or by motion of the state or defense, has reasonable grounds to believe that the defendant is not mentally competent to proceed, the court must promptly commence the process to determine the defendant's mental condition. The court may order the defendant to be evaluated by no more than 3 experts, as needed, and must expeditiously schedule and conduct a competency hearing. Attorneys for the state and for the defendant may be present at any examination by a court-appointed expert. Status hearing(s) must be held no later than 20 days after the motion date and as otherwise necessary to ensure prompt resolution, and absent good cause, a final hearing conducted no later than 45 days from the motion date.

(1) A motion for evaluation made by counsel for the defendant must be written and contain a certificate of counsel that the motion is made in good faith and on reasonable grounds to believe that the defendant may be incompetent to proceed. To the extent that it does not invade the lawyer-client privilege, the motion shall contain a recital of the specific observations of and conversations with the defendant that have formed the basis for the motion.

(2) A motion for the evaluation made by counsel for the state must be written and contain a certificate of counsel that the motion is made in good faith and on reasonable grounds to believe the defendant may be incompetent to proceed and shall include a recital of the specific facts that have formed the basis for the motion, including a recitation of the observations of and statements of the defendant that have caused the state to file the motion.

(3) If the defendant has been released on bail or other release provision, the court may order the defendant to appear at a designated place for evaluation at a specific time as a condition of such release. If the court determines that the defendant will not submit to the evaluation or that the defendant is not likely

Rule 3.210. Incompetence to Proceed: Procedure for Raising the Issue.

to appear for the scheduled evaluation, the court may order the defendant taken into custody until the determination of the defendant's competency to proceed. A motion made for evaluation under this subdivision does not otherwise affect the defendant's right to release.

(4) The order appointing experts must, as described in Rule 3.211:

(A) identify the purpose or purposes of the evaluation, including the nature of the material proceeding(s), and specify the area or areas of inquiry that should be addressed by the evaluator;

(B) specify the legal criteria to be applied; and

(C) specify the date by which the report should be submitted and to whom the report should be submitted.

Committee Notes

1968 Adoption. (a) Same as section 917.01, Florida Statutes, except it was felt that court cannot by rule direct institution officials. Thus words, "he shall report this fact to the court which conducted the hearing. If the officer so reports" and concluding sentence, "No defendant committed by a court to an institution, by reason of the examination referred to in this paragraph, shall be released therefrom, without the consent of the court committing him," should be omitted from the rule but retained by statute.

(b) Same as section 909.17, Florida Statutes.

(c) Same as section 917.02, Florida Statutes.

1972 Amendment. Subdivision (a)(3) refers to Jackson v. Indiana, 406 U.S. 715, 730, 92 S.Ct. 1845, 32 L.Ed.2d 435 (1972); also, United States v. Curry, 410 F.2d 1372 (4th Cir. 1969). Subdivision (d) is added to give the court authority to confine an insane person who is likely to cause harm to others even if the person is otherwise entitled to bail. The amendment does not apply unless the defendant contends that he or she is insane at the time of trial or at the time the offense was committed. The purpose of the amendment is to prevent admittedly insane persons from being at large when there is a likelihood they may injure themselves or others.

1977 Amendment. This language is taken, almost verbatim, from existing rule 3.210(a). The word "insane" is changed to reflect the new terminology, "competence to stand trial." The definition of competence to stand trial is taken verbatim from the United States

Supreme Court formulation of the test in Dusky v. United States, 362 U.S. 402, 80 S.Ct. 788, 4 L.Ed.2d 824 (1960).

(a)(2) The first part of this paragraph is taken, almost verbatim, from the existing rule. The right of counsel for the state to move for such examination has been added.

(b)(1) In order to confine the defendant as incompetent to stand trial, the defendant must be confined under the same standards as those used for civil commitment. These criteria were set forth in the recent U.S. Supreme Court case of Jackson v. Indiana, 406 U.S. 715, 92 S.Ct. 1845, 32 L.Ed.2d 435 (1972), in which it was held to be a denial of equal protection to subject a criminal defendant to a more lenient commitment standard than would be applied to one not charged with a crime. Therefore, the criteria for involuntary civil commitment should be incorporated as the criteria for commitment for incompetence to stand trial.

In this subdivision is found the most difficult of the problems to resolve for the rule. The head-on conflict between the Department of Health and Rehabilitative Services, a part of the executive branch of the government, and the courts occurs when the administrator determines that a defendant no longer should be confined, but the trial judge does not wish the defendant released because the trial judge feels that further commitment is necessary. Under the civil commitment model, the administrator has the power to release a committed patient at such time as the administrator feels the patient no longer meets the standards for commitment. Obviously, since a defendant in a criminal case is under the jurisdiction of the court, such immediate release is unwarranted.

The time period of the initial commitment parallels that of civil commitment.

(b)(2) treats the problem of what the court should do with a defendant who is not competent to stand trial, but who fails to meet the criteria for commitment. If incompetent, but not in need of treatment and not dangerous, then the defendant cannot be committed. The present rule provides for dismissal of the charges immediately. There appears to be no reason why someone in this situation should not be released pending trial on bail, as would other defendants.

The finding of "not guilty by reason of insanity," required under the present rule when a defendant cannot be tried by reason of incompetence, seems inappropriate since such a defense admits the commission of the fact of the crime but denies the defendant's

Rule 3.210. Incompetence to Proceed: Procedure for Raising the Issue.

mental state. Since no such finding has been made (and cannot be made), the verdict entered of not guilty by reason of insanity is not appropriate. Further, it would give a defendant, later competent, a res judicata or double jeopardy defense, the verdict being a final determination of guilt or innocence. It would seem far more appropriate to withdraw the charges. A defendant who regains competence within the period of the statute of limitations could still be tried for the offense, if such trial is warranted.

One of the major problems confronting the institution in which an incompetent person is being held is that of obtaining consent for medical procedures and treatment, not necessarily mental treatment. Generally, under the statute, the patient civilly committed is not thereby deemed incompetent to consent. At the commitment hearing in the civil proceedings, the judge may make the general competency determination. It is recommended that the same process apply in the hearing on competency to stand trial, and that, if the trial judge does not find the defendant incompetent for other purposes, the defendant be legally considered competent for such other purposes.

1980 Amendment.

(a) This provision is identical to that which has been contained in all prior rules and statutes relating to competence to stand trial. No change is suggested.

(b) In order to ensure that the proceedings move quickly the court is required to set a hearing within 20 days. This subdivision should be read in conjunction with rule 3.211 which requires the experts to submit their report to the court at such time as the court shall specify. The court therefore determines the time on which the report is to be submitted. The provision requiring at least 2 but no more than 3 experts is meant to coincide with section 394.02, Florida Statutes (1979), in which the legislature provides for the number of experts to be appointed and that at least 1 of such experts be appointed from a group of certain designated state-related professionals. This legislative restriction on appointment will ensure that the Department of Health and Rehabilitative Services will, to some extent, be involved in the hospitalization decision-making process. Other possible procedures were discussed at great length both among members of the committee and with representatives of the legislature, but it was decided that any more specific procedures should be developed on the local level in the individual circuits and that it would be inappropriate to mandate such specific procedures in a statewide court rule. Since it was felt by the committee to be a critical stage in the proceedings and subject to Sixth Amendment provisions, and since no psychiatrist-patient privilege applies to this stage of the proceeding, the committee felt that attorneys for both sides should have the right to be present at such examinations.

(1) and (2) A motion for examination relative to competency to stand trial should not be a "boiler plate" motion filed in every case. The inclusion of specific facts in the motion will give the trial judge a basis on which to determine whether there is sufficient indication of incompetence to stand trial that experts should be appointed to examine the defendant. Provision was made that conversations and observations need not be disclosed if they were felt to violate the lawyer-client privilege. Observations of the defendant were included in this phrase in that these may, in some cases, be considered "verbal acts."

(3) The mere filing of a motion for examination to determine competence to stand trial should not affect in any way the provision for release of a defendant on bail or other pretrial release provision. If a defendant has been released on bail, the judgment already having been made that he or she is so entitled, and as long as the defendant will continue to appear for appropriate evaluations, the mere fact that the motion was filed should not abrogate the right to bail. Obviously, if other factors would affect the defendant's right to release or would affect the right to release on specific release conditions, those conditions could be changed or the release revoked. By making the requirement that the defendant appear for evaluation a condition of release, the court can more easily take back into custody a defendant who has refused to appear for evaluation, and the defendant can then be evaluated in custody.

1988 Amendment. Title. The title is amended to reflect change in subdivision (a)(1), which broadens the issue of competency in criminal proceedings from the narrow issue of competency to stand trial to competency to proceed at any material stage of a criminal proceeding.

(a) This provision is broadened to prohibit proceeding against a defendant accused of a criminal offense or a violation of probation or community control and is broadened from competency to stand trial to competency to proceed at any material stage of a criminal proceeding as defined in subdivision (1).

Rule 3.210. Incompetence to Proceed: Procedure for Raising the Issue.

(1) This new provision defines a material stage of a criminal proceeding when an incompetent defendant may not be proceeded against. This provision includes competence to be sentenced, which was previously addressed in rule 3.740 and is now addressed with more specificity in the new rule 3.214. Under the Florida Supreme Court decision of Jackson v. State, 452 So.2d 533 (Fla. 1984), this definition would not apply to a motion under rule 3.850.

(2) This new provision allows certain matters in a criminal case to proceed, even if a defendant is determined to be incompetent, in areas not requiring the personal participation of the defendant.

(b) This provision is amended to reflect the changes in subdivision (a) above.

(1) Same as above.

(2) Same as above.

(3) Same as above. This provision also changes the phrase "released from custody on a pretrial release provision" to "released on bail or other release provision" because the term "custody" is subject to several interpretations.

(4) This new provision is designed to specify and clarify in the order appointing experts, the matters the appointed experts are to address, and to specify when and to whom their reports are to be submitted. Court-appointed experts often do not understand the specific purpose of their examination or the specifics of the legal criteria to be applied. Specifying to whom the experts' reports are to be submitted is designed to avoid confusion.

1992 Amendment. The purpose of the amendment is to gender neutralize the wording of the rule.

Introductory Note Relating to Amendments to Rules 3.210 to 3.219. In 1985, the Florida Legislature enacted amendments to part I of chapter 394, the "Florida Mental Health Act," and substantial amendments to chapter 916 entitled "Mentally Deficient and Mentally ill Defendants." The effect of the amendments is to avoid tying mentally ill or deficient defendants in the criminal justice system to civil commitment procedures in the "Baker Act." Reference to commitment of a criminal defendant found not guilty by reason of insanity has been removed from section 394.467, Florida Statutes. Chapter 916 now provides for specific commitment criteria of mentally ill or mentally retarded criminal defendants who are either incompetent to proceed or who have been found not guilty by reason of insanity in criminal proceedings.

In part, the following amendments to rules 3.210 to 3.219 are designed to reflect the 1985 amendments to chapters 394 and 916.

Florida judges on the criminal bench are committing and the Department of Health and Rehabilitative Services (HRS) mental health treatment facilities are admitting and treating those mentally ill and mentally retarded defendants in the criminal justice system who have been adjudged incompetent to stand trial and defendants found to be incompetent to proceed with violation of probation and community control proceedings. Judges are also finding such defendants not guilty by reason of insanity and committing them to HRS for treatment, yet there were no provisions for such commitments in the rules.

Some of the amendments to rules 3.210 to 3.219 are designed to provide for determinations of whether a defendant is mentally competent to proceed in any material stage of a criminal proceeding and provide for community treatment or commitment to HRS when a defendant meets commitment criteria under the provisions of chapter 916 as amended in 1985.

Rule 3.211. Competence to Proceed: Scope of Examination and Report.

(a) Examination by Experts. On appointment by the court, the experts must examine the defendant with respect to the issue of competence to proceed, as specified by the court in its order appointing the experts to evaluate the defendant, and must evaluate the defendant as ordered.

(1) The experts must first consider factors related to the issue of whether the defendant meets the criteria for competence to proceed; that is, whether the defendant has sufficient present ability to consult with counsel with a reasonable degree of rational understanding and whether the defendant has a rational, as well as factual, understanding of the pending proceedings.

(2) In considering the issue of competence to proceed, the examining experts must consider and include in their report:

(A) the defendant's capacity to:

(i) appreciate the charges or allegations against the defendant;

(ii) appreciate the range and nature of possible penalties, if applicable, that may be imposed in the proceedings against the defendant;

(iii) understand the adversary nature of the legal process;

(iv) disclose to counsel facts pertinent to the proceedings at issue;

(v) manifest appropriate courtroom behavior;

(vi) testify relevantly; and

(B) any other factors deemed relevant by the experts.

(b) Factors to Be Evaluated. If the experts should find that the defendant is incompetent to proceed, the experts must report on any recommended treatment for the defendant to attain competence to proceed. In considering the issues relating to treatment, the examining experts must report on:

(1) the mental illness or intellectual disability causing the incompetence;

(2) the completion of a clinical assessment by approved mental health experts trained by the department to ensure safety of the patient and the community;

(3) the treatment or treatments appropriate for the mental illness or intellectual disability of the defendant and an explanation of each of the possible treatment alternatives, including, at a minimum, mental health services, treatment services, rehabilitative services, support services, and case management services as described in s. 394.67, which may be provided by or within multi-disciplinary community treatment teams, such as Florida Assertive Community Treatment, conditional release programs, outpatient services or intensive outpatient treatment programs, and supportive employment and supportive housing opportunities in treating and supporting the recovery of the patient;

(4) the availability of acceptable treatment. If treatment is available in the community, the expert must so state in the report; and

(5) the likelihood of the defendant attaining competence under the treatment recommended, an assessment of the probable duration of the treatment required to restore competence, and

the probability that the defendant will attain competence to proceed in the foreseeable future.

(c) Written Findings of Experts. Any written report submitted by the experts must:

(1) identify the specific matters referred for evaluation;

(2) describe the evaluative procedures, techniques, and tests used in the examination and the purpose or purposes for each;

(3) state the expert's clinical observations, findings, and opinions on each issue referred for evaluation by the court, and indicate specifically those issues, if any, on which the expert could not give an opinion;

(4) identify the sources of information used by the expert and present the factual basis for the expert's clinical findings and opinions; and

(5) include a full and detailed explanation regarding why the alternative treatment options referenced in the evaluation are insufficient to meet the needs of the defendant.

The procedure for determinations of the confidential status of reports is governed by Rule of General Practice and Judicial Administration 2.420.

(d) Limited Use of Competency Evidence.

(1) The information contained in any motion by the defendant for determination of competency to proceed or in any report of experts filed under this rule insofar as the report relates solely to the issues of competency to proceed and commitment, and any information elicited during a hearing on competency to proceed or commitment held under this rule, must be used only in determining the mental competency to proceed or the commitment or other treatment of the defendant.

(2) The defendant waives this provision by using the report, or portions thereof, in any proceeding for any other purpose, in which case disclosure and use of the report, or any portion thereof, are governed by applicable rules of evidence and rules of criminal procedure. If a part of the report is used by the defendant, the state may request the production of any other portion of that report that, in fairness, ought to be considered.

Committee Notes

1980 Adoption. This rule provides for appointment of experts and for the contents of the report which the experts are to render. Since

Rule 3.211. Competence to Proceed: Scope of Examination and Report.

the issue of competency has been raised, the experts will, of course, report on this issue. If there is reason to believe that involuntary hospitalization is also required, the court should order the experts to make this evaluation as well during their initial examination. It was felt, however, that the experts should not inquire into involuntary hospitalization as a matter of course, but only if sufficient reasonable grounds to do so were alleged in the motion, comparing the procedure to that required by the civil commitment process.

(a) Certain factors relating to competency to stand trial have been determined to be appropriate for analysis by examining experts. Often, with different experts involved, the experts do not use the same criteria in reaching their conclusions. The criteria used by experts who testify at the competency and commitment hearings may not be the same as those used by persons involved in the treatment process or later hearings after treatment. This subdivision, therefore, addresses those factors which, at least, should be considered by experts at both ends of the spectrum. Additional factors may be considered, and these factors listed may be addressed in different ways. At least the requirement that these specific factors be addressed will give a common basis of understanding for the experts at the competency hearing, the trial judge, and the experts who will later receive a defendant who is found to be incompetent to stand trial and in need of involuntary hospitalization. The test for determining competency to stand trial is that which has been contained in both the prior rules and statutes developed from Dusky v. United States, 362 U.S. 402, 80 S.Ct. 788, 4 L.Ed.2d 824 (1960).

(1) The factors set forth in this section have been developed by the Department of Health and Rehabilitative Services (HRS) in its Competency Evaluation Instrument, a refinement of the McGarry Competency Evaluation Procedure.

(b) The issue of involuntary hospitalization is to be considered only if the court has ordered the experts to consider this issue; the court would do so if it found that there existed reasonable grounds to believe that the defendant met the criteria for involuntary hospitalization. The factors set forth in order to determine this issue are those that have been developed through prior statutes relating to involuntary hospitalization, from the case of Jackson v. Indiana,

406 U.S. 715, 92 S.Ct. 1845, 32 L.Ed.2d 435 (1972), and In Re: Beverly, 342 So.2d 481 (Fla. 1977).

As to criteria for involuntary hospitalization, see chapter 394, Florida Statutes, or, in the case of mental retardation, see chapter 393, Florida Statutes.

Section 394.467(1), Florida Statutes (1979), prescribes criteria for involuntary hospitalization or placement. In case of mental retardation, section 393.11, Florida Statutes (1979), governs.

(c) In most instances, the issues of incompetency at time of trial and insanity at time of the offense will be raised at the same time or, at least, in the same case. In the event that the 2 are not raised in the same case, there would be no reason for the examining experts to inquire into the mental status of the defendant at the time of the offense itself at the incompetency examination. However, if insanity as a defense is raised, it would be most appropriate for judicial efficiency to have the examining experts inquire into all issues at the same time. This provision permits such inquiry by the experts in the event that notice of intent to rely on the defense of insanity has been filed by the defendant.

(d) This provision is meant to permit local circuits to develop their own forms for such reports if they feel that such forms are appropriate. It does not preclude HRS from suggesting a form that would be of particular assistance to them and requesting its adoption, but adoption is not mandated.

(e) This subdivision provides for the confidentiality of the information obtained by virtue of an examination of the defendant pursuant to this subdivision. Cf. § 90.108, Fla.Stat. (1979); Fla.R.Civ.P. 1.330(6).

Section 916.12, Florida Statutes is a companion statute relating to mental competence to stand trial.

1988 Amendment. Title. The title is amended to reflect changes in rule 3.210.

(a) This subdivision, which was originally an introductory paragraph, is amended to reflect changes in rule 3.210. The deletions related to the extent of the evaluation and when and to whom the experts' reports are to be submitted have been placed in rule 3.210(4) above.

(1) This subdivision, which was formerly subdivision (a), has been amended to reflect changes in rule 3.210 above.

Rule 3.211. Competence to Proceed: Scope of Examination and Report.

(2) This provision has been amended to reflect the changes to rule 3.210. In addition, the 11 factors previously numbered (i) through (xi) have been reduced to 6 factors. Numbers (v), (vi), (vii), (x), and (xi) have been removed. Those 5 factors were felt to not be directly related to the issue of a defendant having the mental capacity to communicate with his or her attorney or to understand the proceedings against him or her and may have had the effect of confusing the issues the experts are to address in assessing a defendant's competency to proceed. The terms "ability" and "capacity" which were used interchangeably in the prior version of this provision have been changed to the single term "capacity" for continuity. A provision has been added which allows the appointed expert to also include any other factors deemed relevant to take into account different techniques and points of view of the experts.

(b) This subdivision, including its 4 subdivisions, is amended to reflect the changes in rule 3.210. It also expands the determination from the limited area of whether an incompetent defendant should be voluntarily committed to treatment to recommended treatment options designed to restore or maintain competence. Subdivision (v) has been deleted because consideration of less restrictive alternatives is addressed in other amendments. [See rule 3.212(c)(3)(iv).] The amendments further reflect 1985 legislative amendments to chapters 394 and 916, Florida Statutes.

(ii) Appropriate treatment may include maintaining the defendant on psychotropic or other medication. See rule 3.215.

(c) This provision is amended to take into account the defense of insanity both at trial and in violation of probation community control hearings.

(d) This provision deletes the old language relating to the use of standardized forms. The new provision, with its 4 subdivisions, outlines in detail what the written report of an expert is to include, to ensure the appointed expert understands what issues are to be addressed, and that the report identifies sources of information, tests or evaluation techniques used, and includes the findings and observations upon which the expert's opinion is based. It requires the expert to specify those issues on which the expert could not render an opinion.

(e) This provision is amended to comply with changes in rule 3.210. In addition, the second paragraph has been expanded to clarify under what circumstances the reports of experts in a competency evaluation may be discovered by the prosecution and used as evidence in a hearing other than the hearing on the issue of a defendant's competency to proceed.

1992 Amendment. The purpose of the amendments is to gender neutralize the wording of the rule.

Introductory Note Relating to Amendments to Rules 3.210 to 3.219. See notes following rule 3.210 for the text of this note.

Rule 3.212. Competence to Proceed: Hearing and Disposition.

(a) Admissibility of Evidence. The experts preparing the reports may be called by either party or the court, and additional evidence may be introduced by either party. The experts appointed by the court are deemed court witnesses whether called by the court or either party and may be examined as such by either party.

(b) Finding of Competence. The court must first consider the issue of the defendant's competence to proceed. If the court finds the defendant competent to proceed, the court must enter its order so finding and proceed.

(c) Commitment on Finding of Incompetence. If the court finds the defendant is incompetent to proceed, or that the defendant is competent to proceed but that the defendant's competence depends on the continuation of appropriate treatment for a mental illness or intellectual disability, the court must consider issues relating to treatment necessary to restore or maintain the defendant's competence to proceed.

> **(1)** The court may order the defendant to undergo treatment if the court finds that the defendant is mentally ill or intellectually disabled and is in need of treatment and that treatment appropriate for the defendant's condition is available. If the court finds that the defendant may be treated in the community on bail or other release conditions, the court may make acceptance of reasonable medical treatment a condition of continuing bail or other release conditions.
>
> **(2)** If the defendant is incarcerated, the court may order treatment to be administered at the custodial facility or may order the defendant transferred to another facility for treatment or may commit the defendant as provided in subdivision (3).

Rule 3.212. Competence to Proceed: Hearing and Disposition.

(3) A defendant may be committed for treatment to restore a defendant's competence to proceed if the court finds that:

(A) the defendant meets the criteria for commitment as set forth by statute;

(B) there is a substantial probability that the mental illness or intellectual disability causing the defendant's incompetence will respond to treatment and that the defendant will regain competency to proceed in the reasonably foreseeable future;

(C) treatment appropriate for restoration of the defendant's competence to proceed is available;

(D) no appropriate treatment alternative less restrictive than that involving commitment is available; and

(E) other mental health services, treatment services, support services, and case management services as described in section 394.67, Florida Statutes, would be inappropriate.

(4) If the court commits the defendant, the order of commitment must contain:

(A) findings of fact relating to the issues of competency and commitment addressing the factors set forth in rule 3.211 when applicable;

(B) copies of the reports of the experts filed with the court under the order of examination;

(C) copies of any other psychiatric, psychological, or social work reports submitted to the court relative to the mental state of the defendant; and

(D) copies of the charging instrument and all supporting affidavits or other documents used in the determination of probable cause.

(5) Before issuing a commitment order, the court must review the examining expert's report to ensure alternative treatment options have been fully considered and found insufficient to meet the needs of the defendant.

(6) The treatment facility must admit the defendant for hospitalization and treatment and may retain and treat the defendant. No later than 60 days from the date of admission, the administrator of the facility must file with the court a report that addresses the issues and considers the factors set forth in rule 3.211, with copies to all parties. If, at any time during the 60 day period or during any period of extended commitment that may be ordered under this rule, the administrator of the facility determines that the defendant no longer meets the criteria for commitment or has become competent to proceed, the administrator must notify the court by such a report, with copies to all parties.

>**(A)** If, during the 60 day period of commitment and treatment or during any period of extended commitment that may be ordered under this rule, counsel for the defendant must have reasonable grounds to believe that the defendant is competent to proceed or no longer meets the criteria for commitment, counsel may move for a hearing on the issue of the defendant's competence or commitment. The motion must contain a certificate of counsel that the motion is made in good faith and on reasonable grounds to believe that the defendant is now competent to proceed or no longer meets the criteria for commitment. To the extent that it does not invade the attorney-client privilege, the motion must contain a recital of the specific observations of and conversations with the defendant that have formed the basis for the motion.

>**(B)** If, on consideration of a motion filed by counsel for the defendant or the prosecuting attorney and any information offered the court in support thereof, the court has reasonable grounds to believe that the defendant may have regained competence to proceed or no longer meets the criteria for commitment, the court must order the administrator of the facility to report to the court on such issues, with copies to all parties, and must order a hearing to be held on those issues.

(7) The court must hold a hearing within 30 days of the receipt of the report from the administrator of the facility. If, following the hearing, the court determines that the defendant continues to be incompetent to proceed and that the defendant meets the criteria for continued commitment or treatment, the court must order continued commitment or treatment for a period not to exceed 1 year. When the defendant is retained by the facility, the same procedure must be repeated prior to the expiration of each additional 1-year period of extended commitment.

Rule 3.212. Competence to Proceed: Hearing and Disposition.

(8) If, at any time after such commitment, the court decides, after hearing, that the defendant is competent to proceed, it must enter its order so finding and proceed.

(9) If, after any such hearing, the court determines that the defendant remains incompetent to proceed but no longer meets the criteria for commitment, the court must proceed as provided in rule 3.212(d).

(d) Release on Finding of Incompetence. If the court decides that a defendant is not mentally competent to proceed and there is a substantial probability that the defendant will gain competency to proceed in the foreseeable future, but does not meet the criteria for commitment, the defendant may be released on appropriate release conditions. The court may order that the defendant receive outpatient treatment at an appropriate local facility and that the defendant report for further evaluation at specified times during the release period as conditions of release. A report must be filed with the court after each evaluation by the persons appointed by the court to make such evaluations, with copies to all parties. The procedure for determinations of the confidential status of reports is governed by Rule of General Practice and Judicial Administration 2.420. If a defendant is found to be mentally incompetent to proceed and there is no substantial probability that the defendant will gain competency to proceed in the foreseeable future, the defendant must be released, or the State must initiate civil commitment proceedings.

Committee Notes

1980 Adoption. This rule sets forth the procedure for the hearing itself. If other experts have been involved who were not appointed pursuant to this rule, provision is made that such experts may then be called by either party. Those experts appointed by the court to conduct the examination, if called by the court or by either party to testify at the hearing, will be regarded as court experts. Either party may then examine such experts by leading questions or may impeach such experts. If a party calls an expert witness other than those appointed by the court pursuant to these rules, the usual evidentiary rules of examining such witnesses shall then apply. Following the hearing, the court may come to one of 3 conclusions: (a) the defendant is competent to stand trial, rule 3.212(a); (b) the defendant is incompetent to stand trial and is in need of involuntary hospitalization, rule 3.212(b); or (c) the defendant is incompetent to stand trial but is not in need of involuntary hospitalization, rule 3.212(c).

(a) This provision has been contained in every prior rule or statute relating to the issues of competency to stand trial and provides that if the defendant is competent the trial shall commence. No change is recommended.

(b) This subdivision provides for the second possible finding of the court, namely that the defendant is found incompetent to stand trial and is in need of involuntary hospitalization. It is designed to track the provisions of chapter 394, Florida Statutes, relating to involuntary hospitalization and the provisions of chapter 393 relating to residential services insofar as they may apply to the defendant under criminal charges. In this way, the procedures to be set up by the institution to which a criminal defendant is sent should not vary greatly from procedures common to the institution in the involuntary hospitalization or residential treatment of those not subject to criminal charges.

The criteria for involuntary hospitalization are set forth in section 394.467(1), Florida Statutes (1979). As to involuntary hospitalization for mental retardation, see section 393.11, Florida Statutes (1979); definition of treatment facility, see section 394.455, Florida Statutes (1979); involuntary admission to residential services, see section 393.11, Florida Statutes (1979).

(2) The requirement that there be certain contents to the order of commitment is set forth in order to give greater assistance to the personnel of the treatment facility. The information to be included in the order should give them the benefit of all information that has been before the trial judge and has been considered by that judge in making the decision to involuntarily hospitalize the defendant. This information should then assist the personnel of the receiving institution in making their initial evaluation and in instituting appropriate treatment more quickly. The last requirement, that of supporting affidavits or other documents used in the determination of probable cause, is to give some indication of the nature of the offense to the examining doctors to enable them to determine when the defendant has reached a level of improvement that he or she can discuss the charge with "a reasonable degree of rational understanding."

(3) This subdivision is designed to correspond with a complementary section of the Florida Statutes. It mandates, as does the statute, that the treatment facility must admit the defendant

Rule 3.212. Competence to Proceed: Hearing and Disposition.

for hospitalization and treatment. The time limitations set forth in this subdivision are designed to coincide with those set forth in chapter 394, Florida Statutes. If, however, the defendant should regain competence or no longer meets hospitalization criteria prior to the expiration of any of the time periods set, the administrator of the facility may report to the court and cause a re-evaluation of the defendant's mental status. At the end of the 6-month period, and every year thereafter, the administrator must report to the court. These time periods are set forth so as to coincide with chapter 394, Florida Statutes.

(i) Permits the defendant's attorney, in an appropriate case, to request a hearing if the attorney believes the defendant to have regained competency. The grounds for such belief are to be contained in the motion, as is a certificate of the good faith of counsel in filing it. If the motion is sufficient to give the court reasonable grounds to believe that the defendant may be competent or no longer meets the criteria for hospitalization, the court can order a report from the administrator and hold a hearing on the issues.

(4) The rule is meant to mandate that the court hold a hearing as quickly as possible, but the hearing must be held at least within 30 days of the receipt of the report from the administrator of the facility.

(c) This rule provides for the disposition of the defendant who falls under the third of the alternatives listed above, that is, one who is incompetent to stand trial but does not meet the provisions for involuntary hospitalization. It is meant to provide as great a flexibility as possible for the trial judge in handling such defendant. As to criteria for involuntary hospitalization, see section 394.467(1), Florida Statutes (1979).

Section 916.13, Florida Statutes complements this rule and provides for the hospitalization of defendants adjudicated incompetent to stand trial.

1988 Amendment. Title. The title has been amended to reflect changes in rules 3.210 and 3.211.

(a) This provision was formerly the introductory paragraph to this rule. It has been labeled subdivision (a) for consistency in form.

(b) This provision was former subdivision (a). It has been amended to reflect changes in rules 3.210 and 3.211. The former subdivisions

(b) and (b)(1) have been deleted because similar language is now found in new subdivision (c).

(c) This new provision, including all its subdivisions, is designed to reflect the commitment criteria in section 916.13(1), Florida Statutes, and to reflect that commitment to the Department of Health and Rehabilitative Services is to be tied to specific commitment criteria when no less restrictive treatment alternative is available.

(1) This provision provides for available community treatment when appropriate.

(2) This provision provides for treatment in a custodial facility or other available community residential program.

(3) This provision, and its subdivisions, outlines when a defendant may be committed and refers to commitment criteria under the provisions of section 916.13(1), Florida Statutes.

(4) This provision, and its subdivisions, was formerly subdivision (b)(2). The language has been amended to reflect changes in chapter 916 relating to the commitment of persons found incompetent to proceed and changes in rules 3.210 and 3.211.

(5) This provision, and its subdivisions, was formerly subdivision (b)(3). The amendments are for the same reasons as (4) above.

(6) This provision was formerly subdivision (b)(4). The amendments are for the same reasons as (4) above.

(7) This provision was formerly subdivision (b)(5). The amendments are for the same reasons as (4) above.

(8) This provision was formerly subdivision (b)(6). The amendments are for the same reasons as (4) above.

(d) The amendments to the provision are for the same reasons as (4) above.

1992 Amendment. The amendments substitute "shall" in place of "may" in subdivision (c)(5)(B) to require the trial court to order the administrator of the facility where an incompetent defendant has been committed to report to the court on the issue of competency when the court has reasonable grounds to believe that the defendant may have regained competence to proceed or no longer meets the criteria for commitment. The amendments also gender neutralize the wording of the rule.

Introductory Note Relating to Amendments to Rules 3.210 to 3.219. See notes following rule 3.210 for the text of this note.

Rule 3.213. Continuing Incompetency to Proceed, Except Incompetency to Proceed with Sentencing; Disposition.

(a) Dismissal without Prejudice during Continuing Incompetency. After a determination that a person is incompetent to stand trial or proceed with a probation or community control violation hearing, the charge(s):

(1) shall be dismissed 1 year after a finding if the charge is a misdemeanor;

(2) shall be dismissed no later than 2 years after a finding if incompetency is due to intellectual disability or autism;

(3) may be dismissed 3 years after a finding, unless a charge is listed in section 916.145, Florida Statutes; or

(4) shall be dismissed after a finding that the defendant has remained incompetent for 5 continuous and uninterrupted years;

provided that the court finds that the defendant remains incompetent to stand trial or proceed with a probation or community control violation hearing unless the court in its order specifies its reasons for believing that the defendant is expected to become competent to proceed. A dismissal under this rule shall be without prejudice to the state to refile the charge(s) should the defendant be declared competent to proceed in the future.

(b) Commitment or Treatment during Continuing Incompetency.

(1) If the defendant meets the criteria for commitment under section 394.467, Florida Statutes, the court shall commit the defendant to the Department of Children and Families for involuntary hospitalization solely under the provisions of law. If the defendant meets the criteria of section 394.4655, Florida Statutes, the court may order that the defendant receive outpatient treatment at any other facility or service on an outpatient basis subject to the provisions of those statutes. In the order of commitment, the judge shall order that the administrator of an inpatient facility notify the state attorney of the committing circuit no less than 30 days prior to the anticipated date of release of the defendant.

(2) If the continuing incompetency is due to intellectual disability or autism, and the defendant either lacks the ability to provide for his or her well-being or is likely to physically injure himself or herself, or others, the defendant may be involuntarily admitted to residential services as provided by law.

(c) Applicability. This rule shall not apply to defendants determined to be incompetent to proceed with sentencing, which is addressed in rule 3.214.

Committee Notes

1980 Adoption. As to involuntary hospitalization, see section 394.467(1), Florida Statutes (1979); as to involuntary admission to residential services, see chapter 393, Florida Statutes (1979).

(b) This provision is meant to deal with the defendant who remains incompetent after 5 years, and who does meet the criteria for involuntary hospitalization. It provides that the criminal charges will be dismissed and the defendant will be involuntarily hospitalized. It further provides that the administrator of the facility must notify the state attorney prior to any release of a defendant committed pursuant to this subdivision.

As to criteria for involuntary hospitalization, see section 394.467(1), Florida Statutes (1979); in case of retardation, see chapter 393, Florida Statutes (1979).

(c) Since commitment criteria for a defendant determined to be incompetent to stand trial are the same as for civil hospitalization, there is no need to continue the difference between felony and misdemeanor procedure.

Section 916.14, Florida Statutes, makes the statute of limitations and defense of former jeopardy inapplicable to criminal charges dismissed because of incompetence of defendant to stand trial.

1988 Amendment. Title. The title has been amended to comply with changes in rule 3.210, but specifically excludes competency to proceed with sentencing, which is addressed in the new rule 3.214.

(a) This provision was amended to reflect changes in rules 3.210 and 3.211. New language is added which specifies that, if charges are dismissed under this rule, it is without prejudice to the state to refile if the defendant is declared competent to proceed in the future. Similar language was previously found in rule 3.214(d), but is more appropriate under this rule.

Rule 3.214. Incompetency to Proceed to Sentencing: Disposition.

(b) This provision has been amended for the same reasons as (a) above.

(c) This new provision specifically exempts this rule from being used against a defendant determined to be incompetent to be sentenced, which is now provided in the new rule 3.214. It is replaced by the new rule 3.214.

1992 Amendment. The purpose of the amendment is to gender neutralize the wording of the rule.

Introductory Note Relating to Amendments to Rules 3.210 to 3.219. See notes following rule 3.210 for the text of this note.

Rule 3.214. Incompetency to Proceed to Sentencing: Disposition.

If a defendant is determined to be incompetent to proceed after being found guilty of an offense or violation of probation or community control or after voluntarily entering a plea to an offense or violation of probation or community control, but prior to sentencing, the court shall postpone the pronouncement of sentence and proceed pursuant to rule 3.210 (et seq.) and the following rules.

Committee Notes

1988 Amendment. Title. This new rule replaces the former rule 3.740. It was felt to be more appropriately addressed in this sequence. The former rule 3.214 is now renumbered 3.215. The former rule 3.740 used the inappropriate phrase "(p)rocedures when insanity is alleged as cause for not pronouncing sentence." Insanity is an affirmative defense to a criminal charge. The more correct term is "incompetence to proceed to sentencing."

(a) This new provision reiterates amendments to rule 3.210 and provides that sentencing shall be postponed for a defendant incompetent to proceed with disposition of a criminal matter-to include a finding of guilt at trial, after entry of a voluntary plea, or after a violation of probation or community control proceeding.

Introductory Note Relating to Amendments to Rules 3.210 to 3.219. See notes following rule 3.210 for the text of this note.

Rule 3.215. Effect of Adjudication of Incompetency to Proceed: Psychotropic Medication.

(a) Former Jeopardy. If the defendant is declared incompetent to stand trial during trial and afterwards declared competent to stand trial, the defendant's other uncompleted trial shall not constitute former jeopardy.

(b) Limited Application of Incompetency Adjudication. An adjudication of incompetency to proceed shall not operate as an adjudication of incompetency to consent to medical treatment or for any other purpose unless such other adjudication is specifically set forth in the order.

(c) Psychotropic Medication. A defendant who, because of psychotropic medication, is able to understand the proceedings and to assist in the defense shall not automatically be deemed incompetent to proceed simply because the defendant's satisfactory mental condition is dependent on such medication, nor shall the defendant be prohibited from proceeding solely because the defendant is being administered medication under medical supervision for a mental or emotional condition.

(1) Psychotropic medication is any drug or compound affecting the mind, behavior, intellectual functions, perception, moods, or emotion and includes anti-psychotic, anti-depressant, anti-manic, and anti-anxiety drugs.

(2) If the defendant proceeds to trial with the aid of medication for a mental or emotional condition, on the motion of defense counsel, the jury shall, at the beginning of the trial and in the charge to the jury, be given explanatory instructions regarding such medication.

Committee Notes

1980 Adoption. (c) As to psychotropic medications, see section 916.12(2), Florida Statutes (1980).

(d) This subdivision is intended to provide specific exceptions to the speedy trial rule.

1988 Amendment. Title. This rule was formerly rule 3.214.

The amendments to this rule, including the title, are designed to reflect amendments to rules 3.210 and 3.211.

(d) Matters contained in former subsection (d) are covered by the provisions of rule 3.191. That subsection has therefore been deleted.

1992 Amendment. The purpose of the amendment is to gender neutralize the wording of the rule.

Introductory Note Relating to Amendments to Rules 3.210 to 3.219. See notes following rule 3.210 for the text of this note.

Rule 3.216. Insanity At Time of Offense or Probation or Community Control Violation: Notice and Appointment of Experts.

(a) Expert to Aid Defense Counsel. When in any criminal case a defendant is adjudged to be indigent or partially indigent, and is not represented by the public defender or regional counsel, and counsel has reason to believe that the defendant may be incompetent to proceed or that the defendant may have been insane at the time of the offense or probation or community control violation, counsel may so inform the court who shall appoint 1 expert to examine the defendant in order to assist counsel in the preparation of the defense. The expert shall report only to the attorney for the defendant and matters related to the expert shall be deemed to fall under the lawyer-client privilege.

(b) Notice of Intent to Rely on Insanity Defense. When in any criminal case it shall be the intention of the defendant to rely on the defense of insanity either at trial or probation or community control violation hearing, no evidence offered by the defendant for the purpose of establishing that defense shall be admitted in the case unless advance notice in writing of the defense shall have been given by the defendant as hereinafter provided.

(c) Time for Filing Notice. The defendant shall give notice of intent to rely on the defense of insanity no later than 15 days after the arraignment or the filing of a written plea of not guilty in the case when the defense of insanity is to be relied on at trial or no later than 15 days after being brought before the appropriate court to answer to the allegations in a violation of probation or community control proceeding. If counsel for the defendant shall have reasonable grounds to believe that the defendant may be incompetent to proceed, the notice shall be given at the same time that the motion for examination into the defendant's competence is filed. The notice shall contain a statement of particulars showing the nature of the insanity the defendant expects to prove and the names and addresses of the witnesses by whom the defendant expects to show insanity, insofar as is possible.

(d) Court-Ordered Evaluations. On the filing of such notice and on motion of the state, the court shall order the defendant to be examined by the state's mental health expert(s) as to the sanity or insanity of the defendant at the time of the commission of the alleged offense or probation or community control violation.

Attorneys for the state and defendant may be present at the examination.

(e) Time for Filing Notice of Intent to Rely on a Mental Health Defense Other than Insanity. The defendant shall give notice of intent to rely on any mental health defense other than insanity as soon as a good faith determination has been made to utilize the defense but in no event later than 30 days prior to trial. The notice shall contain a statement of particulars showing the nature of the defense the defendant expects to prove and the names and addresses of the witnesses by whom the defendant expects to prove the defense, insofar as possible. If expert testimony will be presented, the notice shall indicate whether the expert has examined the defendant.

(f) Court-Ordered Experts for Other Mental Health Defenses. If the notice to rely on any mental health defense other than insanity indicates the defendant will rely on the testimony of an expert who has examined the defendant, the court shall upon motion of the state order the defendant be examined by one qualified expert for the state as to the mental health defense raised by the defendant. Upon a showing of good cause, the court may order additional examinations upon motion by the state or the defendant. Attorneys for the state and defendant may be present at the examination. When the defendant relies on the testimony of an expert who has not examined the defendant, the state shall not be entitled to a compulsory examination of the defendant.

(g) Waiver of Time to File. On good cause shown for the omission of the notice of intent to rely on the defense of insanity or any mental health defense, the court may in its discretion grant the defendant 10 days to comply with the notice requirement. If leave is granted and the defendant files the notice, the defendant is deemed unavailable to proceed. If the trial has already commenced, the court, only on motion of the defendant, may declare a mistrial in order to permit the defendant to raise the defense of insanity pursuant to this rule. Any motion for mistrial shall constitute a waiver of the defendant's right to any claim of former jeopardy arising from the uncompleted trial.

(h) Evaluating Defendant after Pretrial Release. If the defendant has been released on bail or other release conditions, the court may order the defendant to appear at a designated place for evaluation at a specific time as a condition of the release provision. If the court determines that the defendant will not submit to the

Rule 3.216. Insanity At Time of Offense or Probation or Community Control Violation: Notice and Appointment of Experts.

evaluation provided for herein or that the defendant is not likely to appear for the scheduled evaluation, the court may order the defendant taken into custody until the evaluation is completed. A motion made for evaluation under this subdivision shall not otherwise affect the defendant's right to pretrial release.

(i) Evidence. Any experts appointed by the court may be summoned to testify at the trial, and shall be deemed court witnesses whether called by the court or by either party. Other evidence regarding the defendant's insanity or mental condition may be introduced by either party. At trial, in its instructions to the jury, the court shall include an instruction on the consequences of a verdict of not guilty by reason of insanity.

Committee Notes

1980 Adoption. (a) This subdivision is based on Pouncy v. State, 353 So.2d 640 (Fla. 3d DCA 1977), and provides that an expert may be provided for an indigent defendant. The appointment of the expert will in this way allow the public defender or court-appointed attorney to screen possible incompetency or insanity cases and give a basis for determining whether issues of incompetency or insanity ought to be raised before the court; it will also permit the defense attorney to specify in greater detail in the statement of particulars the nature of the insanity that attorney expects to prove, if any, and the basis for the raising of that defense.

(b) Essentially the same as in prior rules; provides that written notice must be given in advance by the defendant.

(c) Since counsel for indigents often are not appointed until arraignment and since it is sometimes difficult for a defendant to make a determination on whether the defense of insanity should be raised prior to arraignment, a 15-day post-arraignment period is provided for the filing of the notice. The defendant must raise incompetency at the same time as insanity, if at all possible. With the appointment of the expert to assist, the defendant should be able to raise both issues at the same time if grounds for both exist. The remainder of the rule, providing for the statement to be included in the notice, is essentially the same as that in prior rules.

(d) The appointment of experts provision is designed to track, insofar as possible, the provisions for appointment of experts contained in the rules relating to incompetency to stand trial and in the Florida Statutes relating to appointment of expert witnesses.

Insofar as possible, the single examination should include incompetency, involuntary commitment issues where there are reasonable grounds for their consideration, and issues of insanity at time of the offense. Judicial economy would mandate such a single examination where possible.

(g) In order to obtain more standardized reports, specific items relating to the examination are required of the examining experts. See note to rule 3.211(a).

(h) Essentially the substance of prior rule 3.210(e)(4) and (5), with some changes. Both prior provisions are combined into a single provision; speedy trial time limits are no longer set forth, but waiver of double jeopardy is mandated.

(i) Same as rule 3.210(b)(3), relating to incompetency to stand trial. See commentary to that rule.

(j) A restatement of former rule 3.210(e)(7). The provision that experts called by the court shall be deemed court witnesses is new. The former provision relating to free access to the defendant is eliminated as unnecessary.

As to appointment of experts, see section 912.11, Florida Statutes.

1988 Amendment. The amendments to this rule, including the title, provide for the affirmative defense of insanity in violation of probation or community control proceedings as well as at trial.

1992 Amendment. The purpose of the amendment is to gender neutralize the wording of the rule.

1996 Amendment. Subdivisions (e) and (f) were added to conform to State v. Hickson, 630 So.2d 172 (Fla. 1993). These amendments are not intended to expand existing case law.

Introductory Note Relating to Amendments to Rules 3.210 to 3.219. See notes following rule 3.210 for the text of this note.

Rule 3.217. Judgment of Not Guilty by Reason of Insanity; Disposition of Defendant.

(a) Verdict of Not Guilty by Reason of Insanity. When a person is found by the jury or the court not guilty of the offense or is found not to be in violation of probation or community control by reason of insanity, the jury or judge, in giving the verdict or finding of not guilty judgment, shall state that it was given for that reason.

(b) Treatment, Commitment, or Discharge after Acquittal. When a person is found not guilty of the offense or is found not to be in violation of probation or community control by reason of insanity, if the court then determines that the defendant presently meets the criteria set forth by law, the court shall commit the defendant to the Department of Children and Families or shall order outpatient treatment at any other appropriate facility or service, or shall discharge the defendant. Any order committing the defendant or requiring outpatient treatment or other outpatient service shall contain:

(1) findings of fact relating to the issue of commitment or other court-ordered treatment;

(2) copies of any reports of experts filed with the court; and

(3) any other psychiatric, psychological, or social work report submitted to the court relative to the mental state of the defendant.

Committee Notes

1980 Adoption.

(a) Same substance as in prior rule.

(b) The criteria for commitment are set forth in chapter 394, Florida Statutes. This rule incorporates those statutory criteria by reference and then restates the other alternatives available to the judge under former rule 3.210.

See section 912.18, Florida Statutes, for criteria.

(1) This subdivision is equivalent to rule 3.212(b)(2); see commentary to that rule.

1988 Amendment. The amendments to this rule provide for evaluation of a defendant found not guilty by reason of insanity in violation of probation or community control proceedings as well as at trial. The amendments further reflect 1985 amendments to chapter 916, Florida Statutes.

1992 Amendment. The purpose of the amendment is to gender neutralize the wording of the rule.

Introductory Note Relating to Amendments to Rules 3.210 to 3.219. See notes following rule 3.210 for the text of this note.

Rule 3.218. Commitment of a Defendant Found Not Guilty by Reason of Insanity.

(a) Commitment; 6-Month Report. The Department of Children and Families shall admit to an appropriate facility a defendant found not guilty by reason of insanity under rule 3.217 and found to meet the criteria for commitment for hospitalization and treatment and may retain and treat the defendant. No later than 6 months from the date of admission, the administrator of the facility shall file with the court a report, and provide copies to all parties, which shall address the issues of further commitment of the defendant. If at any time during the 6-month period, or during any period of extended hospitalization that may be ordered under this rule, the administrator of the facility shall determine that the defendant no longer meets the criteria for commitment, the administrator shall notify the court by such a report and provide copies to all parties. The procedure for determinations of the confidential status of reports is governed by Rule of General Practice and Judicial Administration 2.420.

(b) Right to Hearing if Committed upon Acquittal. The court shall hold a hearing within 30 days of the receipt of any report from the administrator of the facility on the issues raised thereby, and the defendant shall have a right to be present at the hearing. If the court determines that the defendant continues to meet the criteria for continued commitment or treatment, the court shall order further commitment or treatment for a period not to exceed 1 year. The same procedure shall be repeated before the expiration of each additional 1-year period in which the defendant is retained by the facility.

(c) Evidence to Determine Continuing Insanity. Before any hearing held under this rule, the court may, on its own motion, and shall, on motion of counsel for the state or defendant, appoint no fewer than 2 nor more than 3 experts to examine the defendant relative to the criteria for continued commitment or placement of the defendant and shall specify the date by which the experts shall report to the court on these issues and provide copies to all parties.

Committee Notes

1980 Adoption. This provision provides for hospitalization of a defendant found not guilty by reason of insanity and is meant to track similar provisions in the rules relating to competency to stand trial and the complementary statutes. It provides for an initial 6-month period of commitment with successive 1-year periods; it provides for reports to the court and for the appointment of experts to examine the defendant when such hearings are necessary. The underlying rationale of this rule is to make standard, insofar as possible, the commitment process, whether it be for incompetency to stand trial or following a judgment of not guilty by reason of insanity.

For complementary statute providing for hospitalization of defendant adjudicated not guilty by reason of insanity, see section 912.15, Florida Statutes.

1988 Amendment. The amendments to this rule, including the title, provide for commitment of defendants found not guilty by reason of insanity in violation of probation or community control proceedings, as well as those so found at trial. The amendments further reflect 1985 amendments to chapter 916, Florida Statutes.

Introductory Note Relating to Amendments to Rules 3.210 to 3.219. See notes following rule 3.210 for the text of this note.

Rule 3.219. Conditional Release.

(a) Release Plan. The committing court may order a conditional release of any defendant who has been committed according to a finding of incompetency to proceed or an adjudication of not guilty by reason of insanity based on an approved plan for providing appropriate outpatient care and treatment. When the administrator shall determine outpatient treatment of the defendant to be appropriate, the administrator may file with the court, and provide copies to all parties, a written plan for outpatient treatment, including recommendations from qualified professionals. The plan may be submitted by the defendant. The plan shall include:

(1) special provisions for residential care, adequate supervision of the defendant, or both;

(2) provisions for outpatient mental health services; and

(3) if appropriate, recommendations for auxiliary services such as vocational training, educational services, or special medical care.

In its order of conditional release, the court shall specify the conditions of release based on the release plan and shall direct the appropriate agencies or persons to submit periodic reports to the court regarding the defendant's compliance with the conditions of the release, and progress in treatment, and provide copies to all parties. The procedure for determinations of the confidential status of reports is governed by Rule of General Practice and Judicial Administration 2.420.

(b) Defendant's Failure to Comply. If it appears at any time that the defendant has failed to comply with the conditions of release, or that the defendant's condition has deteriorated to the point that inpatient care is required, or that the release conditions should be modified, the court, after hearing, may modify the release conditions or, if the court finds the defendant meets the statutory criteria for commitment, may order that the defendant be recommitted to the Department of Children and Families for further treatment.

(c) Discharge. If at any time it is determined after hearing that the defendant no longer requires court-supervised follow-up care, the court shall terminate its jurisdiction in the cause and discharge the defendant.

Committee Notes

1980 Adoption. This rule implements the prior statutory law permitting conditional release.

For complementary statute providing for conditional release, see section 916.17, Florida Statutes.

1988 Amendment. The amendments to this rule are designed to reflect amendments to rules 3.210, 3.211, and 3.218 as well as 1985 amendments to chapter 916, Florida Statutes.

(b) This provision has been amended to permit the court to recommit a conditionally released defendant to HRS under the provisions of chapter 916 only if the court makes a finding that the defendant currently meets the statutory commitment criteria found in section 916.13(1), Florida Statutes.

1992 Amendment. The purpose of the amendment is to gender neutralize the wording of the rule.

Introductory Note Relating to Amendments to Rules 3.210 to 3.219. See notes following rule 3.210 for the text of this note.

VI. Discovery

Rule 3.220. Discovery.

(a) Notice of Discovery. After the filing of the charging document, a defendant may elect to participate in the discovery process provided by these rules, including the taking of discovery depositions, by filing with the court and serving on the prosecuting attorney a "Notice of Discovery" which binds both the prosecution

Rule 3.220. Discovery.

and defendant to all discovery procedures contained in these rules. Participation by a defendant in the discovery process, including the taking of any deposition by a defendant or the filing of a public records request under chapter 119, Florida Statutes, for law enforcement records relating to the defendant's pending prosecution, which are nonexempt as a result of a codefendant's participation in discovery, is an election to participate in discovery and triggers a reciprocal discovery obligation for the defendant. If any defendant knowingly or purposely shares in discovery obtained by a codefendant, the defendant is deemed to have elected to participate in discovery.

(b) Prosecutor's Discovery Obligation.

(1) Within 15 days after service of the Notice of Discovery, the prosecutor must serve a written Discovery Exhibit which must disclose to the defendant and permit the defendant to inspect, copy, test, and photograph the following information and material within the state's possession or control, except that any property or material that portrays sexual performance by a child, constitutes generated child pornography, or constitutes child pornography may not be copied, photographed, duplicated, or otherwise reproduced so long as the state attorney makes the property or material reasonably available to the defendant or the defendant's attorney:

(A) a list of the names and addresses of all persons known to the prosecutor to have information that may be relevant to any offense charged or any defense thereto, or to any similar fact evidence to be presented at trial under section 90.404(2), Florida Statutes. The names and addresses of persons listed must be clearly designated in the following categories:

(i) Category A. These witnesses must include (1) eye witnesses, (2) alibi witnesses and rebuttal to alibi witnesses, (3) witnesses who were present when a recorded or unrecorded statement was taken from or made by a defendant or codefendant, which must be separately identified within this category, (4) investigating officers, (5) witnesses known by the prosecutor to have any material information that tends to negate the guilt of the defendant as to any offense charged, (6) child hearsay witnesses, (7) expert witnesses who have not provided a written report and a curriculum vitae or who are going to testify, and (8) informant witnesses, whether in custody, who offer testimony concerning the statements of a defendant about the issues for which the defendant is being tried.

(ii) Category B. All witnesses not listed in either Category A or Category C.

(iii) Category C. All witnesses who performed only ministerial functions or whom the prosecutor does not intend to call at trial and whose involvement with and knowledge of the case is fully set out in a police report or other statement furnished to the defense;

(B) the statement of any person whose name is furnished in compliance with the preceding subdivision. The term "statement" as used herein includes a written statement made by the person and signed or otherwise adopted or approved by the person and also includes any statement of any kind or manner made by the person and written or recorded or summarized in any writing or recording. The term "statement" is specifically intended to include all police and investigative reports of any kind prepared for or in connection with the case, but must not include the notes from which those reports are compiled;

(C) any written or recorded statements and the substance of any oral statements made by the defendant, including a copy of any statements contained in police reports or report summaries, together with the name and address of each witness to the statements;

(D) any written or recorded statements and the substance of any oral statements made by a codefendant;

(E) those portions of recorded grand jury minutes that contain testimony of the defendant;

(F) any tangible papers or objects that were obtained from or belonged to the defendant;

(G) whether the state has any material or information that has been provided by a confidential informant;

(H) whether there has been any electronic surveillance, including wiretapping, of the premises of the defendant or of conversations to which the defendant was a party and any documents relating thereto;

(I) whether there has been any search or seizure and any documents relating thereto;

(J) reports or statements of experts made in connection with the particular case, including results of physical or mental examinations and of scientific tests, experiments, or comparisons;

(K) any tangible papers or objects that the prosecuting attorney intends to use in the hearing or trial and that were not obtained from or that did not belong to the defendant;

(L) any tangible paper, objects, or substances in the possession of law enforcement that could be tested for DNA; and

(M) whether the state has any material or information that has been provided by an informant witness, including:

>**(i)** the substance of any statement allegedly made by the defendant about which the informant witness may testify;
>
>**(ii)** a summary of the criminal history record of the informant witness;
>
>**(iii)** the time and place under which the defendant's alleged statement was made;
>
>**(iv)** whether the informant witness has received, or expects to receive, anything in exchange for his or her testimony;
>
>**(v)** the informant witness's prior history of cooperation, in return for any benefit, as known to the prosecutor.

(2) If the court determines, in camera, that any police or investigative report contains irrelevant, sensitive information or information interrelated with other crimes or criminal activities and the disclosure of the contents of the police report may seriously impair law enforcement or jeopardize the investigation of the other crimes or activities, the court may prohibit or partially restrict the disclosure.

(3) The court may prohibit the state from introducing into evidence any of the foregoing material not disclosed, so as to secure and maintain fairness in the just determination of the cause.

(4) As soon as practicable after the filing of the charging document the prosecutor must disclose to the defendant any material information within the state's possession or control that tends to negate the guilt of the defendant as to any offense charged, regardless of whether the defendant has incurred reciprocal discovery obligations.

(c) Disclosure to Prosecution.

(1) After the filing of the charging document and subject to constitutional limitations, the court may require a defendant to:

(A) appear in a lineup;

(B) speak for identification by witnesses to an offense;

(C) be fingerprinted;

(D) pose for photographs not involving re-enactment of a scene;

(E) try on articles of clothing;

(F) permit the taking of specimens of material under the defendant's fingernails;

(G) permit the taking of samples of the defendant's blood, hair, and other materials of the defendant's body that involves no unreasonable intrusion thereof;

(H) provide specimens of the defendant's handwriting; and

(I) submit to a reasonable physical or medical inspection of the defendant's body.

(2) If the personal appearance of a defendant is required for the foregoing purposes, reasonable notice of the time and location of the appearance must be given by the prosecuting attorney to the defendant and his or her counsel. Provisions may be made for appearances for such purposes in an order admitting a defendant to bail or providing for pretrial release.

(d) Defendant's Obligation.

(1) If a defendant elects to participate in discovery, either through filing the appropriate notice or by participating in any discovery process, including the taking of a discovery deposition, the following disclosures must be made:

(A) Within 15 days after receipt by the defendant of the Discovery Exhibit furnished by the prosecutor under subdivision (b)(1)(A) of this rule, the defendant must furnish to the prosecutor a written list of the names and addresses of all witnesses whom the defendant expects to call as witnesses at the trial or hearing. When the prosecutor subpoenas a witness whose name has been furnished by the defendant, except for trial subpoenas, the rules applicable to the taking of depositions apply.

(B) Within 15 days after receipt of the prosecutor's Discovery Exhibit the defendant must serve a written Discovery Exhibit which must disclose to and permit the prosecutor to inspect, copy, test, and photograph the following information and material that is in the defendant's possession or control:

(i) the statement of any person listed in subdivision (d)(1)(A), other than that of the defendant;

Rule 3.220. Discovery.

(ii) reports or statements of experts, that the defendant intends to use as a witness at a trial or hearing, made in connection with the particular case, including results of physical or mental examinations and of scientific tests, experiments, or comparisons; and

(iii) any tangible papers or objects that the defendant intends to use in the hearing or trial.

(2) The prosecutor and the defendant must perform their obligations under this rule in a manner mutually agreeable or as ordered by the court.

(3) The filing of a motion for protective order by the prosecutor will automatically stay the times provided for in this subdivision. If a protective order is granted, the defendant may, within 2 days thereafter, or at any time before the prosecutor furnishes the information or material that is the subject of the motion for protective order, withdraw the defendant's notice of discovery and not be required to furnish reciprocal discovery.

(e) Restricting Disclosure. The court on its own initiative or on motion of counsel must deny or partially restrict disclosures authorized by this rule if it finds there is a substantial risk to any person of physical harm, intimidation, bribery, economic reprisals, or unnecessary annoyance or embarrassment resulting from the disclosure, that outweighs any usefulness of the disclosure to either party.

(f) Additional Discovery. On a showing of materiality, the court may require such other discovery to the parties as justice may require.

(g) Matters Not Subject to Disclosure.

(1) *Work Product.* Disclosure must not be required of legal research or of records, correspondence, reports, or memoranda to the extent that they contain the opinions, theories, or conclusions of the prosecuting or defense attorney or members of their legal staffs.

(2) *Informants.* Disclosure of a confidential informant must not be required unless the confidential informant is to be produced at a hearing or trial or a failure to disclose the informant's identity will infringe the constitutional rights of the defendant.

(h) Discovery Depositions.

(1) *Generally.* At any time after the filing of the charging document, any party may take the deposition on oral examination of any person authorized by this rule. A party taking a deposition must give reasonable written notice to each

other party and make a good faith effort to coordinate the date, time, and location of the deposition to accommodate the schedules of other parties and the witness to be deposed. The notice must state the time and the location where the deposition is to be taken, the name of each person to be examined, and a certificate of counsel that a good faith effort was made to coordinate the deposition schedule. Unless a provision of this rule conflicts with the Florida Rules of Civil Procedure, the procedure for taking the deposition, including the scope of the examination, and the issuance of a subpoena for deposition by an attorney of record in the action, is the same as that provided in the Florida Rules of Civil Procedure and section 48.031, Florida Statutes. To protect deponents and the rights of the parties and to ensure compliance with statutes, the court may enter orders, including but not limited to the orders allowed by rule 3.220(e) and (*l*), on motion of a party, the deponent, or on its own motion, for good cause shown. Any deposition taken under this rule may be used by any party for the purpose of contradicting or impeaching the testimony of the deponent as a witness. The trial court or the clerk of the court may, on application by a pro se litigant or the attorney for any party, issue subpoenas for the persons whose depositions are to be taken. In any case, including multiple defendants or consolidated cases, no person may be deposed more than once except by consent of the parties or by order of the court issued on good cause shown. A witness who refuses to obey a duly served subpoena may be adjudged in contempt of the court from which the subpoena issued.

(A) The defendant may, without leave of court, take the deposition of any witness listed by the prosecutor as a Category A witness or listed by a co-defendant as a witness to be called at a joint trial or hearing. After receipt by the defendant of the Discovery Exhibit, the defendant may, without leave of court, take the deposition of any unlisted witness who may have information relevant to the offense charged. The prosecutor may, without leave of court, take the deposition of any witness listed by the defendant to be called at a trial or hearing.

(B) No party may take the deposition of a witness listed by the prosecutor as a Category B witness except upon leave of court with good cause shown. In determining whether to allow a deposition, the court should consider the

Rule 3.220. Discovery.

consequences to the defendant, the complexities of the issues involved, the complexity of the testimony of the witness (e.g., experts), and the other opportunities available to the defendant to discover the information sought by deposition.

(C) A witness listed by the prosecutor as a Category C witness is not subject to deposition unless the court determines that the witness should be listed in another category.

(D) No deposition may be taken in a case in which the defendant is charged only with a misdemeanor or a criminal traffic offense when all other discovery provided by this rule has been complied with unless good cause can be shown to the trial court. In determining whether to allow a deposition, the court should consider the consequences to the defendant, the complexity of the issues involved, the complexity of the witness's testimony (e.g., experts), and the other opportunities available to the defendant to discover the information sought by deposition. However, this prohibition against the taking of depositions does not apply if following the furnishing of discovery by the defendant the state then takes the statement of a listed defense witness under section 27.04, Florida Statutes.

(2) *Transcripts.* No transcript of a deposition for which the state may be obligated to expend funds may be ordered by a party unless it is in compliance with general law.

(3) *Location of Deposition.* Unless the deposition will be taken by communication technology, depositions of witnesses residing:

(A) in the county in which the trial is to take place must be taken in the building in which the trial will be held, such other location as is agreed on by the parties, or a location designated by the court; or

(B) outside the county in which the trial is to take place must be taken in a court reporter's office in the county or state in which the witness resides, such other location as is agreed on by the parties, or a location designated by the court.

(4) *Visual Recording and Photographs.* For deponents 18 years of age or older, a discovery deposition must not be visually recorded unless ordered by the court for good cause shown or upon the consent of the parties and the deponent. For deponents less than 18 years of age, a discovery deposition must be audio-visually recorded unless otherwise ordered by the court. No deponent may be photographed during a discovery deposition.

(5) *Depositions of Law Enforcement Officers.* Subject to the general provisions of subdivision (h)(1), law enforcement officers must appear for deposition, without subpoena, on written notice of taking deposition delivered at the physical address of the law enforcement agency or department, or an e-mail or other address designated by the law enforcement agency or department, 5 days before the date of the deposition. Any physical address or e-mail address designated by a law enforcement agency or department for service of notice of deposition must be provided by the prosecuting attorney with discovery. Law enforcement officers who fail to appear for deposition after being served notice as required by the rule may be adjudged in contempt of court.

(6) *Witness Coordinating Office/Notice of Taking Deposition.* If a witness coordinating office has been established in the jurisdiction under applicable Florida Statutes, the deposition of any witness should be coordinated through that office. The witness coordinating office should attempt to schedule the depositions of a witness at a time and location convenient for the witness and acceptable to the parties.

(7) *Defendant's Physical Presence.* A defendant may not be physically present at a deposition except on stipulation of the parties or as provided by this rule. The court may order the physical presence of the defendant on a showing of good cause. The court may consider:

    (A) the need for the physical presence of the defendant to obtain effective discovery;

    (B) the intimidating effect of the defendant's presence on the witness, if any;

    (C) any cost or inconvenience which may result; and

    (D) any alternative communication technology available.

(8) Telephonic Statements. On stipulation of the parties and the consent of the witness, the statement of any witness may be taken by telephone in lieu of the deposition of the witness. In such case, the witness need not be under oath. The statement, however, must be recorded and may be used for impeachment at trial as a prior inconsistent statement under the Florida Evidence Code.

Rule 3.220. Discovery.

(i) Investigations Not to Be Impeded. Except as is otherwise provided as to matters not subject to disclosure or restricted by protective orders, neither the counsel for the parties nor other prosecution or defense personnel may advise persons having relevant material or information, except the defendant, to refrain from discussing the case with opposing counsel or showing opposing counsel any relevant material, nor may they otherwise impede opposing counsel's investigation of the case.

(j) Continuing Duty to Disclose. If, subsequent to compliance with the rules, a party discovers additional witnesses or material that the party would have been under a duty to disclose or produce at the time of the previous compliance, the party must promptly disclose or produce the witnesses or material in the same manner as required under these rules for initial discovery. This duty includes any additional recorded or unrecorded statements of any person disclosed under subdivisions (b)(1)(A) or (d)(1)(A) of this rule that materially alter a written or recorded statement previously provided under these rules.

(k) Court May Alter Times. The court may alter the times for compliance with any discovery under these rules on good cause shown.

(l) Protective Orders.

    (1) Motion to Restrict Disclosure of Matters. On a showing of good cause, the court must at any time order that specified disclosures be restricted, deferred, or exempted from discovery, that certain matters not be inquired into, that the scope of the deposition be limited to certain matters, that a deposition be sealed and after being sealed be opened only by order of the court, or make such other order as is appropriate to protect a witness from harassment, unnecessary inconvenience, or invasion of privacy, including prohibiting the taking of a deposition. All material and information to which a party is entitled, however, must be disclosed in time to permit the party to make beneficial use of it.

    (2) Motion to Terminate or Limit Examination. At any time during the taking of a deposition, on motion of a party or of the deponent, and on a showing that the examination is being conducted in bad faith or in such manner as to unreasonably annoy, embarrass, or oppress the deponent or party, the court in which the action is pending or the circuit court where the deposition is being taken may:

        (A) terminate the deposition;

(B) limit the scope and manner of the taking of the deposition;
(C) limit the time of the deposition;
(D) continue the deposition to a later time;
(E) order the deposition to be taken in open court; and
(F) impose any sanction authorized by this rule.

If the order terminates the deposition, it may be resumed thereafter only on the order of the court in which the action is pending. On demand of any party or deponent, the taking of the deposition must be suspended for the time necessary to make a motion for an order.

(m) In Camera and Ex Parte Proceedings.

(1) Any person may move for an order denying or regulating disclosure of sensitive matters. The court may consider the matters contained in the motion in camera.

(2) On request, the court must allow the defendant to make an ex parte showing of good cause for taking the deposition of a Category B witness.

(3) A record must be made of proceedings authorized under this subdivision. If the court enters an order granting relief after an in camera inspection or ex parte showing, the entire record of the proceeding must be sealed and preserved and be made available to the appellate court in the event of an appeal.

(n) Sanctions.

(1) If, at any time during the course of the proceedings, it is brought to the attention of the court that a party has failed to comply with an applicable discovery rule or with an order issued under an applicable discovery rule, the court may order the party to comply with the discovery or inspection of materials not previously disclosed or produced, grant a continuance, grant a mistrial, prohibit the party from calling a witness not disclosed or introducing in evidence the material not disclosed, or enter such other order as it deems just under the circumstances.

(2) Willful violation by counsel or a party not represented by counsel of an applicable discovery rule, or an order issued under an applicable discovery rule, subjects counsel or the unrepresented party to appropriate sanctions by the court. The sanctions may include, but are not limited to, contempt proceedings against the attorney or unrepresented party, as well as the assessment of costs incurred by the opposing party, when appropriate.

(3) Every request for discovery or response or objection, including a notice of deposition made by a party represented by an attorney, must be signed by at least 1 attorney of record, as defined by Florida Rule of General Practice and Judicial Administration 2.505, in the attorney's individual name, whose address must be stated. A party who is not represented by an attorney must sign the request, response, or objection and list his or her address. The signature of the attorney constitutes a certification that the document complies with Florida Rule of General Practice and Judicial Administration 2.515. The signature of the attorney or party constitutes a certification that the signer has read the request, response, or objection and that to the best of the signer's knowledge, information, or belief formed after a reasonable inquiry it is:

(A) consistent with these rules and warranted by existing law or a good faith argument for the extension, modification, or reversal of existing law;

(B) not interposed for any improper purpose, such as to harass or to cause unnecessary delay or needless increase in the cost of litigation; and

(C) not unreasonable or unduly burdensome or expensive, given the needs of the case and the importance of the issues at stake in the litigation.

If a request, response, or objection is not signed, it must be stricken unless it is signed promptly after the omission is called to the attention of the party making the request, response, or objection, and a party may not be obligated to take any action with respect to it until it is signed.

If a certification is made in violation of this rule, the court, on motion or on its own initiative, must impose on the person who made the certification, the firm or agency with which the person is affiliated, the party on whose behalf the request, response, or objection is made, or any or all of the above an appropriate sanction, which may include an order to pay the amount of the reasonable expenses incurred because of the violation, including a reasonable attorney's fee.

(o) Pretrial Conference.

(1) The trial court may hold 1 or more pretrial conferences to consider such matters as will promote a fair and expeditious trial. The defendant must be present at any pretrial conference, unless the defendant's presence is waived in writing or on the record by the defendant or by the defendant's counsel with the defendant's consent.

(2) The court may set, and on the request of any party must set, a discovery schedule, including a discovery cut-off date, at the pretrial conference.

Committee Notes

1968 Adoption. (a)(1) This is substantially the same as section 925.05, Florida Statutes.

(a)(2) This is new and allows a defendant rights which he did not have, but must be considered in light of subdivision (c).

(a)(3) This is a slight enlargement upon the present practice; however, from a practical standpoint, it is not an enlargement, but merely a codification of section 925.05, Florida Statutes, with respect to the defendant's testimony before a grand jury.

(b) This is a restatement of section 925.04, Florida Statutes, except for the change of the word "may" to "shall."

(c) This is new and affords discovery to the state within the trial judge's discretion by allowing the trial judge to make discovery under (a)(2) and (b) conditioned upon the defendant giving the state some information if the defendant has it. This affords the state some area of discovery which it did not previously have with respect to (b). A question was raised concerning the effect of (a)(2) on FBI reports and other reports which are submitted to a prosecutor as "confidential" but it was agreed that the interests of justice would be better served by allowing this rule and that, after the appropriate governmental authorities are made aware of the fact that their reports may be subject to compulsory disclosure, no harm to the state will be done.

(d) and (e) This gives the defendant optional procedures. (d) is simply a codification of section 906.29, Florida Statutes, except for the addition of "addresses." The defendant is allowed this procedure in any event. (e) affords the defendant the additional practice of obtaining all of the state's witnesses, as distinguished from merely those on whose evidence the information, or indictment, is based, but only if the defendant is willing to give the state a list of all defense witnesses, which must be done to take advantage of this rule. The confidential informant who is to be used as a witness must be disclosed; but it was expressly viewed that this should not otherwise overrule present case law on the subject of disclosure of

Rule 3.220. Discovery.

confidential informants, either where disclosure is required or not required.

(f) This is new and is a compromise between the philosophy that the defendant should be allowed unlimited discovery depositions and the philosophy that the defendant should not be allowed any discovery depositions at all. The purpose of the rule is to afford the defendant relief from situations when witnesses refuse to "cooperate" by making pretrial disclosures to the defense. It was determined to be necessary that the written signed statement be a criterion because this is the only way witnesses can be impeached by prior contradictory statements. The word "cooperate" was intentionally left in the rule, although the word is a loose one, so that it can be given a liberal interpretation, i.e., a witness may claim to be available and yet never actually submit to an interview. Some express the view that the defendant is not being afforded adequate protection because the cooperating witness will not have been under oath, but the subcommittee felt that the only alternative would be to make unlimited discovery depositions available to the defendant which was a view not approved by a majority of the subcommittee. Each minority is expressed by the following alternative proposals:

Alternative Proposal (1): When a person is charged with an offense, at any time after the filing of the indictment, information, or affidavit upon which the defendant is to be tried, such person may take the deposition of any person by deposition upon oral examination for the purpose of discovery. The attendance of witnesses may be compelled by the use of subpoenas as provided by law. The deposition of a person confined in prison may be taken only by leave of court on such terms as the court prescribes. The scope of examination and the manner and method of taking such deposition shall be as provided in the Florida Rules of Civil Procedure and the deposition may be used for the purpose of contradicting or impeaching the testimony of a deponent as a witness.

Alternative Proposal (2): If a defendant signs and files a written waiver of his or her privilege against self-incrimination and submits to interrogation under oath by the prosecuting attorney, then the defendant shall be entitled to compulsory process for any or all witnesses to enable the defendant to interrogate them under oath, before trial, for discovery purposes.

A view was expressed that some limitation should be placed on the state's rights under sections 27.04 and 32.20, Florida Statutes, which allow the prosecutor to take all depositions unilaterally at any time. It was agreed by all members of the subcommittee that this right should not be curtailed until some specific time after the filing of an indictment, information, or affidavit, because circumstances sometimes require the filing of the charge and a studied marshalling of evidence thereafter. Criticism of the present practice lies in the fact that any time up to and during the course of the trial the prosecutor can subpoena any person to the privacy of the prosecutor's office without notice to the defense and there take a statement of such person under oath. The subcommittee was divided, however, on the method of altering this situation and the end result was that this subcommittee itself should not undertake to change the existing practice, but should make the Supreme Court aware of this apparent imbalance.

(g) This is new and is required in order to make effective the preceding rules.

(h) This is new and, although it encompasses relief for both the state and the defense, its primary purpose is to afford relief in situations when witnesses may be intimidated and a prosecuting attorney's heavy docket might not allow compliance with discovery within the time limitations set forth in the rules. The words, "sufficient showing" were intentionally included in order to permit the trial judge to have discretion in granting the protective relief. It would be impossible to specify all possible grounds which can be the basis of a protective order. This verbiage also permits a possible abuse by a prosecution-minded trial judge, but the subcommittee felt that the appellate court would remedy any such abuse in the course of making appellate decisions.

(i) This is new and, although it will entail additional expense to counties, it was determined that it was necessary in order to comply with the recent trend of federal decisions which hold that due process is violated when a person who has the money with which to resist criminal prosecution gains an advantage over the person who is not so endowed. Actually, there is serious doubt that the intent of this subdivision can be accomplished by a rule of procedure; a statute is needed. It is recognized that such a statute may be unpopular with the legislature and not enacted. But, if this subdivision has not given effect there is a likelihood that a constitutional infirmity (equal protection of the law) will be found and either the entire rule with all subdivisions will be held void or confusion in application will result.

Rule 3.220. Discovery.

(j) This provision is necessary since the prosecutor is required to assume many responsibilities under the various subdivisions under the rule. There are no prosecuting attorneys, either elected or regularly assigned, in justice of the peace courts. County judge's courts, as distinguished from county courts, do not have elected prosecutors. Prosecuting attorneys in such courts are employed by county commissions and may be handicapped in meeting the requirements of the rule due to the irregularity and uncertainty of such employment. This subdivision is inserted as a method of achieving as much uniformity as possible in all of the courts of Florida having jurisdictions to try criminal cases.

1972 Amendment. The committee studied the ABA Standards for Criminal Justice relating to discovery and procedure before trial. Some of the standards are incorporated in the committee's proposal, others are not. Generally, the standards are divided into 5 parts:

Part I deals with policy and philosophy and, while the committee approves the substance of Part I, it was determined that specific rules setting out this policy and philosophy should not be proposed.

Part II provides for automatic disclosures (avoiding judicial labor) by the prosecutor to the defense of almost everything within the prosecutor's knowledge, except for work product and the identity of confidential informants. The committee adopted much of Part II, but felt that the disclosure should not be automatic in every case; the disclosure should be made only after request or demand and within certain time limitations. The ABA Standards do not recommend reciprocity of discovery, but the committee deemed that a large degree of reciprocity is in order and made appropriate recommendations.

Part III of the ABA Standards recommends some disclosure by the defense (not reciprocal) to which the state was not previously entitled. The committee adopted Part III and enlarged upon it.

Part IV of the Standards sets forth methods of regulation of discovery by the court. Under the Standards the discovery mentioned in Parts II and III would have been automatic and without the necessity of court orders or court intervention. Part III provides for procedures of protection of the parties and was generally incorporated in the recommendations of the committee.

Part V of the ABA Standards deals with omnibus hearings and pretrial conferences. The committee rejected part of the Standards dealing with omnibus hearings because it felt that it was superfluous under Florida procedure. The Florida committee determined that a trial court may, at its discretion, schedule a hearing for the purposes enumerated in the ABA Omnibus Hearing and that a rule authorizing it is not necessary. Some of the provisions of the ABA Omnibus Hearing were rejected by the Florida committee, i.e., stipulations as to issues, waivers by defendant, etc. A modified form of pretrial conference was provided in the proposals by the Florida committee.

(a)(1)(i) Same as ABA Standard 2.1(a)(i) and substance of Standard 2.1(e). Formerly Florida Rule of Criminal Procedure 3.220(e) authorized exchange of witness lists. When considered with proposal 3.220(a)(3), it is seen that the proposal represents no significant change.

(ii) This rule is a modification of Standard 2.1(a)(ii) and is new in Florida, although some such statements might have been discoverable under rule 3.220(f). Definition of "statement" is derived from 18 U.S.C. § 3500.

Requiring law enforcement officers to include irrelevant or sensitive material in their disclosures to the defense would not serve justice. Many investigations overlap and information developed as a byproduct of one investigation may form the basis and starting point for a new and entirely separate one. Also, the disclosure of any information obtained from computerized records of the Florida Crime Information Center and the National Crime Information Center should be subject to the regulations prescribing the confidentiality of such information so as to safeguard the right of the innocent to privacy.

(iii) Same as Standard 2.1(a)(ii) relating to statements of accused; words "known to the prosecutor, together with the name and address of each witness to the statement" added and is new in Florida.

(iv) From Standard 2.1(a)(ii). New in Florida.

(v) From Standard 2.1(a)(iii) except for addition of words, "that have been recorded" which were inserted to avoid any inference that the proposed rule makes recording of grand jury testimony mandatory. This discovery was formerly available under rule 3.220(a)(3).

(vi) From Standard 2.1(a)(v). Words, "books, papers, documents, photographs" were condensed to "papers or objects" without intending to change their meaning. This was previously available under rule 3.220(b).

Rule 3.220. Discovery.

(vii) From Standard 2.1(b)(i) except word "confidential" was added to clarify meaning. This is new in this form.

(viii) From Standard 2.1(b)(iii) and is new in Florida in this form. Previously this was disclosed upon motion and order.

(ix) From Standard 2.3(a), but also requiring production of "documents relating thereto" such as search warrants and affidavits. Previously this was disclosed upon motion and order.

(x) From Standard 2.1(a)(iv). Previously available under rule 3.220(a)(2). Defendant must reciprocate under proposed rule 3.220(b)(4).

(xi) Same committee note as (b) under this subdivision.

(2) From Standard 2.1(c) except omission of words "or would tend to reduce his punishment therefor" which should be included in sentencing.

(3) Based upon Standard 2.2(a) and (b) except Standards required prosecutor to furnish voluntarily and without demand while this proposal requires defendant to make demand and permits prosecutor 15 days in which to respond.

(4) From Standards 2.5(b) and 4.4. Substance of this proposal previously available under rule 3.220(h).

(5) From Standard 2.5. New in Florida.

(b)(1) From Standard 3.1(a). New in Florida.

(2) From Standard 3.1(b). New in Florida.

(3) Standards did not recommend that defendant furnish prosecution with reciprocal witness list; however, formerly, rule 3.220(e) did make such provision. The committee recommended continuation of reciprocity.

(4) Standards did not recommend reciprocity of discovery. Previously, Florida rules required some reciprocity. The committee recommended continuation of former reciprocity and addition of exchanging witness' statement other than defendants'.

(c) From Standard 2.6. New in Florida, but generally recognized in decisions.

(d) Not recommended by Standards. Previously permitted under rule 3.220(f) except for change limiting the place of taking the deposition and eliminating requirement that witness refuse to give voluntary signed statement.

(e) From Standard 4.1. New in Florida.

(f) Same as rule 3.220(g).

(g) From Standard 4.4 and rule 3.220(h).

(h) From Standard 4.4 and rule 3.220(h).

(i) From Standard 4.6. Not previously covered by rule in Florida, but permitted by decisions.

(j)(1) From Standard 4.7(a). New in Florida except court discretion permitted by rule 3.220(g).

(2) From Standard 4.7(b). New in Florida.

(k) Same as prior rule.

(l) Modified Standard 5.4. New in Florida.

1977 Amendment. The proposed change only removes the comma which currently appears after (a)(1).

1980 Amendment. The intent of the rule change is to guarantee that the accused will receive those portions of police reports or report summaries which contain any written, recorded, or oral statements made by the accused.

1986 Amendment. The showing of good cause under (d)(2) of this rule may be presented ex parte or in camera to the court.

1989 Amendment. 3.220(a). The purpose of this change is to ensure reciprocity of discovery. Under the previous rule, the defendant could tailor discovery, demanding only certain items of discovery with no requirement to reciprocate items other than those demanded. A defendant could avoid reciprocal discovery by taking depositions, thereby learning of witnesses through the deposition process, and then deposing those witnesses without filing a demand for discovery. With this change, once a defendant opts to use any discovery device, the defendant is required to produce all items designated under the discovery rule, whether or not the defendant has specifically requested production of those items.

Former subdivision (c) is relettered (b). Under (b)(1) the prosecutor's obligation to furnish a witness list is conditioned upon the defendant filing a "Notice of Discovery."

Former subdivision (a)(1)(i) is renumbered (b)(1)(i) and, as amended, limits the ability of the defense to take depositions of those persons designated by the prosecutor as witnesses who should not be deposed because of their tangential relationship to the case. This does not preclude the defense attorney or a defense investigator from interviewing any witness, including a police witness, about the witness's knowledge of the case.

This change is intended to meet a primary complaint of law enforcement agencies that depositions are frequently taken of

Rule 3.220. Discovery.

persons who have no knowledge of the events leading to that charge, but whose names are disclosed on the witness list. Examples of these persons are transport officers, evidence technicians, etc.

In order to permit the defense to evaluate the potential testimony of those individuals designated by the prosecutor, their testimony must be fully set forth in some document, generally a police report. (a)(1)(ii) is renumbered (b)(1)(ii). This subdivision is amended to require full production of all police incident and investigative reports, of any kind, that are discoverable, provided there is no independent reason for restricting their disclosure. The term "statement" is intended to include summaries of statements of witnesses made by investigating officers as well as statements adopted by the witnesses themselves.

The protection against disclosure of sensitive information, or information that otherwise should not be disclosed, formerly set forth in (a)(1)(i), is retained, but transferred to subdivision (b)(1)(xii).

The prohibition sanction is not eliminated, but is transferred to subdivision (b)(1)(xiii). "Shall" has been changed to "may" in order to reflect the procedure for imposition of sanctions specified in Richardson v. State, 246 So. 2d 771 (Fla. 1971).

The last phrase of renumbered subdivision (b)(2) is added to emphasize that constitutionally required Brady material must be produced regardless of the defendant's election to participate in the discovery process.

Former subdivision (b) is relettered (c).

Former subdivisions (b)(3) and (4) are now included in new subdivision (d). An introductory phrase has been added to subdivision (d). Subdivision (d) reflects the change in nomenclature from a "Demand for Discovery" to the filing of a "Notice of Discovery."

As used in subdivision (d), the word "defendant" is intended to refer to the party rather than to the person. Any obligations incurred by the "defendant" are incurred by the defendant's attorney if the defendant is represented by counsel and by the defendant personally if the defendant is not represented.

The right of the defendant to be present and to examine witnesses, set forth in renumbered subdivision (d)(1), refers to the right of the defense, as party to the action. The term refers to the attorney for the defendant if the defendant is represented by counsel. The right of the defendant to be physically present at the deposition is controlled by new subdivision (h)(6).

Renumbered subdivision (d)(2), as amended, reflects the new notice of discovery procedure. If the defendant elects to participate in discovery, the defendant is obligated to furnish full reciprocal disclosure.

Subdivision (e) was previously numbered (a)(4). This subdivision has been modified to permit the remedy to be sought by either prosecution or defense.

Subdivision (f) was previously numbered (a)(5) and has been modified to permit the prosecutor, as well as the defense attorney, to seek additional discovery.

Former subdivision (c) is relettered (g).

Former subdivision (d) is relettered (h). Renumbered subdivision (h)(1) has been amended to reflect the restrictions on deposing a witness designated by the prosecution under (b)(1)(i) (designation of a witness performing ministerial duties only or one who will not be called at trial).

(h)(1)(i) is added to provide that a deposition of a witness designated by the prosecutor under (b)(1)(i) may be taken only upon good cause shown by the defendant to the court.

(h)(1)(ii) is added to provide that abuses by attorneys of the provisions of (b)(1)(i) are subject to stringent sanctions.

New subdivision (h)(1)(iii) abolishes depositions in misdemeanor cases except when good cause is shown.

A portion of former subdivision (d)(1) is renumbered (h)(3). This subdivision now permits the administrative judge or chief judge, in addition to the trial judge, to designate the place for taking the deposition.

New subdivision (h)(4) recognizes that children and some adults are especially vulnerable to intimidation tactics. Although it has been shown that such tactics are infrequent, they should not be tolerated because of the traumatic effect on the witness. The videotaping of the deposition will enable the trial judge to control such tactics. Provision is also made to protect witnesses of fragile emotional strength because of their vulnerability to intimidation tactics.

New subdivision (h)(5) emphasizes the necessity for the establishment, in each jurisdiction, of an effective witness coordinating office. The Florida Legislature has authorized the establishment of such office through section 43.35, Florida Statutes.

Rule 3.220. Discovery.

This subdivision is intended to make depositions of witnesses and law enforcement officers as convenient as possible for the witnesses and with minimal disruption of law enforcement officers' official duties.

New subdivision (h)(6) recognizes that one of the most frequent complaints from child protection workers and from rape victim counselors is that the presence of the defendant intimidates the witnesses. The trauma to the victim surpasses the benefit to the defense of having the defendant present at the deposition. Since there is no right, other than that given by the rules of procedure, for a defendant to attend a deposition, the Florida Supreme Court Commission on Criminal Discovery believes that no such right should exist in those cases. The "defense," of course, as a party to the action, has a right to be present through counsel at the deposition. In this subdivision, the word "defendant" is meant to refer to the person of the defendant, not to the defense as a party. See comments to rules 3.220(d) and 3.220(d)(1).

Although defendants have no right to be present at depositions and generally there is no legitimate reason for their presence, their presence is appropriate in certain cases. An example is a complex white collar fraud prosecution in which the defendant must explain the meaning of technical documents or terms. Cases requiring the defendant's presence are the exception rather than the rule. Accordingly, (h)(6)(i)-(ii) preclude the presence of defendants at depositions unless agreed to by the parties or ordered by the court. These subdivisions set forth factors that a court should take into account in considering motions to allow a defendant's presence.

New subdivision (h)(7) permits the defense to obtain needed factual information from law enforcement officers by informal telephone deposition. Recognizing that the formal deposition of a law enforcement officer is often unnecessary, this procedure will permit such discovery at a significant reduction of costs.

Former subdivisions (e), (f), and (g) are relettered (i), (j) and (k), respectively.

Former subdivision (h) is relettered (1) and is modified to emphasize the use of protective orders to protect witnesses from harassment or intimidation and to provide for limiting the scope of the deposition as to certain matters.

Former subdivision (i) is relettered (m).

Former subdivision (j) is relettered (n).

Renumbered (n)(2) is amended to provide that sanctions are mandatory if the court finds willful abuse of discovery. Although the amount of sanction is discretionary, some sanction must be imposed.

(n)(3) is new and tracks the certification provisions of federal procedure. The very fact of signing such a certification will make counsel cognizant of the effect of that action.

Subdivision (k) is relettered (o).

Subdivision (l) is relettered (p).

1992 Amendment. The proposed amendments change the references to "indictment or information" in subdivisions (b)(1), (b)(2), (c)(1), and (h)(1) to "charging document." This amendment is proposed in conjunction with amendments to rule 3.125 to provide that all individuals charged with a criminal violation would be entitled to the same discovery regardless of the nature of the charging document (i.e., indictment, information, or notice to appear).

1996 Amendment. This is a substantial rewording of the rule as it pertains to depositions and pretrial case management. The amendment was in response to allegations of discovery abuse and a call for a more cost conscious approach to discovery by the Florida Supreme Court. In felony cases, the rule requires prosecutors to list witnesses in categories A, B, and C. Category A witnesses are subject to deposition as under the former rule. Category B witnesses are subject to deposition only upon leave of court. Category B witnesses include, but are not limited to, witnesses whose only connection to the case is the fact that they are the owners of property; transporting officers; booking officers; records and evidence custodians; and experts who have filed a report and curriculum vitae and who will not offer opinions subject to the Frye test. Category C witnesses may not be deposed. The trial courts are given more responsibility to regulate discovery by pretrial conference and by determining which category B witnesses should be deposed in a given case.

The rule was not amended for the purpose of prohibiting discovery. Instead, the rule recognizes that many circuits now have "early resolution" or "rocket dockets" in which "open file discovery" is used to resolve a substantial percentage of cases at or before arraignment. The committee encourages that procedure. If a case cannot be resolved early, the committee believes that resolution of typical cases will occur after the depositions of the most essential witnesses (category A) are taken. Cases which do not resolve after the depositions of Category A, may resolve if one or more category B witnesses are deposed. If the case is still unresolved, it is probably going to be a case that needs to be tried. In that event, judges may determine which additional depositions, if any, are necessary for pretrial preparation. A method for making that determination is provided in the rule.

Additionally, trial judges may regulate the taking of depositions in a number of ways to both facilitate resolution of a case and protect a witness from unnecessary inconvenience or harassment. There is a provision for setting a discovery schedule, including a discovery cut-off date as is common in civil practice. Also, a specific method is provided for application for protective orders.

One feature of the new rules relates to the deposition of law enforcement officers. Subpoenas are no longer required.

The rule has standardized the time for serving papers relating to discovery at fifteen days.

Discovery in misdemeanor cases has not been changed. (b)(1)(A)(i) An investigating officer is an officer who has directed the collection of evidence, interviewed material witnesses, or who was assigned as the case investigator.

(h)(1) The prosecutor and defense counsel are encouraged to be present for the depositions of essential witnesses, and judges are encouraged to provide calendar time for the taking of depositions so that counsel for all parties can attend. This will 1) diminish the potential for the abuse of witnesses, 2) place the parties in a position to timely and effectively avail themselves of the remedies and sanctions established in this rule, 3) promote an expeditious and timely resolution of the cause, and 4) diminish the need to order transcripts of the deposition, thereby reducing costs.

1998 Amendment. This rule governs only the location of depositions. The procedure for procuring out-of-state witneses for depositions is governed by statute.

Court Commentary

1996 Amendment. The designation of a witness who will present similar fact evidence will be dependent upon the witness's relationship to the similar crime, wrong, or act about which testimony will be given rather than the witness's relationship to the crime with which the defendant is currently charged.

1999/2000 Amendment. This rule does not affect requests for nonexempt law enforcement records as provided in chapter 119, Florida Statutes, other than those that are nonexempt as a result of a codefendant's participation in discovery. See Henderson v. State, 745 So.2d 319 (Fla. Feb. 18, 1999).

2014 Amendment. The amendment to subdivision (b)(1)(A)(i)(8) is not intended to limit in any manner whatsoever the discovery obligations under the other provisions of the rule. With respect to subdivision (b)(l)(M)(iv), the Florida Innocence Commission recognized the impossibility of listing in the body of the rule every possible permutation expressing a benefit by the state to the informant witness. Although the term "anything" is not defined in the rule, the following are examples of benefits that may be considered by the trial court in determining whether the state has complied with its discovery obligations. The term "anything" includes, but is not limited to, any deal, promise, inducement, pay, leniency, immunity, personal advantage, vindication, or other benefit that the prosecution, or any person acting on behalf of the prosecution, has knowingly made or may make in the future.

2018 Amendment. The amendments to subdivision (j) are a clarification of the rule based on Scipio v. State, 928 So. 2d 1138 (Fla. 2006), and Washington v. State, 151 So. 3d 544 (Fla. 1st DCA 2014).

VII. Substitution of Judge

Rule 3.231. Substitution of Judge.

If by reason of death or disability the judge before whom a trial has commenced is unable to proceed with the trial, or posttrial proceedings, another judge, certifying that he or she has become familiar with the case, may proceed with the disposition of the case, except in death penalty sentencing proceedings. In death penalty sentencing proceedings, a successor judge who did not hear the evidence during the penalty phase of the trial shall conduct a new sentencing proceeding before a new jury.

Committee Notes

1972 Adoption. New. Follows ABA Standard 4.3, Trial by Jury. Inserted to provide for substitution of trial judge in specified instances.

VIII. Change of Venue

Rule 3.240. Change of Venue.

(a) Grounds for Motion. The state or the defendant may move for a change of venue on the ground that a fair and impartial trial cannot be had in the county where the case is pending for any reason other than the interest and prejudice of the trial judge.

(b) Contents of Motion. Every motion for change of venue shall be in writing and be accompanied by:

    (1) affidavits of the movant and 2 or more other persons setting forth facts on which the motion is based; and

    (2) a certificate by the movant's counsel that the motion is made in good faith.

(c) Time for Filing. A motion for change of venue shall be filed no less than 10 days before the time the case is called for trial unless good cause is shown for failure to file within such time.

(d) Action on Motion. The court shall consider the affidavits filed by all parties and receive evidence on every issue of fact necessary to its decision. If the court grants the motion it shall make an order removing the cause to the court having jurisdiction to try such offense in some other convenient county where a fair and impartial trial can be had.

(e) Defendant in Custody. If the defendant is in custody, the order shall direct that the defendant be forthwith delivered to the custody of the sheriff of the county to which the cause is removed.

(f) Transmittal of Documents. The clerk shall docket the order of removal and transmit to the court to which the cause is removed a certified copy of the order of removal and of the record and proceedings and of the undertakings of the witnesses and the accused.

(g) Attendance by Witnesses. When the cause is removed to another court, witnesses who have been lawfully subpoenaed or ordered to appear at the trial shall, on notice of such removal, attend the court to which the cause is removed at the time specified in the order of removal. A witness who refuses to obey a duly served subpoena may be adjudged in contempt of court.

(h) Multiple Defendants. If there are several defendants and an order is made removing the cause on the application of 1 or more but not all of them, the other defendants shall be tried and all proceedings had against them in the county in which the cause is pending in all respects as if no order of removal had been made as to any defendant.

(i) Action of Receiving Court. The court to which the cause is removed shall proceed to trial and judgment therein as if the cause had originated in that court. If it is necessary to have any of the original pleadings or other documents before that court, the court from which the cause is removed shall at any time on application of the prosecuting attorney or the defendant order such documents or pleadings to be transmitted by the clerk, a certified copy thereof being retained.

(j) Prosecuting Attorney's Obligation. The prosecuting attorney of the court to which the cause is removed may amend the information, or file a new information. Any such new information shall be entitled in the county to which the cause is removed, but the allegations as to the place of commission of the crime shall refer to the county in which the crime was actually committed.

Committee Notes

1968 Adoption. (a) through (d) substantially same as sections 911.02 through 911.05, Florida Statutes. Language is simplified and requirement pertaining to cases in criminal courts of record that removal be to adjoining county is omitted. Modern communications and distribution of television and press makes old requirements impractical. Designation of county left to discretion of the trial judge.

(e) through (i) same as corresponding sections 911.06 through 911.10, Florida Statutes.

1972 Amendment. Same as prior rule.

IX. The Trial

Rule 3.250. Accused as Witness.

In all criminal prosecutions the accused may choose to be sworn as a witness in the accused's own behalf and shall in that case be subject to examination as other witnesses, but no accused person shall be compelled to give testimony against himself or herself, nor shall any prosecuting attorney be permitted before the jury or court to comment on the failure of the accused to testify in his or her own behalf.

Committee Notes

1968 Adoption. Same as section 918.09, Florida Statutes.

1972 Amendment. Same as prior rule. The committee considered The Florida Bar proposed amendment to this rule, but makes no recommendation with respect thereto.

Rule 3.251. Right to Trial by Jury.

In all criminal prosecutions the accused shall have the right to a speedy and public trial by an impartial jury in the county where the crime was committed.

Committee Notes

1972 Adoption. Substance of Art. I, §16, Florida Constitution.

Rule 3.260. Waiver of Jury Trial.

A defendant may in writing waive a jury trial with the consent of the state.

Committee Notes

1968 Adoption. This is the same as Federal Rule of Criminal Procedure 23(a). This changes existing law by providing for consent of state.

1972 Amendment. Changes former rule by deleting "the approval of the Court," thus making trial by judge mandatory where both parties agree. The committee felt that the matter of withdrawal of a waiver was a matter within the inherent discretion of the trial judge and that no rule is required.

Rule 3.270. Number of Jurors.

Twelve persons shall constitute a jury to try all capital cases, and 6 persons shall constitute a jury to try all other criminal cases.

Committee Notes

1968 Adoption. Except for substituting the word "persons" for "men," the suggested rule is a transcription of section 913.10, Florida Statutes. The standing committee on Florida court rules raised the question as to whether this rule is procedural or substantive and directed the subcommittee to call this fact to the attention of the Supreme Court.

1972 Amendment. Same as prior rule.

Rule 3.280. Alternate Jurors.

(a) Selection. The court may direct that jurors, in addition to the regular panel, be called and impanelled to sit as alternate jurors. Alternate jurors, in the order in which they are impanelled, shall replace jurors who, prior to the time the jury retires to consider its verdict, become unable or disqualified to perform their duties. Alternate jurors shall be drawn in the same manner, have the same qualifications, be subject to the same examination, take the same oath, and have the same functions, powers, facilities, and privileges as the principal jurors. Except as hereinafter provided regarding capital cases, an alternate juror who does not replace a principal juror shall be discharged at the same time the jury retires to consider its verdict.

(b) Responsibilities. At the conclusion of the guilt or innocence phase of the trial, each alternate juror will be excused with instructions to remain in the courtroom. The jury will then retire to consider its verdict, and each alternate will be excused with appropriate instructions that the alternate juror may have to return for an additional hearing should the defendant be convicted of a capital offense.

Committee Notes

1968 Adoption. Save for certain rewording, the suggested rule is a transcription of section 913.10(2), Florida Statutes, except that the provisions for the challenging of the alternate jurors has been included more appropriately in the rule relating to challenges.

1972 Amendment. Same as prior rule.

1977 Amendment. This rule clarifies any ambiguities as to what should be done with alternate jurors at the conclusion of a capital case and whether they should be available for the penalty phase of the trial. The change specifies that they will not be instructed as to any further participation until the other jurors who are deliberating on guilt or innocence are out of the courtroom, in order not to influence the deliberating jurors or in any way convey that the trial judge feels that a capital conviction is imminent.

Rule 3.281. List of Prospective Jurors.

Upon request, any party shall be furnished by the clerk of the court with a list containing names and addresses of prospective jurors summoned to try the case together with copies of all jury questionnaires returned by the prospective jurors.

Committee Notes

1972 Adoption. ABA Standard 2.2. The furnishing of such a list should result in considerable time being saved at voir dire. Also includes those questionnaires authorized by section 40.101, Florida Statutes, although the statute itself provides for such disclosure.

Rule 3.290. Challenge to Panel.

The state or defendant may challenge the panel. A challenge to the panel may be made only on the ground that the prospective jurors were not selected or drawn according to law. Challenges to the panel shall be made and decided before any individual juror is examined, unless otherwise ordered by the court. A challenge to the panel shall be in writing and shall specify the facts constituting the ground of the challenge. Challenges to the panel shall be tried by the court. Upon the trial of a challenge to the panel the witnesses may be examined on oath by the court and may be so examined by either party. If the challenge to the panel is sustained, the court shall discharge the panel. If the challenge is not sustained, the individual jurors shall be called.

Committee Notes

1968 Adoption. This is a transcription of section 913.01, Florida Statutes.

1972 Amendment. Same as prior rule 3.300; order of rule changed to improve chronology.

Rule 3.300. Voir Dire Examination, Oath, and Excusing of Member.

(a) Oath. The prospective jurors shall be sworn collectively or individually, as the court may decide. The form of oath shall be as follows:

"Do you solemnly swear (or affirm) that you will answer truthfully all questions asked of you as prospective jurors, so help you God?"

If any prospective juror affirms, the clause "so help you God" shall be omitted.

(b) Examination. The court may then examine each prospective juror individually, or may examine the prospective jurors collectively. Counsel for both the state and defendant shall have the right to examine jurors orally on their voir dire. The order in which the parties may examine each juror shall be determined by the court. The right of the parties to conduct an examination of each juror orally shall be preserved.

(c) Prospective Jurors Excused. If, after the examination of any prospective juror, the court is of the opinion that the juror is not qualified to serve as a trial juror, the court shall excuse the juror from the trial of the cause. If, however, the court does not excuse the juror, either party may then challenge the juror, as provided by law or by these rules.

Committee Notes

1968 Adoption.

(a) Save for the inclusion of the form of oath, the suggested rule is a transcription of a part of section 913.02(1), Florida Statutes. The form of oath paraphrases in pertinent part the oath set out in section 913.11, Florida Statutes.

(b) The suggested rule is a transcription of the remainder of section 913.02(1), Florida Statutes.

(c) Substantially same as section 913.02(2), Florida Statutes.

1972 Amendment. (a) The language relating to competence to serve as jurors deleted as superfluous, (c) amended for clarification by inserting the clause "that such juror is not qualified to serve as a trial juror" for the clause "that such juror is incompetent."

1980 Amendment. As to examination by parties, this brings rule 3.300(b) into conformity with Florida Rule of Civil Procedure 1.431(b). This rule also allows the court to examine each prospective juror individually or collectively.

Rule 3.310. Time for Challenge.

The state or defendant may challenge an individual prospective juror before the juror is sworn to try the cause; except that the Court may, for good cause, permit a challenge to be made after the juror is sworn, but before any evidence is presented.

Committee Notes

1968 Adoption. Save for the heading and for the inclusion of the phrase, "for cause or peremptorily," the suggested rule is a transcription of the provisions of section 913.04, Florida Statutes.

1972 Amendment. Prior rule amended only by deleting some language felt by the committee to be superfluous.

Rule 3.315. Exercise of Challenges.

On the motion of any party, all challenges shall be addressed to the court outside the hearing of the jury panel in a manner selected by the court so that the jury panel is not aware of the nature of the challenge, the party making the challenge, or the basis of the court's ruling on the challenge, if for cause.

Committee Notes

1980 Adoption. With the exception of "Upon the motion of any party," the language is taken directly from Florida Rule of Civil Procedure 1.431(c)(3). This rule had no counterpart in the criminal rules.

Rule 3.320. Manner of Challenge.

A challenge to an individual juror may be oral. When a juror is challenged for cause the ground of the challenge shall be stated.

Committee Notes

1968 Adoption. Save for the heading and the insertion of the word "the," the suggested rule is a transcription of the provisions of section 913.05, Florida Statutes. The phrase "for cause or peremptorily" has been added.

1972 Amendment. Same as prior rule [but some terminology has been changed].

Rule 3.330. Determination of Challenge for Cause.

The court shall determine the validity of a challenge of an individual juror for cause. In making such determination the juror challenged and any other material witnesses, produced by the parties, may be examined under oath by either party. The court may consider also any other evidence material to such challenge.

Committee Notes

1968 Adoption. The suggested rule is essentially a transcription of sections 913.06 and 913.07, Florida Statutes, except for the first and last sentences.

1972 Amendment. Same as prior rule [but some terminology has been changed].

Rule 3.340. Effect of Sustaining Challenge.

If a challenge for cause of an individual juror is sustained, the juror shall be discharged from the trial of the cause. If a peremptory challenge to an individual juror is made, the juror shall be discharged likewise from the trial of the cause.

Committee Notes

1968 Adoption. The first sentence of the suggested rule except for the inclusion of the words "for cause" is a transcription of section 913.09, Florida Statutes. The last sentence has been added.

1972 Amendment. Same as prior rule.

Rule 3.350. Peremptory Challenges.

(a) Number. Each party shall be allowed the following number of peremptory challenges:

>**(1) Felonies Punishable by Death or Imprisonment for Life.** Ten, if the offense charged is punishable by death or imprisonment for life;

>**(2) All Other Felonies.** Six, if the offense charged is a felony not punishable by death or imprisonment for life.

>**(3) Misdemeanors.** Three, if the offense charged is a misdemeanor.

(b) Codefendants. If 2 or more defendants are jointly tried, each defendant shall be allowed the number of peremptory challenges specified above, and in such case the state shall be allowed as many challenges as are allowed to all of the defendants.

(c) Multiple Counts and Multiple Charging Documents. If an indictment or information contains 2 or more counts or if two or more indictments or informations are consolidated for trial, the

Rule 3.350. Peremptory Challenges.

defendant shall be allowed the number of peremptory challenges that would be permissible in a single case, but in the interest of justice the judge may use judicial discretion in extenuating circumstances to grant additional challenges to the accumulate maximum based on the number of charges or cases included when it appears that there is a possibility that the state or the defendant may be prejudiced. The state and the defendant shall be allowed an equal number of challenges.

(d) Alternate Jurors. If 1 or 2 alternate jurors are called, each party is entitled to 1 peremptory challenge, in addition to those otherwise allowed by law, for each alternate juror so called. The additional peremptory challenge may be used only against the alternate juror and the other peremptory challenges allowed by law shall not be used against the alternate juror.

(e) Additional Challenges. The trial judge may exercise discretion to allow additional peremptory challenges when appropriate.

Committee Notes

1968 Adoption. The suggested rule is a transcription of section 913.08, Florida Statutes, excluding subdivision (5), which is lifted from section 913.10(2), Florida Statutes, and included since the several provisions relate to peremptory challenges. The question was raised regarding multiple counts or consolidation in their relation to the number of challenges. It was decided not to imply approval of multiple counts or consolidation. The standing committee on Florida court rules raised the question as to whether or not this rule is procedural or substantive and directed the subcommittee to call this fact to the attention of the supreme court.

1972 Amendment. Substantially same as prior rule; introductory language modernized.

1977 Amendment. This proposed rule amends rule 3.350(e) to allow the defendant and the state an equal number of peremptory challenges and to permit the court to grant additional challenges to both parties where it appears that the state would otherwise be prejudiced.

1992 Amendment. The amendment adds (e) that specifically sets out the trial court's discretion to allow peremptory challenges in addition to those provided for in the rule. This amendment was one of several proposed by the jury management committee that provided for a reduction in the number of peremptory challenges allowed by the rule. The majority of the criminal procedure rules committee, while recommending against adoption of the remaining proposals of the jury management committee, nevertheless felt it would be appropriate to add (e) to clarify that the trial court's discretion is not limited to those situations set out in (c) of the rule (i.e., multiple counts or informations or indictments consolidated for trial).

Rule 3.360. Oath of Trial Jurors.

The following oath shall be administered to the jurors:

"Do you solemnly swear (or affirm) that you will well and truly try the issues between the State of Florida and the defendant and render a true verdict according to the law and the evidence, so help you God?"

If any juror affirms, the clause "so help you God" shall be omitted.

Committee Notes

1968 Adoption. The suggested rule is a transcription of section 913.11, Florida Statutes.

1972 Adoption. Language of prior rule amended slightly to modernize.

Rule 3.361. Witness Attendance and Subpoenas.

(a) Subpoenas Generally. Subpoenas for testimony before the court and subpoenas for production of tangible evidence before the court may be issued by the clerk of the court or by any attorney of record in an action.

(b) Subpoena for Testimony or Production of Tangible Evidence.

(1) A subpoena for testimony or production of tangible evidence before the court shall state the name of the court and the title of the action and shall command each person to whom it is directed to attend and give testimony or produce the evidence at a time and place specified in the subpoena.

(2) On oral request of an attorney, the clerk shall issue a subpoena for testimony before the court or a subpoena for the production of tangible evidence before the court, signed and sealed but otherwise in blank, and the subpoena shall be filled in by the attorney before service.

(c) For Production of Tangible Evidence.

(1) If a subpoena commands a person or entity to produce books, papers, documents, or tangible things, the person or entity may move the court to quash or modify the subpoena before the time specified in the subpoena for compliance.

(2) The court may (A) quash or modify the subpoena if it is unreasonable and oppressive, or (B) require the person in whose behalf the subpoena is issued to advance the reasonable cost of producing the books, papers, documents, or tangible things.

(d) Attendance and Enforcement. A witness subpoenaed for testimony before the court or for production of tangible evidence before the court shall appear and remain in attendance until excused by the court or by all parties. A witness who refuses to obey a subpoena or who departs without being excused properly may be held in contempt.

X. Conduct to Trial; Jury Instructions

Rule 3.370. Regulation and Separation of Jurors.

(a) During Trial. After the jurors have been sworn they shall hear the case as a body and, within the discretion of the trial judge, may be sequestered. In capital cases, absent a showing of prejudice, the trial court may order that between the guilt and penalty phases of the trial the jurors may separate for a definite time to be fixed by the court and then reconvene before the beginning of the penalty phase.

(b) After Submission of Cause. Unless the jurors have been kept together during the trial the court may, after the final submission of the cause, order that the jurors may separate for a definite time to be fixed by the court and then reconvene in the courtroom before retiring for consideration of their verdict.

(c) During Deliberations. Absent exceptional circumstances of emergency, accident, or other special necessity or unless sequestration is waived by the state and the defendant, in all capital cases in which the death penalty is sought by the state, once the jurors have retired for consideration of their verdict, they must be sequestered until such time as they have reached a verdict or have otherwise been discharged by the court. In all other cases, the court, in its discretion, either on the motion of counsel or on the court's initiative, may order that the jurors be permitted to separate. If jurors are allowed to separate, the trial judge shall give appropriate cautionary instructions.

Committee Notes

1968 Adoption. (a) Taken from section 919.01, Florida Statutes.

(b) Taken from section 919.02, Florida Statutes.

1972 Amendment. (a) and (b) substantially the same as former rule 3.380, except that some language has been modernized. New provision permits nonsequestered jury to separate after receiving case for consideration.

Former rule 3.370 has been deleted as its substance is now contained in new Rules 3.150 through 3.153 on Joinder and Severance.

Rule 3.371. Juror Questions of Witnesses.

(a) Judicial Discretion. At the discretion of the presiding trial judge, jurors may be allowed to submit questions of witnesses during the trial.

(b) Procedure. The trial judge shall utilize the following procedure if a juror indicates that the juror wishes to ask a question:

(1) the questions must be submitted in writing;

(2) the trial judge shall review the question outside the presence of the jury;

(3) counsel shall have an opportunity to object to the question outside the presence of the jury;

(4) counsel shall be allowed to ask follow up questions; and

(5) the jury must be advised that if a question submitted by a juror is not allowed for any reason, the juror must not discuss it with the other jurors and must not hold it against either party.

Rule 3.372. Juror Notebooks.

In its discretion, the court may authorize documents and exhibits to be included in notebooks for use by the jurors during trial to aid them in performing their duties.

Rule 3.380. Motion for Judgment of Acquittal.

(a) Timing. If, at the close of the evidence for the state or at the close of all the evidence in the cause, the court is of the opinion that the evidence is insufficient to warrant a conviction, it may, and on the motion of the prosecuting attorney or the defendant shall, enter a judgment of acquittal.

(b) Waiver. A motion for judgment of acquittal is not waived by subsequent introduction of evidence on behalf of the defendant. The motion must fully set forth the grounds on which it is based.

(c) Renewal. If the jury returns a verdict of guilty or is discharged without having returned a verdict, the defendant's motion may be made or renewed within 10 days after the reception of a verdict and the jury is discharged or such further time as the court may allow.

Committee Notes

1968 Adoption. Substantially same as section 918.08, Florida Statutes, except as follows:

(a) The existing statutory practice of granting directed verdicts is abolished in favor of the federal practice of having the judge enter a judgment of acquittal.

(b) The wording was changed to comply with the judgment of acquittal theory. A majority of the committee felt that the substance of the existing statute was all right, but a minority felt that the language should be changed so that a defendant would waive an erroneous denial of his motion for judgment of acquittal by introducing evidence. This point was raised in Wiggins v. State, 101 So.2d 833 (Fla. 1st DCA 1958), wherein the court said that this statute is "ineptly worded."

1972 Amendment. (a) and (b) same as prior rule 3.660, transferred to better follow trial chronology. (c) provides time period for renewal of motion and is new.

1980 Amendment. This brings rule 3.380(c) into conformity with Florida Rule of Civil Procedure 1.480(b) as it relates to the number of days (10) within which a party, either in a civil or criminal case, may make or renew a motion for judgment of acquittal. There appears to be no sound reason for the distinction between the criminal rule (4 days or such greater time as the court may allow, not to exceed 15 days) and the civil rule (10 days).

Rule 3.381. Final Arguments.

In all criminal trials, excluding the sentencing phase of a capital case, at the close of all the evidence, the prosecuting attorney shall be entitled to an initial closing argument and a rebuttal closing argument before the jury or the court sitting without a jury. Failure of the prosecuting attorney to make a closing argument shall not deprive the defense of its right to make a closing argument or the prosecuting attorney's right to then make a rebuttal argument. If the defendant does not present a closing argument, the prosecuting attorney will not be permitted a rebuttal argument.

Rule 3.390. Jury Instructions.

(a) Subject of Instructions. The Florida Standard Jury Instructions in Criminal Cases appearing on The Florida Bar's website may be used, as provided in Florida Rule of General Practice and Judicial Administration 2.570, by the presiding judge in instructing the jury in a criminal case. The presiding judge shall instruct the jury only on the law of the case before or after the argument of counsel and may provide appropriate instructions during the trial. If the instructions are given prior to final argument, the presiding judge shall give the jury final procedural instructions after final arguments are concluded and prior to deliberations. Except in capital cases, the judge shall not instruct the jury on the sentence that may be imposed for the offense for which the accused is on trial.

(b) Form of Instructions. The instruction to a jury shall be orally delivered and shall also be in writing. All written instructions shall also be filed in the cause.

(c) Written Request. At the close of the evidence, or at such earlier time during the trial as the court reasonably directs any party may file written requests that the court instruct the jury on the law as set forth in the requests. The court shall inform counsel of its proposed action on the request and of the instructions that will be given prior to their argument to the jury.

(d) Objections. No party may raise on appeal the giving or failure to give an instruction unless the party objects thereto before the jury retires to consider its verdict, stating distinctly the matter to which the party objects and the grounds of the objection. Opportunity shall be given to make the objection out of the presence of the jury.

(e) Transcript and Review. When an objection is made to the giving of or failure to give an instruction, no exception need be made to the court's ruling thereon in order to have the ruling reviewed, and the grounds of objection and ruling thereon shall be taken by the court reporter and, if the jury returns a verdict of guilty, transcribed by the court reporter and filed in the cause.

Committee Notes

1972 Adoption. The committee adopted section 918.10, Florida Statutes, with only minor modification as to terminology.

1988 Amendment. To assist the jury in understanding the jury instructions.

1992 Amendment. Suggested change in wording to make (d) clearer and easier to understand and also so it more closely follows its federal counterpart, Federal Rule of Criminal Procedure 30.

Rule 3.391. Selection of Foreperson of Jury.

The court shall instruct the jurors to select one of their number foreperson.

Committee Notes

1968 Adoption. This rule was inserted in order to clarify the system of selecting jury foreman.

1972 Amendment. Same as former rule 3.390.

Rule 3.400. Materials to the Jury Room.

(a) Discretionary Materials. The court may permit the jury, upon retiring for deliberation, to take to the jury room:

(1) a copy of the charges against the defendant;

(2) forms of verdict approved by the court, after being first submitted to counsel;

(3) all things received in evidence other than depositions. If the thing received in evidence is a public record or a private document which, in the opinion of the court, ought not to be taken from the person having it in custody, a copy shall be taken or sent instead of the original.

(b) Mandatory Materials. The court must provide the jury, upon retiring for deliberation, with a written copy of the instructions given to take to the jury room.

Committee Notes

1968 Adoption. (1) and (2) same as section 919.04(1) and (2), Florida Statutes.

Section (3) was changed from the existing section 919.04(3) by adding to the things which should not be taken with or sent to the jury, written or recorded statements or confessions. It was felt by the committee that the present practice of allowing such things to be taken with the jury is unfair and emphasizes such statements or confessions to the jury. Since they are always read to the jury they should receive no additional emphasis than the testimony of any witness from the stand. [Court did not approve this change; the proposal was not adopted; and F.S.A. § 919.04(3) was transferred unchanged to Rule 1.400(c).]

1972 Amendment. (a) permits a copy of the indictment or information to be taken to the jury room. The committee deliberated at length about this provision but finally approved same. (b), (c), and (d) are same as former rule 3.400(a), (b), and (c) [but some terminology has been changed].

Rule 3.410. Jury Request to Review Evidence or for Additional Instructions.

(a) If after they have retired to consider their verdict, jurors request additional instructions or to have any testimony read or played back to them they may be conducted into the courtroom by the officer who has them in charge and the court may give them the additional instructions or may order the testimony read or played back to them. The instructions shall be given and the testimony presented only after notice to the prosecuting attorney and to counsel for the defendant. All testimony read or played back must be done in open court in the presence of all parties. In its discretion, the court may respond in writing to the inquiry without having the jury brought before the court, provided the parties have received the opportunity to place objections on the record and both the inquiry and response are made part of the record.

(b) In a case in which the jury requests to have the transcripts of trial testimony, the following procedures must be followed:

>**(1)** The trial judge must deny the requests for transcripts.

>**(2)** The trial judge must instruct jurors that they can, however, request to have any testimony read or played back, which may or may not be granted at the court's discretion.

>**(3)** In cases in which jurors make only a general request for transcripts, as opposed to identifying any particular witness' testimony that they wish to review, the trial judge must instruct jurors that, if they request a read or play back, they must specify the particular trial testimony they wish to have read or played back.

(c) If, after being properly instructed in accordance with subdivision (b), the jurors request a read or play back of any trial testimony, the trial judge must follow the procedures set forth in subdivision (a).

Committee Notes

1968 Adoption. Same as section 919.05, Florida Statutes.

1972 Amendment. This is the same as former rule 3.410, except that the former rule made it mandatory for the trial judge to give additional instructions upon request. The committee feels that this should be discretionary.

Rule 3.420. Recall of Jury for Additional Instructions.

The court may recall the jurors after they have retired to consider their verdict to give them additional instructions or to correct any erroneous instructions given them. The additional or corrective instructions may be given only after notice to the prosecuting attorney and to counsel for the defendant.

Committee Notes

1968 Adoption. Same as section 919.06, Florida Statutes.

1972 Amendment. Same as former rule.

Rule 3.430. Jury Not Recallable to Hear Additional Evidence.

After the jurors have retired to consider their verdict the court shall not recall the jurors to hear additional evidence.

Committee Notes

1968 Adoption. Same as section 919.07, Florida Statutes.

1972 Amendment. Same as prior rule.

XI. The Verdict

Rule 3.440. Rendition of Verdict; Reception and Recording.

When the jurors have agreed upon a verdict they shall be conducted into the courtroom by the officer having them in charge. The court shall ask the foreperson if an agreement has been reached on a verdict. If the foreperson answers in the affirmative, the judge shall call on the foreperson to deliver the verdict in writing to the clerk. The court may then examine the verdict and correct it as to matters of form with the unanimous consent of the jurors. The clerk shall then read the verdict to the jurors and, unless disagreement is expressed by one or more of them or the jury is polled, the verdict shall be entered of record, and the jurors discharged from the cause. No verdict may be rendered unless all of the trial jurors concur in it.

Committee Notes

1968 Adoption. Same as section 919.09, Florida Statutes.

1972 Amendment. Same as prior rule.

Rule 3.450. Polling the Jury.

On the motion of either the state or the defendant or on its own motion, the court shall cause the jurors to be asked severally if the verdict rendered is their verdict. If a juror dissents, the court must direct that the jury be sent back for further consideration. If there is no dissent the verdict shall be entered of record and the jurors discharged. However, no motion to poll the jury shall be entertained after the jury is discharged or the verdict recorded.

Committee Notes

1968 Adoption. Same as section 919.10, Florida Statutes, except elimination of polling jury after directed verdict in view of innovation of "judgment of acquittal."

1972 Amendment. Same as prior rule.

Rule 3.451. Judicial Comment on Verdict.

While it is appropriate for the court to thank jurors at the conclusion of a trial for their public service, the court shall not praise or criticize their verdict.

Committee Notes

1972 Adoption. From ABA Standard 5.6, Trial by Jury.

Rule 3.470. Proceedings on Sealed Verdict.

The court may, with the consent of the prosecuting attorney and the defendant, direct the jurors that if they should agree upon a verdict during a temporary adjournment of the court, the foreperson and each juror shall sign the same, and the verdict shall be sealed in an envelope and delivered to the officer having charge of the jury, after which the jury may separate until the court reconvenes. When the court authorizes the rendition of a sealed verdict, it shall admonish the jurors not to make any disclosure, of any kind, concerning it or to speak with other persons concerning the case, until their verdict shall have been rendered in open court. The officer shall deliver the sealed verdict to the clerk. When the jurors have reassembled in open court, the envelope shall be opened by the court or clerk, and must be received in the same manner as unsealed verdicts.

Committee Notes

1968 Adoption of Rule 3.470. Same as section 919.12, Florida Statutes.

1968 Adoption of Rule 3.480. Same as section 919.13, Florida Statutes.

1972 Amendment. Former rule 3.480 has been deleted, its substance now contained in rule 3.470. Substantially same as former rules 3.470 and 3.480.

Rule 3.490. Determination of Degree of Offense.

If the indictment or information charges an offense divided into degrees, the jury may find the defendant guilty of the offense charged or any lesser degree supported by the evidence. The judge shall not instruct on any degree as to which there is no evidence.

Committee Notes

1968 Adoption. Same as 919.14.

1972 Amendment. Same as prior rule except references to affidavit have been deleted.

Rule 3.500. Verdict of Guilty Where More Than One Count.

If different offenses are charged in the indictment or information on which the defendant is tried, the jurors shall, if they convict the defendant, make it appear by their verdict on which counts or of which offenses they find the defendant guilty.

Committee Notes

1968 Adoption. Same as section 919.15, Florida Statutes.

1972 Amendment. Amended to modernize the language of the rule. Substantially the same as prior rule.

Rule 3.505. Inconsistent Verdicts.

The state need not elect between inconsistent counts, but the trial court shall submit to the jury verdict forms as to each count with instructions applicable to returning its verdicts from the inconsistent counts.

Committee Notes

1977 Adoption. Although there appears to be no rule or statute relating to "election," many Florida cases refer to the fact that the trial court is required to make the state elect, before or during trial, between inconsistent counts. Many times the circumstances show conclusively that the accused is guilty of one or the other of inconsistent offenses. Since the evidence is then inconsistent with any reasonable hypothesis of innocence, the circumstantial rule is satisfied and the evidence should support a verdict of guilty as to either offense. In such a case the state should not be required to elect. This new rule is intended to lead to uniformity throughout the state on this issue and is more consonant with rule 3.140(k)(5).

Rule 3.510. Determination of Attempts and Lesser Included Offenses.

On an indictment or information on which the defendant is to be tried for any offense the jury may convict the defendant of:

(a) an attempt to commit the offense if such attempt is an offense and is supported by the evidence. The judge shall not instruct the jury if there is no evidence to support the attempt and the only evidence proves a completed offense; or

(b) any offense that as a matter of law is a necessarily included offense or a lesser included offense of the offense charged in the indictment or information and is supported by the evidence. The judge shall not instruct on any lesser included offense as to which there is no evidence.

Committee Notes

1968 Adoption. Same as section 919.16, Florida Statutes. The standing committee on Florida court rules raised the question as to whether this rule is procedural or substantive and directed the subcommittee to call this fact to the attention of the supreme court.

1972 Amendment. Same as prior rule except that references to affidavit have been deleted.

Rule 3.520. Verdict in Case of Joint Defendants.

On the trial of 2 or more defendants jointly the jurors may render a verdict as to any defendant in regard to whom the jurors agree.

Committee Notes

1968 Adoption. Same as section 919.17, Florida Statutes.

1972 Amendment. Same as prior rule.

Rule 3.530. Reconsideration of Ambiguous or Defective Verdict.

If a verdict is so defective that the court cannot determine from it whether the jurors intended to acquit the defendant or to convict the defendant of an offense for which judgment could be entered under the indictment or information on which the defendant is tried, or cannot determine from it on what count or counts the jurors intended to acquit or convict the defendant, the court shall, with proper instructions, direct the jurors to reconsider the verdict, and the verdict shall not be received until it shall clearly appear therefrom whether the jurors intended to convict or acquit the defendant and on what count or counts they intended to acquit or convict the defendant. If the jury persists in rendering a defective verdict, the court shall declare a mistrial.

Committee Notes

1968 Adoption. Same as section 919.18, Florida Statutes.

1972 Amendment. Same as prior rule.

Rule 3.540. When Verdict May Be Rendered.

A verdict may be rendered and additional or corrective instructions given on any day, including Sunday or any legal holiday.

Committee Notes

1968 Adoption. Same as section 919.19, Florida Statutes.

1972 Amendment. Same as prior rule.

Rule 3.550. Disposition of Defendant.

If a verdict of guilty is rendered the defendant shall, if in custody, be remanded. If the defendant is at large on bail, the defendant may be taken into custody and committed to the proper official or remain at liberty on the same or additional bail as the court may direct.

Committee Notes

1968 Adoption. Same as section 919.20, Florida Statutes.

Rule 3.560. Discharge of Jurors.

After the jurors have retired to consider their verdict, the court shall discharge them from the cause when:

(a) their verdict has been received;

(b) on the expiration of such time as the court deems proper, if the court finds there is no reasonable probability that the jurors can agree on a verdict; or

(c) a necessity exists for their discharge.

The court may in any event discharge the jurors from the cause if the prosecuting attorney and the defendant consent to the discharge.

Committee Notes

1968 Adoption. Same as section 919.21, Florida Statutes, except (4) omitted.

1972 Amendment. Same as prior rule.

Rule 3.570. Irregularity in Rendition, Reception, and Recording of Verdict.

No irregularity in the rendition or reception of a verdict may be raised unless it is raised before the jury is discharged. No irregularity in the recording of a verdict shall affect its validity unless the defendant was in fact prejudiced by the irregularity.

Committee Notes

1968 Adoption. Rule 3.570 is same as section 919.22, Florida Statutes. Section 919.23, Florida Statutes, was not included in the rules. This deals with the recommendation of mercy and it was felt that this was not procedural but substantive and not within the scope of the rulemaking power of the supreme court.

1972 Amendment. Same as prior rule.

Rule 3.575. Motion to Interview Juror.

A party who has reason to believe that the verdict may be subject to legal challenge may move the court for an order permitting an interview of a juror or jurors to so determine. The motion shall be filed within 10 days after the rendition of the verdict, unless good cause is shown for the failure to make the motion within that time. The motion shall state the name of any juror to be interviewed and the reasons that the party has to believe that the verdict may be subject to challenge. After notice and hearing, the trial judge, upon a finding that the verdict may be subject to challenge, shall enter an order permitting the interview, and setting therein a time and a place for the interview of the juror or jurors, which shall be conducted in the presence of the court and the parties. If no reason is found to believe that the verdict may be subject to challenge, the court shall enter its order denying permission to interview.

Court Commentary

2004 Amendment. This rule does not abrogate Rule Regulating The Florida Bar 4-3.5(d)(4), which allows an attorney to interview a juror to determine whether the verdict may be subject to legal challenge after filing a notice of intention to interview.

XII. Post-Trial-Motions

Rule 3.580. Court May Grant New Trial.

When a verdict has been rendered against the defendant or the defendant has been found guilty by the court, the court on motion of the defendant, or on its own motion, may grant a new trial or arrest judgment.

Committee Notes

1968 Adoption. Same as section 920.01, Florida Statutes, except arrest of judgment is added.

1972 Amendment. Same as prior rule.

Rule 3.590. Time for and Method of Making Motions; Procedure; Custody Pending Hearing.

(a) Time for Filing in Noncapital Cases. In cases in which the state does not seek the death penalty, a motion for new trial or a motion in arrest of judgment, or both, may be made, either orally in open court or in writing and filed with the clerk's office, within 10 days after the rendition of the verdict or the finding of the court. A timely motion may be amended to state new grounds without leave of court prior to expiration of the 10-day period and in the discretion of the court at any other time before the motion is determined.

(b) Time for Filing in Capital Cases Where the Death Penalty Is an Issue. A motion for new trial or a motion in arrest of judgment, or both, or for a new penalty phase hearing may be made within 10 days after written final judgment of conviction and sentence of life imprisonment or death is filed. The motion may address grounds which arose in the guilt phase and the penalty phase of the trial. Separate motions for the guilt phase and the penalty phase may be filed. The motion or motions may be amended without leave of court prior to the expiration of the 10-day period, and in the discretion of the court, at any other time before the motion is determined.

(c) Oral Motions. When the defendant has been found guilty by a jury or by the court, the motion may be dictated into the record, if a court reporter is present, and may be argued immediately after the return of the verdict or the finding of the court. The court may immediately rule on the motion.

(d) Written Motions. The motion may be in writing, filed with the clerk; it shall state the grounds on which it is based. A copy of a written motion shall be served on the prosecuting attorney. When the court sets a time for the hearing thereon, the clerk may notify counsel for the respective parties or the attorney for the defendant may serve notice of hearing on the prosecuting attorney.

(e) Custody Pending Motion. A defendant who is not already at liberty on bail shall remain in custody and not be allowed liberty on bail unless the court, on good cause shown if the offense for which the defendant is convicted is bailable, permits the defendant to be released on bail until the court disposes of the motion. If the defendant is already at liberty on bail that is deemed by the court to be good and sufficient, the court may permit the defendant to continue at large on such bail until the motion for new trial is heard and the court disposes of the motion.

Committee Notes

1968 Adoption. (a) The same as the first part of section 920.02(3), Florida Statutes, except that the statutory word "further" is changed to "greater" in the rule and provision for motion in arrest of judgment is added.

(b) Substantially the same as first part of section 920.02(2), Florida Statutes. The rule omits the requirement that the defendant be sentenced immediately on the denial of a motion for new trial (the court might wish to place the defendant on probation or might desire to call for a presentence investigation). The rule also omits the statute's requirement that an order of denial be dictated to the court reporter, because the clerk is supposed to be taking minutes at this stage.

NOTE: The provisions of the last part of section 920.02(2), Florida Statutes, as to supersedeas and appeal are not incorporated into this rule; such provisions are not germane to motions for new trial or arrest of judgment.

(c) Substantially same as section 920.03, Florida Statutes.

(d) Substantially same as last part of section 920.02(3), Florida Statutes, except that the last sentence of the rule is new.

NOTE: The provisions of section 920.02(4), Florida Statutes, relating to supersedeas on appeal and the steps that are necessary to obtain one, are not incorporated into a rule. The provisions of section 920.02(4) do not belong in a group of rules dealing with motions for new trial.

1972 Amendment. Substantially the same as prior rule.

1980 Amendment. This brings rule 3.590(a) into conformity with Florida Rule of Civil Procedure 1.530(b) as it relates to the time within which a motion for new trial or in arrest of judgment may be filed. It also allows the defendant in a criminal case the opportunity to amend the motion. The opportunity to amend already exists in a civil case. No sound reason exists to justify the disparities in the rules.

2006 Amendment. This amendment provides the time limitations and procedures for moving for new trial, arrest of judgment or a new penalty phase in capital cases in which the death penalty is an issue. The motion may be made within ten days after written final judgment of conviction and sentence of life imprisonment or death is filed.

Rule 3.600. Grounds for New Trial.

(a) Grounds for Granting. The court shall grant a new trial only if:

(1) the jurors decided the verdict by lot;

(2) the verdict is contrary to law or the weight of the evidence; or

(3) new and material evidence, which, if introduced at the trial would probably have changed the verdict or finding of the court, and which the defendant could not with reasonable diligence have discovered and produced at the trial, has been discovered.

(b) Grounds for Granting if Prejudice is Established. The court shall grant a new trial if substantial rights of the defendant were prejudiced because:

(1) the defendant was not present at any proceeding at which the defendant's presence is required by these rules;

(2) the jury received any evidence out of court, other than that resulting from an authorized view of the premises;

(3) the jurors, after retiring to deliberate upon the verdict, separated without leave of court;

(4) any juror was guilty of misconduct;

(5) the prosecuting attorney was guilty of misconduct;

(6) the court erred in the decision of any matter of law arising during the course of the trial;

(7) the court erroneously instructed the jury on a matter of law or refused to give a proper instruction requested by the defendant; or

(8) for any other cause not due to the defendant's own fault, the defendant did not receive a fair and impartial trial.

(c) Evidence. When a motion for new trial calls for a decision on any question of fact, the court may consider evidence on such motion by affidavit or otherwise.

Committee Notes

1968 Adoption. Same as sections 920.04 and 920.05, Florida Statutes, except that the last paragraph of section 920.05 is omitted from the rule. The provision of the omitted paragraph that a new trial shall be granted to a defendant who has not received a fair and impartial trial through no personal fault is inserted in the rule as subdivision (b)(8). The provision of the omitted paragraph of the statute which requires a new trial when the sentence exceeds the penalty provided by law is omitted from the rule because no defendant is entitled to a new trial merely because an excessive sentence has been pronounced. The standing committee on Florida court rules questioned whether this rule is procedural or substantive and directed the subcommittee to call this fact to the attention of the supreme court.

(c) Same as second paragraph of section 920.07, Florida Statutes.

1972 Amendment. Same as prior rule.

Rule 3.610. Motion for Arrest of Judgment; Grounds.

The court shall grant a motion in arrest of judgment only if:

(a) the indictment or information on which the defendant was tried is so defective that it will not support a judgment of conviction;

(b) the court is without jurisdiction of the cause;

(c) the verdict is so uncertain that it does not appear therefrom that the jurors intended to convict the defendant of an offense for which the defendant could be convicted under the indictment or information; or

(d) the defendant was convicted of an offense for which the defendant could not be convicted under the indictment or information.

Committee Notes

1968 Adoption. Note that (a)(1) of the rule revamps section 920.05(2)(a) through (d), Florida Statutes, in an effort to better take into account the fact that an accusatorial writ that would not withstand a motion to quash (dismiss) might well support a judgment of conviction if no such motion is filed. See Sinclair v. State, 46 So.2d 453 (1950).

Note also that, where appropriate, the rule mentions "affidavit" in addition to "indictment" and "information." The standing committee on Florida court rules questioned whether this rule is procedural or substantive and directed the subcommittee to call this fact to the attention of the supreme court.

1972 Amendment. Same as prior rule. References to trial affidavit deleted.

Rule 3.620. When Evidence Sustains Only Conviction of Lesser Offense.

When the offense is divided into degrees or necessarily includes lesser offenses and the court, on a motion for new trial, is of the opinion that the evidence does not sustain the verdict but is sufficient to sustain a finding of guilt of a lesser degree or of a lesser offense necessarily included in the one charged, the court shall not grant a new trial but shall find or adjudge the defendant guilty of the lesser degree or lesser offense necessarily included in the charge, unless a new trial is granted by reason of some other prejudicial error.

Committee Notes

1968 Adoption. Substantially the same as section 920.06, Florida Statutes.

1972 Amendment. Same as prior rule.

Rule 3.630. Sentence Before or After Motion Filed.

The court in its discretion may sentence the defendant either before or after the filing of a motion for new trial or arrest of judgment.

Committee Notes

1968 Adoption. Same as first paragraph of section 920.07, Florida Statutes. Provision for arrest of judgment is added.

1972 Amendment. Same as prior rule.

Rule 3.640. Effect of Granting New Trial.

When a new trial is granted, the new trial shall proceed in all respects as if no former trial had occurred except that when an offense is divided into degrees or the charge includes a lesser offense, and the defendant has been found guilty of a lesser degree or lesser included offense, the defendant cannot thereafter be prosecuted for a higher degree of the same offense or for a higher offense than that of which the defendant was convicted.

Committee Notes

1968 Adoption. Based on section 920.09, Florida Statutes. The second paragraph of the existing statute allows the testimony of an absent witness, given at a former trial, to be used only if the witness is absent from the state or dead. This has been enlarged to include absent witnesses who are physically incapacitated to attend court or who have become mentally incapacitated to testify since the former trial.

1972 Committee Note. Same as prior rule.

XIII. Judgment

Rule 3.650. Judgment Defined.

The term "judgment" means the adjudication by the court that the defendant is guilty or not guilty.

Committee Notes

1968 Adoption. Substantially the same as section 921.01, Florida Statutes.

1972 Amendment. Same as prior rule.

Rule 3.670. Rendition of Judgment.

(a) If the defendant is found not guilty, a judgment of not guilty must be rendered in open court and in writing, signed by a judge, filed, and recorded.

(b) If the defendant is found guilty, a judgment of guilty must be rendered in open court and in writing, signed by the judge, filed, and recorded. However, where allowed by law, the judge may withhold an adjudication of guilt. In the case of a felony, the judge may withhold an adjudication of guilt only if the judge places the defendant on probation.

(c) When a judge renders a final judgment of conviction, withholds adjudication of guilt after a verdict of guilty, imposes a sentence, grants probation, or revokes probation, the judge must forthwith inform the defendant concerning the rights of appeal therefrom, including the time allowed by law for taking an appeal.

(d) Within 15 days after the signed written judgment and sentence is filed with the clerk of court, the clerk of the court must serve on counsel for the defendant and counsel for the state a copy of the judgment of conviction and sentence entered, noting thereon the date of service by a certificate of service. If it is the practice of the trial court or the clerk of court to hand deliver copies of the judgment and sentence at the time of sentencing and copies are in fact hand delivered at that time, hand delivery must be noted in the court file, but no further service is required and the certificate of service need not be included on the hand-delivered copy.

Committee Notes

1968 Adoption. To the same effect as section 921.02, Florida Statutes, except the portion reading "in writing, signed by the judge" which was added. Last sentence was added to permit the judge to operate under section 948.01(3), Florida Statutes.

The Florida law forming the basis of this proposal is found in article V, sections 4 and 5, Constitution of Florida, concerning the right of appeal from a judgment of conviction; section 924.06, Florida Statutes, specifying when a defendant may take an appeal; section 924.09, Florida Statutes, and Florida Criminal Appellate Rule 6.2 concerning the time for taking appeals by a defendant in criminal cases; and section 948.011, Florida Statutes, providing for a sentence of a fine and probation as to imprisonment.

The purpose of the proposed rule is to provide assurance that a defendant, represented or unrepresented by counsel, will have authoritative and timely notice of the right to appeal.

1972 Amendment. Same as prior rule [but some terminology has been changed].

2005 Amendment. Amended to conform with section 775.08435, Florida Statutes (2004), effective July 1, 2004 (ch. 2004-60, Laws of Fla.).

Rule 3.680. Judgment on Informal Verdict.

If a verdict is rendered from which it can be clearly understood that the jurors intended to acquit the defendant, a judgment of not guilty shall be rendered thereon even though the verdict is defective. No judgment of guilty shall be rendered on a verdict unless the jurors clearly express in it a finding of guilt of the defendant.

Committee Notes

1968 Adoption. Same as section 921.02, Florida Statutes.
1972 Amendment. Same as prior rule.

Rule 3.690. Judgment of Not Guilty; Defendant Discharged and Sureties Exonerated.

When a judgment of not guilty is entered, the defendant, if in custody, shall be immediately discharged unless the defendant is in custody on some other charge. If the defendant is at large on bail, the defendant's sureties shall be exonerated and, if money or bonds have been deposited as bail, the money or bonds shall be refunded.

Committee Notes

1968 Adoption. Same as section 921.04, Florida Statutes.

1972 Amendment. Same as prior rule.

Rule 3.691. Post-Trial Release.

(a) When Authorized. A defendant who has been adjudicated guilty of the commission of any non-capital offense for which bail is not prohibited under section 903.133, Florida Statutes, may be released, pending review of the conviction, at the discretion of either the trial or appellate court, applying the principles enunciated in Younghans v. State, 90 So. 2d 308 (Fla. 1956). No defendant may be admitted to bail on appeal from a conviction of a felony unless the defendant establishes that the appeal is taken in good faith, on grounds fairly debatable, and not frivolous. However, in no case shall bail be granted if the defendant has previously been convicted of a felony, the commission of which occurred prior to the commission of the subsequent felony, and the defendant's civil rights have not been restored or if other felony charges are pending against the defendant and probable cause has been found that the defendant has committed the felony or felonies at the time the request for bail is made.

(b) Written Findings. In any case in which the court has the discretion to release the defendant pending review of the conviction and, after the defendant's conviction, denies release, it shall state in writing its reasons for the denial.

(c) Review of Denial. An order by a trial court denying bail to a defendant pursuant to the provisions of subdivision (a) may be reviewed by motion to the appellate court and the motion shall be advanced on the calendar of the appellate court for expeditious review.

(d) Conditions of Release. If the defendant is released after conviction and pending appeal, the conditions shall be:

(1) the defendant will duly prosecute the appeal; and

(2) the defendant will surrender himself or herself in execution of the judgment or sentence on its being affirmed or modified or on the appeal being dismissed; or in case the judgment is reversed and the cause remanded for a new trial, the defendant will appear in the court to which the cause may be remanded for a new trial, that the defendant will appear in the court to which the cause may be remanded and submit to the orders and process thereof and will not depart the jurisdiction of the court without leave.

(e) Approval of Bond. The court shall approve the sufficiency and adequacy of the bond, its security, and sureties, prior to the release of the defendant. However, in no case may an original appearance bond be continued for an appeal.

Committee Notes

1977 Amendment. Chapter 76-138, section 2, Laws of Florida, by appropriate vote, repealed the provisions of rule 3.691, insofar as they were inconsistent with the legislative act. This rule has been amended to include the provisions of Chapter 76-138, Laws of Florida.

Rule 3.692. Petition to Seal or Expunge.

(a) Requirements of Petition. The completed petition, sworn statement, and certificate of eligibility shall be served on the prosecuting attorney and the arresting authority; however, it is not necessary to make any agency other than the state a party.

(1) All relief sought by reason of sections 943.0585, Florida Statutes, shall be by written petition, filed with the clerk. The petition must be accompanied by:

(A) a valid certificate of eligibility issued by the Florida Department of Law Enforcement; and

(B) a sworn statement by the petitioner attesting that the petitioner:

(i) satisfies the eligibility requirement in section 943.0585(1), Florida Statutes;

(ii) is eligible for an expunction to the best of the petitioner's knowledge; and

Rule 3.692. Petition to Seal or Expunge.

(iii) does not have any other petition to seal or expunge a criminal history record pending before any court.

The completed petition, sworn statement, and certificate of eligibility shall be served on the prosecuting attorney and the arresting authority; however, it is not necessary to make any agency other than the state a party.

(2) All relief sought pursuant to section 943.059, Florida Statutes, shall be by written petition, filed with the clerk. The petition must be accompanied by:

(A) a valid certificate of eligibility issued by the Florida Department of Law Enforcement; and

(B) a sworn statement by the petitioner attesting that the petitioner:

(i) satisfies the eligibility requirement in section 943.059(1), Florida Statutes;

(ii) is eligible for a sealing to the best of the petitioner's knowledge; and

(iii) does not have any other petition to seal or expunge a criminal history record pending before the court.

(b) State's Response; Evidence. The prosecuting attorney and arresting agency may respond to the petition and sworn statement. The court may receive evidence on any issue of fact necessary to rule on the petition.

(c) Written Order. If the petition is granted, the court shall enter its written order so stating and further setting forth the records and agencies or departments to which it is directed. Any request for expunging or sealing of a criminal history record may be denied at the sole discretion of the court. The court may not order a criminal justice agency to expunge or seal a criminal history record until the petitioner has applied for and received a certificate of eligibility.

(d) Clerk's Duties.

(1) On receipt of an order sealing or expunging non judicial criminal history records, the clerk shall:

(A) furnish a certified copy thereof to each agency or department named therein except the court;

(B) certify copies of the order to the appropriate state attorney, or statewide prosecutor, and the arresting agency; and

(C) certify a copy of the order to any other agency that the records of the court reflect has received the criminal history record from the court.

(2) In regard to the official records of the court, including the court file of the cause, the clerk shall:

(A) remove from the official records of the court, excepting the court file, all entries and records subject to the order, provided that, if it is not practical to remove the entries and records, the clerk shall make certified copies thereof and then expunge by appropriate means the original entries and records;

(B) seal the entries and records, or certified copies thereof, together with the court file and retain the same in a nonpublic index, subject to further order of the court (see Johnson v. State, 336 So. 2d 93 (Fla. 1976)); and

(C) in multi-defendant cases, make a certified copy of the contents of the court file that shall be sealed under subdivision (d)(2)(B). Thereafter, all references to the petitioner shall be expunged from the original court file.

(e) Costs. Petitioner shall bear all costs of certified copies unless petitioner is indigent.

Committee Notes

1984 Amendment. Substantially the same as the former rule. The statutory reference in (1) was changed to cite the current statute and terminology was changed accordingly. Subdivision (f) of the former rule was deleted because it dealt with substantive matters covered by section 943.058, Florida Statutes (1981).

2000 Amendment. Substantially the same as the former rule, but references to certificate of eligibility for obtaining nonjudicial criminal history records were added pursuant to State v. D.H.W., 686 So. 2d 1331 (Fla. 1996).

2019 Amendment. Subdivisions addressing human trafficking were moved to rule 3.693.

Rule 3.693. Petition to Seal or Expunge; Human Trafficking.

(a) Requirements of Petition.

(1) A person who is a victim of human trafficking may petition for the expunction of a criminal history record pursuant to

Rule 3.693. Petition to Seal or Expunge; Human Trafficking.

section 943.0583, Florida Statutes. The petition shall be in writing and filed with the clerk of court in any county in the circuit in which the petitioner was arrested. The petition need not be filed in the court where the petitioner's criminal proceeding originally occurred. The petition must be initiated by the petitioner with due diligence after the victim has ceased to be a victim of human trafficking or has sought services for victims of human trafficking. The petition to expunge is complete only when accompanied by:

 (A) the petitioner's sworn statement attesting that the petitioner is eligible for such an expunction to the best of his or her knowledge or belief; and

 (B) official documentation of the petitioner's status as a victim of human trafficking, if any exists.

The petition to expunge need not be accompanied by a certificate of eligibility from the Florida Department of Law Enforcement. The completed petition, sworn statement, and any other official documentation of the petitioner's status as a victim of human trafficking, shall be served on the prosecuting attorney and the arresting authority; however, it is not necessary to make any agency other than the state a party.

(b) State's Response; Evidence. The prosecuting attorney and arresting agency may respond to the petition. Official documentation of the victim's status creates a presumption that his or her participation in the offense was a result of having been a victim of human trafficking but is not required for granting a petition under section 943.0583, Florida Statutes. A determination made without such official documentation must be made by a showing of clear and convincing evidence. Determination of the petition under section 943.0583, Florida Statutes, should be by a preponderance of the evidence.

(c) Written Order. If the petition is granted, the court shall enter its written order so stating and further setting forth the records and agencies or departments to which it is directed.

(d) Clerk's Duties.

 (1) On the receipt of an order sealing or expunging nonjudicial criminal history records, the clerk shall:

  (A) furnish a certified copy thereof to each agency or department named therein except the court;

(B) certify copies of the order to the appropriate prosecuting attorney and the arresting agency; and

(C) certify a copy of the order to any other agency which the records of the court reflect has received the criminal history record from the court.

(2) In regard to the official records of the court, including the court file of the cause, the clerk shall:

(A) remove from the official records of the court, excepting the court file, all entries and records subject to the order, provided that, if it is not practical to remove the entries and records, the clerk shall make certified copies thereof and then expunge by appropriate means the original entries and records;

(B) seal the entries and records, or certified copies thereof, together with the court file and retain the same in a nonpublic index, subject to further order of the court (see Johnson v. State, 336 So.2d 93 (Fla. 1976)); and

(C) in multi-defendant cases, make a certified copy of the contents of the court file that shall be sealed under subdivision (d)(2)(B).

Thereafter, all references to the petitioner shall be expunged from the original court file.

Committee Notes

2019 Amendment. Rule 3.693 was previously a part of rule 3.692.

Rule 3.694. Petition to Seal or Expunge; Lawful Self-Defense Expunction.

(a) Requirements of Petition. All relief sought by reason of section 943.0578, Florida Statutes, shall be by written petition, filed with the clerk. The petition must be accompanied by:

(1) a valid certificate of eligibility for expunction issued by the Florida Department of Law Enforcement pursuant to this section; and

(2) the petitioner's sworn statement attesting that the petitioner is eligible for such an expunction to the best of his or her knowledge or belief.

In judicial proceedings under this section, the completed petition to expunge shall be served upon the appropriate state attorney or the statewide prosecutor and upon the arresting agency; however, it is not necessary to make any agency other than the state a party.

(b) State's Response. The appropriate state attorney or the statewide prosecutor and the arresting agency may respond to the court regarding the completed petition to expunge.

(c) Written Order. If the petition is granted, the court shall enter its written order so stating and further setting forth the records and agencies or departments to which it is directed. Any request for expunging or sealing of a criminal history record may be denied at the sole discretion of the court. The court may not order a criminal justice agency to expunge or seal a criminal history record until the petitioner has applied for and received a certificate of eligibility.

(d) Clerk's Duties.

(1) On the receipt of an order sealing or expunging nonjudicial criminal history records, the clerk shall:

(A) furnish a certified copy thereof to each agency or department named therein except the court;

(B) certify copies of the order to the appropriate prosecuting attorney and the arresting agency; and

(C) certify a copy of the order to any other agency which the records of the court reflect has received the criminal history record from the court.

(2) In regard to the official records of the court, including the court file of the cause, the clerk shall:

(A) remove from the official records of the court, excepting the court file, all entries and records subject to the order, provided that, if it is not practical to remove the entries and records, the clerk shall make certified copies thereof and then expunge by appropriate means the original entries and records;

(B) seal the entries and records, or certified copies thereof, together with the court file and retain the same in a nonpublic index, subject to further order of the court (see Johnson v. State, 336 So. 2d 93 (Fla. 1976)); and

(C) in multi-defendant cases, make a certified copy of the contents of the court file that shall be sealed under subdivision (d)(2)(B). Thereafter, all references to the petitioner shall be expunged from the original court file.

(e) Costs. Petitioner shall bear all costs of certified copies unless petitioner is indigent.

Committee Notes

2019 Amendment. New rule to address section 943.0578, Florida Statutes.

XIV. Sentence

Rule 3.700. Sentence Defined; Pronouncement and Entry; Sentencing Judge.

(a) Sentence Defined. The term sentence means the pronouncement by the court of the penalty imposed on a defendant for the offense of which the defendant has been adjudged guilty.

(b) Pronouncement and Entry. Every sentence or other final disposition of the case shall be pronounced in open court, including, if available at the time of sentencing, the amount of jail time credit the defendant is to receive. The final disposition of every case shall be entered in the minutes in courts in which minutes are kept and shall be docketed in courts that do not maintain minutes.

(c) Sentencing Judge.

(1) Noncapital Cases. In any case, other than a capital case, in which it is necessary that sentence be pronounced by a judge other than the judge who presided at trial or accepted the plea, the sentencing judge shall not pass sentence until the judge becomes acquainted with what transpired at the trial, or the facts, including any plea discussions, concerning the plea and the offense.

(2) Capital Cases. In any capital case in which it is necessary that sentence be pronounced by a judge other than the judge who presided at the capital trial, the sentencing judge shall conduct a new sentencing proceeding before a jury prior to passing sentence.

Committee Notes

1968 Adoption. This rule is a revamped version of section 921.05, Florida Statutes.

1972 Amendment. Subdivisions (a) and (b) are substantially the same as in former rule. Subdivision (c) was added to emphasize that the sentencing procedure should be conducted by the trial judge or the judge taking the plea. The rule makes provision for emergency situations when such judge is unavailable.

Rule 3.701. Sentencing Guidelines.

(a) Use with Forms. This rule is to be used in conjunction with forms 3.988(a)-(i).

(b) Statement of Purpose. The purpose of sentencing guidelines is to establish a uniform set of standards to guide the sentencing judge in the sentence decision-making process. The guidelines represent a synthesis of current sentencing theory and historic sentencing practices throughout the state. Sentencing guidelines are intended to eliminate unwarranted variation in the sentencing process by reducing the subjectivity in interpreting specific offense-related and offender-related criteria and in defining their relative importance in the sentencing decision. The sentencing guidelines embody the following principles:

(1) Sentencing should be neutral with respect to race, gender, and social and economic status.

(2) The primary purpose of sentencing is to punish the offender. Rehabilitation and other traditional considerations continue to be desired goals of the criminal justice system but must assume a subordinate role.

(3) The penalty imposed should be commensurate with the severity of the convicted offense and the circumstances surrounding the offense.

(4) The severity of the sanction should increase with the length and nature of the offender's criminal history.

(5) The sentence imposed by the sentencing judge should reflect the length of time to be served, shortened only by the application of gain time.

(6) While the sentencing guidelines are designed to aid the judge in the sentencing decision and are not intended to usurp judicial discretion, departures from the presumptive sentences established in the guidelines shall be articulated in writing and made when circumstances or factors reasonably justify the aggravation or mitigation of the sentence. The level of proof necessary to establish facts supporting a departure from a sentence under the guidelines is a preponderance of the evidence.

(7) Because the capacities of state and local correctional facilities are finite, use of incarcerative sanctions should be limited to those persons convicted of more serious offenses to those who have longer criminal histories. To ensure such usage of finite resources, sanctions used in sentencing convicted felons should be the least restrictive necessary to achieve the purposes of the sentence.

(c) Offense Categories. Offenses have been grouped into 9 offense categories encompassing the following statutes:

Category 1: Murder, manslaughter: Chapter 782 (except subsection 782.04(1)(a)), subsection 316.193(3)(c)3, and subsection 327.351(2).

Category 2: Sexual offenses: Section 775.22, chapters 794 and 800, section 826.04, and section 491.0112.

Category 3: Robbery: Section 812.13, and sections 812.133 and 812.135.

Category 4: Violent personal crimes: Section 231.06, chapters 784 and 836, section 843.01, and subsection 381.411(4).

Category 5: Burglary: Chapter 810, section 817.025, and subsection 806.13(3).

Category 6: Thefts, forgery, fraud: Sections 192.037 and 206.56, chapters 322 and 409, section 370.142, section 415.111, chapter 443, section 493.3175, sections 494.0018, 496.413, and 496.417, chapter 509, subsection 517.301(1)(a), subsections 585.145(3) and 585.85(2), section 687.146, and chapters 812 (except section 812.13), 815, 817, 831, and 832.

Category 7: Drugs: Section 499.005 and chapter 893.

Category 8: Weapons: Chapter 790 and section 944.40.

Category 9: All other felony offenses.

(d) General Rules and Definitions.

(1) One guideline scoresheet shall be utilized for each defendant covering all offenses pending before the court for sentencing. The state attorney's office will prepare the scoresheets and present them to defense counsel for review as to accuracy in all cases unless the judge directs otherwise. The sentencing judge shall approve all scoresheets.

(2) "Conviction" means a determination of guilt resulting from plea or trial, regardless of whether adjudication was withheld or whether imposition of sentence was suspended.

(3) "Primary offense" is defined as the offense at conviction that, when scored on the guidelines scoresheet, recommends the most severe sanction. In the case of multiple offenses, the primary offense is determined in the following manner:

(A) A separate guidelines scoresheet shall be prepared scoring each offense at conviction as the "primary offense at conviction" with the other offenses at conviction scored as "additional offenses at conviction."

(B) The guidelines scoresheet that recommends the most severe sentence range shall be the scoresheet to be utilized by the sentencing judge pursuant to these guidelines.

(4) All other offenses for which the offender is convicted and that are pending before the court for sentencing at the same time shall be scored as additional offenses based upon their degree and the number of counts of each.

(5) "Prior record" refers to any past criminal conduct on the part of the offender, resulting in conviction, prior to the commission of the primary offense. Prior record includes all prior Florida, federal, out-of-state, military, and foreign convictions, as well as convictions for violation of municipal or county ordinances that bring within the municipal or county code the violation of a state statute or statutes. Provided, however, that:

(A) Entries in criminal histories that show no disposition, disposition unknown, arrest only, or other nonconviction disposition shall not be scored.

(B) When scoring federal, foreign, military, or out-of-state convictions, assign the score for the analogous or parallel Florida statute.

(C) When unable to determine whether an offense at conviction is a felony or misdemeanor, the offense should be scored as a misdemeanor. When the degree of the felony is ambiguous or impossible to determine, score the offense as a third-degree felony.

(D) Prior record shall include criminal traffic offenses, which shall be scored as misdemeanors.

(E) Convictions that do not constitute violations of a parallel or analogous state criminal statute shall not be scored.

(F) An offender's prior record shall not be scored if the offender has maintained a conviction-free record for a period of 10 consecutive years from the most recent date of release from confinement, supervision, or sanction, whichever is later, to the date of the primary offense.

(G) All prior juvenile dispositions that are the equivalent of convictions as defined in subdivision (d)(2), occurring within 3 years of the commission of the primary offense and that would have been criminal if committed by an adult, shall be included in prior record.

(6) "Legal status at time of offense" is defined as follows: Offenders on parole, probation, or community control; offenders in custody serving a sentence; escapees; fugitives who have fled to avoid prosecution or who have failed to appear for a criminal judicial proceeding or who have violated conditions of a supersedeas bond; and offenders in pretrial intervention or diversion programs. Legal status points are to be assessed where these forms of legal constraint existed at the time of the commission of offenses scored as primary or additional offenses at conviction. Legal status points are to be assessed only once whether there are one or more offenses at conviction.

(7) Victim injury shall be scored for each victim physically injured during a criminal episode or transaction, and for each count resulting in such injury whether there are one or more victims.

(8) The recommended sentences provided in the guideline grids are assumed to be appropriate for the composite score of the offender. A range is provided to permit some discretion. The permitted ranges allow the sentencing judge additional discretion when the particular circumstances of a crime or defendant make it appropriate to increase or decrease the recommended sentence without the requirement of finding reasonable justification to do so and without the requirement of a written explanation.

(9) For those offenses having a mandatory penalty, a scoresheet should be completed and the guideline sentence calculated. If the recommended sentence is less than the mandatory penalty, the mandatory sentence takes precedence. If the guideline sentence exceeds the mandatory sentence, the guideline sentence should be imposed.

(10) If the composite score for a defendant charged with a single offense indicates a guideline sentence that exceeds the maximum sentence provided by statute for that offense, the statutory maximum sentence should be imposed.

(11) Departures from the recommended or permitted guideline sentence should be avoided unless there are circumstances or factors that reasonably justify aggravating or mitigating the sentence. Any sentence outside the permitted guideline range must be accompanied by a written statement delineating the reasons for the departure. Reasons for deviating from the guidelines shall not include factors relating to prior arrests without conviction or the instant offenses for which convictions have not been obtained.

(12) A sentence must be imposed for each offense. However, the total sentence cannot exceed the total guideline sentence unless a written reason is given. Where the offender is being sentenced for a capital felony and other noncapital felonies that arose out of the same criminal episode or transaction, the sentencing court may impose any sentence authorized by law for the noncapital felonies.

(13) Community control is a form of intensive supervised custody in the community involving restriction of the freedom of the offender. When community control is imposed, it shall not exceed the term provided by general law.

(14) Sentences imposed after revocation of probation or community control must be in accordance with the guidelines. The sentence imposed after revocation of probation or community control may be included within the original cell (guidelines range) or may be increased to the next higher cell (guidelines range) without requiring a reason for departure.

(15) Categories 3, 5, and 6 contain an additional factor to be scored under the heading of Prior Record: Prior convictions for similar offenses. Prior convictions scored under this factor should be calculated in addition to the general prior record score. Scoring is limited to prior felony convictions included within the category.

Rule 3.702. Sentencing Guidelines (1994).

(a) Use. This rule is to be used in conjunction with the forms located at rule 3.990. This rule is intended to implement the 1994 revised sentencing guidelines in strict accordance with chapter 921, Florida Statutes, as revised by chapter 93-406, Laws of Florida.

(b) Purpose and Construction. The purpose of the 1994 revised sentencing guidelines and the principles they embody are set out in subsection 921.001(4). Existing caselaw construing the application of sentencing guidelines that is in conflict with the provisions of this rule or the statement of purpose or the principles embodied by the 1994 sentencing guidelines set out in subsection 921.001(4) is superseded by the operation of this rule.

(c) Offense Severity Ranking. Felony offenses subject to the 1994 revised sentencing guidelines are listed in a single offense severity ranking chart located at section 921.0012. The offense severity ranking chart employs 10 offense levels, ranked from least severe to most severe. Each felony offense is assigned to a level according to the severity of the offense, commensurate with the harm or potential for harm to the community that is caused by the offense. Felony offenses not listed in section 921.0012 are to be assigned a severity level as described in section 921.0013.

(d) General Rules and Definitions.

(1) A comprehensive guidelines scoresheet shall be prepared for each defendant covering all offenses pending before the court for sentencing, including offenses for which the defendant has been adjudicated an habitual felony offender or an habitual violent felony offender. The office of the state attorney or the probation services office, or both where appropriate, will prepare the scoresheets and present them to defense counsel for review as to accuracy. Where the defendant is alleged to have violated probation or community control and probation services will recommend revocation, probation services shall prepare a comprehensive guidelines scoresheet for use at sentencing after revocation of probation or community control. The sentencing judge shall review the scoresheet for accuracy.

(2) "Conviction" means a determination of guilt resulting from plea or trial, regardless of whether adjudication was withheld or whether imposition of sentence was suspended.

(3) "Primary offense" is the offense pending for sentencing that results in the highest number of total sentence points. Only one offense may be scored as the primary offense.

(4) "Additional offense" is any offense, other than the primary offense, pending before the court for sentencing. Sentence points for additional offenses are determined by the severity level and the number of offenses at a particular severity level. Misdemeanors are scored at level "M" regardless of degree.

Rule 3.702. Sentencing Guidelines (1994).

(5) "Victim injury" is scored for physical injury or death suffered by a person as a direct result of any offense pending before the court for sentencing. If an offense pending before the court for sentencing involves sexual penetration, victim injury is to be scored. If an offense pending before the court for sentencing involves sexual contact, but no penetration, victim injury shall be scored. If the victim of an offense involving sexual penetration or sexual contact without penetration suffers any physical injury as a direct result of an offense pending before the court for sentencing, that physical injury is to be scored separately and in addition to any points scored for the sexual contact or sexual penetration.

Victim injury shall be scored for each victim physically injured and for each offense resulting in physical injury whether there are one or more victims. However, if the victim injury is the result of a crime of which the defendant has been acquitted, it shall not be scored.

(6) Attempts, conspiracies, and solicitations charged under chapter 777 are scored at severity levels below the level at which the completed offense is located. Attempts and solicitations are scored 2 severity levels below the completed offense. Criminal conspiracies are scored 1 severity level below the completed offense.

(7) "Total offense score" results from adding the sentence points for primary offense, additional offense, and victim injury.

(8) "Prior record" refers to any conviction for an offense committed by the defendant prior to the commission of the primary offense. Prior record shall include convictions for offenses committed by the defendant as an adult or as a juvenile, convictions by federal, out-of-state, military or foreign courts, and convictions for violations of county or municipal ordinances that incorporate by reference a penalty under state law. Federal, out-of-state, military, or foreign convictions are scored at the severity level at which the analogous or parallel Florida crime is located.

> **(A)** Convictions for offenses committed more than 10 years prior to the date of the commission of the primary offense are not scored as prior record if the defendant has not been convicted of any other crime for a period of 10 consecutive years from the most recent date of release from

confinement, supervision, or other sanction, whichever is later, to the date of the commission of the primary offense.

(B) Juvenile dispositions of offenses committed by the defendant within 3 years prior to the date of the commission of the primary offense are scored as prior record if the offense would have been a crime if committed by an adult. Juvenile dispositions of sexual offenses committed by the defendant more than 3 years prior to the date of the primary offense are to be scored as prior record if the defendant has not maintained a conviction-free record, either as an adult or as a juvenile, for a period of 3 consecutive years from the most recent date of release from confinement, supervision, or sanction, whichever is later, to the date of commission of the primary offense.

(C) Entries in criminal histories that show no disposition, disposition unknown, arrest only, or a disposition other than conviction shall not be scored. Criminal history records expunged or sealed under section 943.058 or other provisions of law, including former sections 893.14 and 901.33, shall be scored as prior record where the defendant whose record has been expunged or sealed is before the court for sentencing.

(D) Any uncertainty in the scoring of the defendant's prior record shall be resolved in favor of the defendant, and disagreement as to the propriety of scoring specific entries in the prior record shall be resolved by the sentencing judge.

(E) When unable to determine whether the conviction to be scored as prior record is a felony or a misdemeanor, the conviction should be scored as a misdemeanor. When the degree of felony is ambiguous or the severity level cannot be determined, the conviction should be scored at severity level 1.

(9) "Legal status violations" occur when a defendant, while under any of the forms of legal status listed in subsection 921.0011(3), commits an offense that results in conviction. Legal status violations receive a score of 4 sentence points and are scored when the offense committed while under legal status is before the court for sentencing. Points for a legal status violation are to be assessed only once regardless of the existence of more than one form of legal status at the time an offense is

Rule 3.702. Sentencing Guidelines (1994).

committed or the number of offenses committed while under any form of legal status.

(10) "Release program violations" occur when the defendant is found to have violated a condition of a release program designated in subsection 921.0011(6). Six points shall be assessed for each violation up to a maximum of 18 points in the case of multiple violations. Where there are multiple violations, points in excess of 6 may be assessed only for each successive violation that follows the reinstatement or modification of the release program and are not to be assessed for violation of several conditions of a single release program order.

(11) "Total prior record score" results from adding sentence points for prior record, legal status violations, and release program violations.

(12) Possession of a firearm, destructive device, semiautomatic weapon, or a machine gun during the commission or attempt to commit a crime will result in additional sentence points. Eighteen sentence points shall be assessed where the defendant is convicted of committing or attempting to commit any felony other than those enumerated in subsection 775.087(2) while having in his or her possession a firearm as defined in subsection 790.001(6) or a destructive device as defined in subsection 790.001(4). Twenty-five sentence points shall be assessed where the offender is convicted of committing or attempting to commit any felony other than those enumerated in subsection 775.087(2) while having in his or her possession a semiautomatic weapon as defined in subsection 775.087(2) or a machine gun as defined in subsection 790.001(9).

(13) "Subtotal sentence points" result from adding the total offense score, the total prior record score, and any additional points for possession of a firearm, destructive device, semiautomatic weapon, or machine gun.

(14) If the primary offense is drug trafficking under section 893.135, the subtotal sentence points may be multiplied, at the discretion of the sentencing court, by a factor of 1.5. If the primary offense is a violation of the Law Enforcement Protection Act under subsections 775.0823(2), (3), (4), or (5), the subtotal sentence points shall be multiplied by a factor of 2. If the primary offense is a violation of subsection 775.087(2)(a)(2) or subsections 775.0823(6) or (7), the subtotal sentence points shall be multiplied by a factor of 1.5. If both enhancements are applicable, only the enhancement with the higher multiplier is to be used.

(15) "Total sentence points" result from the enhancement, if applicable, of the subtotal sentence points. If no enhancement is applicable, the subtotal sentence points are the total sentence points.

(16) "Presumptive sentence" is determined by the total sentence points. If the total sentence points are less than or equal to 40, the recommended sentence, absent a departure, shall not be state prison. However, the sentencing court may increase sentence points less than or equal to 40 by up to and including 15 percent to arrive at total sentence points in excess of 40. If the total sentence points are greater than 40 but less than or equal to 52, the decision to sentence the defendant to state prison or a nonstate prison sanction is left to the discretion of the sentencing court. If the total sentence points are greater than 52, the sentence, absent a departure, must be to state prison.

A state prison sentence is calculated by deducting 28 points from the total sentence points where total sentence points exceed 40. The resulting number represents state prison months. State prison months may be increased or decreased by up to and including 25 percent at the discretion of the sentencing court. State prison months may not be increased where the sentencing court has exercised discretion to increase total sentence points under 40 points to achieve a state prison sentence. The sentence imposed must be entered on the scoresheet.

(17) For those offenses having a mandatory penalty, a scoresheet should be completed and the guidelines presumptive sentence calculated. If the presumptive sentence is less than the mandatory penalty, the mandatory sentence takes precedence. If the presumptive sentence exceeds the mandatory sentence, the presumptive sentence should be imposed.

(18) Departure from the recommended guidelines sentence provided by the total sentence points should be avoided unless there are circumstances or factors that reasonably justify aggravating or mitigating the sentence. A state prison sentence that deviates from the recommended prison sentence by more than 25 percent, a state prison sentence where the total sentence points are equal to or less than 40, or a sentence other

Rule 3.702. Sentencing Guidelines (1994).

than state prison where the total sentence points are greater than 52 must be accompanied by a written statement delineating the reasons for departure. Circumstances or factors that can be considered include, but are not limited to, those listed in subsections 921.0016(3) and (4). Reasons for departing from the recommended guidelines sentence shall not include circumstances or factors relating to prior arrests without conviction or charged offenses for which convictions have not been obtained.

(A) If a sentencing judge imposes a sentence that departs from the recommended guidelines sentence, the reasons for departure shall be orally articulated at the time sentence is imposed. Any departure sentence must be accompanied by a written statement, signed by the sentencing judge, delineating the reasons for departure. The written statement shall be filed in the court file within 15 days of the date of sentencing. A written transcription of orally stated reasons for departure articulated at the time sentence was imposed is sufficient if it is signed by the sentencing judge and filed in the court file within 15 days of the date of sentencing. The sentencing judge may also list the written reasons for departure in the space provided on the guidelines scoresheet and shall sign the scoresheet.

(B) The written statement delineating the reasons for departure shall be made a part of the record. The written statement, if it is a separate document, must accompany the guidelines scoresheet required to be provided to the Department of Corrections pursuant to subsection 921.0014(5).

(19) The sentencing court shall impose or suspend sentence for each separate count, as convicted. The total sentence shall be within the guidelines sentence unless a departure is ordered.

If a split sentence is imposed, the incarcerative portion of the sentence must not deviate more than 25 percent from the recommended guidelines prison sentence. The total sanction (incarceration and community control or probation) shall not exceed the term provided by general law or the guidelines recommended sentence where the provisions of subsection 921.001(5) apply.

(20) Sentences imposed after revocation of probation or community control must be in accordance with the guidelines.

Cumulative incarceration imposed after revocation of probation or community control is subject to limitations imposed by the guidelines. A violation of probation or community control may not be the basis for a departure sentence.

Committee Notes

1993 Adoption.

(d)(1) If sentences are imposed under section 775.084 and the sentencing guidelines, a scoresheet listing only those offenses sentenced under the sentencing guidelines must be prepared and utilized in lieu of the comprehensive scoresheet.

Due to ethical considerations, defense counsel may not be compelled to submit or sign a scoresheet.

(d)(3) The primary offense need not be the highest ranked offense pending for sentencing where scoring the less severe offense as the primary offense will result in higher total sentence points. This can occur where the multipliers for drug trafficking or violations of the Law Enforcement Protection Act are applied or where past convictions can be included as prior record that could not be scored if the offense ranked at a higher severity level was the primary offense.

(d)(16) The presumptive sentence is assumed to be appropriate for the composite score of the defendant. Where the total sentence points do not exceed 40, the court has the flexibility to impose any lawful term of probation with or without a period of incarceration as a condition of probation, a county jail term alone, or any nonincarcerative disposition. Any sentence may include a requirement that a fine be paid.

Rule 3.703. Sentencing Guidelines (1994 as amended).

(a) Use. This rule is to be used in conjunction with the forms located at rule 3.992. This rule implements the 1998 Criminal Punishment Code, in compliance with chapter 921, Florida Statutes. This rule applies to offenses committed on or after October 1, 1998, or as otherwise required by law.

(b) Purpose and Construction. The purpose of the 1998 Criminal Punishment Code, and the principles it embodies, are set out in subsection 921.002(1), Florida Statutes. Existing case law construing the application of sentencing guidelines will continue as

Rule 3.703. Sentencing Guidelines (1994 as amended).

precedent unless in conflict with the provisions of this rule or the 1998 Criminal Punishment Code.

(c) Offense Severity Ranking.

(1) Felony offenses subject to the 1998 Criminal Punishment Code are listed in a single offense severity ranking chart located at section 921.0022, Florida Statutes. The offense severity ranking chart employs 10 offense levels, ranked from least severe to most severe. Each felony offense is assigned to a level according to the severity of the offense, commensurate with the harm or potential for harm to the community that is caused by the offense, as determined by statute. The numerical statutory reference in the left column of the chart and the felony degree designations in the middle column of the chart determine whether felony offenses are specifically listed in the offense severity ranking chart and the appropriate severity level. The language in the right column is merely descriptive.

(2) Felony offenses not listed in section 921.0022 are assigned a severity level in accordance with section 921.0023, Florida Statutes, as follows:

(A) a felony of the third degree within offense level 1;

(B) a felony of the second degree within offense level 4;

(C) a felony of the first degree within offense level 7;

(D) a felony of the first degree punishable by life within offense level 9; or

(E) a life felony within offense level 10.

An offense does not become unlisted and subject to the provisions of section 921.0023 because of a reclassification of the degree of felony under section 775.0845, section 775.087, section 775.0875, or section 794.023, Florida Statutes, or any other law that provides an enhanced penalty for a felony offense.

(d) General Rules and Definitions.

(1) One or more Criminal Punishment Code scoresheets must be prepared for each offender covering all offenses pending before the court for sentencing, including offenses for which the offender may qualify as an habitual felony offender, an habitual violent felony offender, a violent career criminal, or a prison releasee reoffender. The office of the prosecuting attorney must prepare the scoresheets and present them to defense counsel for review as to accuracy. If sentences are imposed under section 775.084, or section 775.082(9), Florida Statutes, and the Criminal Punishment Code, a scoresheet listing only those

offenses sentenced under the Criminal Punishment Code must be filed in addition to any sentencing documents filed under section 775.084 or section 775.082(9).

(2) One scoresheet must be prepared for all offenses committed under any single version or revision of the guidelines or Criminal Punishment Code pending before the court for sentencing.

(3) If an offender is before the court for sentencing for more than 1 felony and the felonies were committed under more than 1 version or revision of the guidelines or Criminal Punishment Code, separate scoresheets must be prepared and used at sentencing. The sentencing court may impose such sentence concurrently or consecutively.

(4) The sentencing judge must review the scoresheet for accuracy and sign it.

(5) Felonies, except capital felonies, with continuing dates of enterprise are to be sentenced under the guidelines or Criminal Punishment Code in effect on the beginning date of the criminal activity.

(6) "Conviction" means a determination of guilt that is the result of a plea or trial, regardless of whether adjudication is withheld.

(7) "Primary offense" means the offense at conviction pending before the court for sentencing for which the total sentence points recommend a sanction that is as severe as, or more severe than, the sanction recommended for any other offense committed by the offender and pending before the court at sentencing. Only 1 count of 1 offense before the court for sentencing may be classified as the primary offense.

(8) "Additional offense" means any offense other than the primary offense for which an offender is convicted and which is pending before the court for sentencing at the time of the primary offense.

(9) "Victim injury" is scored for physical injury or death suffered by a person as a direct result of any offense pending before the court for sentencing. Except as otherwise provided by law, the sexual penetration and sexual contact points will be scored as follows. Sexual penetration points are scored if an offense pending before the court for sentencing involves sexual penetration. Sexual contact points are scored if an offense pending before the court for sentencing involves sexual contact, but no penetration. If the victim of an offense involving sexual penetration or sexual contact without penetration suffers any physical injury as a direct result of an offense pending before the court for sentencing, that physical injury must be scored in addition to any points scored for the sexual contact or sexual penetration.

Victim injury must be scored for each victim physically injured and for each offense resulting in physical injury whether there are 1 or more victims. However, victim injury must not be scored for an offense for which the offender has not been convicted.

Victim injury resulting from 1 or more capital offenses before the court for sentencing must not be included upon any scoresheet prepared for non-capital offenses also pending before the court for sentencing. This does not prohibit the scoring of victim injury as a result of the non-capital offense or offenses before the court for sentencing.

(10) Unless specifically provided otherwise by statute, attempts, conspiracies, and solicitations must be indicated in the space provided on the Criminal Punishment Code scoresheet and must be scored at 1 severity level below the completed offense.

Attempts, solicitations, and conspiracies of third-degree felonies located in offense severity levels 1 and 2 must be scored as misdemeanors. Attempts, solicitations, and conspiracies of third-degree felonies located in offense severity levels 3, 4, 5, 6, 7, 8, 9, and 10 must be scored as felonies 1 offense level beneath the incomplete or inchoate offense.

(11) An increase in offense severity level may result from a reclassification of felony degrees under sections 775.0845, 775.087, 775.0875, or 794.023, Florida Statutes. Any such increase must be indicated in the space provided on the Criminal Punishment Code scoresheet.

(12) A single assessment of 30 prior serious felony points is added if the offender has a primary offense or any additional offense ranked in level 8, 9, or 10 and 1 or more prior serious felonies. A 'prior serious felony' is an offense in the offender's prior record ranked in level 8, 9, or 10 and for which the offender is serving a sentence of confinement, supervision, or other sanction or for which the offender's date of release from confinement, supervision, or other sanction, whichever is later, is within 3 years before the date the primary offense or any additional offenses were committed. Out of state convictions

wherein the analogous or parallel Florida offenses are located in offense severity level 8, 9, or 10 must be considered prior serious felonies.

(13) If the offender has 1 or more prior capital felonies, points must be added to the subtotal sentence points of the offender equal to twice the number of points the offender receives for the primary offense and any additional offense. Out-of-state convictions wherein the analogous or parallel Florida offenses are capital offenses must be considered capital offenses for purposes of operation of this section.

(14) "Prior record" refers to any conviction for an offense committed by the offender prior to the commission of the primary offense. Prior record includes convictions for offenses committed by the offender as an adult or as a juvenile, convictions by federal, out of state, military, or foreign courts and convictions for violations of county or municipal ordinances that incorporate by reference a penalty under state law. Federal, out of state, military or foreign convictions are scored at the severity level at which the analogous or parallel Florida crime is located.

(A) Convictions for offenses committed more than 10 years before the date of the commission of the primary offense must not be scored as prior record if the offender has not been convicted of any other crime for a period of 10 consecutive years from the most recent date of release from confinement, supervision, or other sanction, whichever is later, to the date of the commission of the primary offense.

(B) Juvenile dispositions of offenses committed by the offender within 5 years before the date of the commission of the primary offense must be scored as prior record if the offense would have been a crime if committed by an adult. Juvenile dispositions of sexual offenses committed by the offender more than 5 years before the date of the primary offense must be scored as prior record if the offender has not maintained a conviction-free record, either as an adult or as a juvenile, for a period of 5 consecutive years from the most recent date of release from confinement, supervision, or sanction, whichever is later, to the date of commission of the primary offense.

(C) Entries in criminal histories that show no disposition, disposition unknown, arrest only, or a disposition other than conviction must not be scored. Criminal history

Rule 3.703. Sentencing Guidelines (1994 as amended).

records expunged or sealed under section 943.058, Florida Statutes, or other provisions of law, including former sections 893.14 and 901.33, Florida Statutes, must be scored as prior record where the offender whose record has been expunged or sealed is before the court for sentencing.

(D) Any uncertainty in the scoring of the offender's prior record must be resolved in favor of the offender and disagreement as to the propriety of scoring specific entries in the prior record must be resolved by the sentencing judge.

(E) When unable to determine whether the conviction to be scored as prior record is a felony or a misdemeanor, the conviction must be scored as a misdemeanor. When the degree of felony is ambiguous or the severity level cannot be determined, the conviction must be scored at severity level 1.

(15) "Legal status points" are assessed when an offender:

(A) escapes from incarceration;

(B) flees to avoid prosecution;

(C) fails to appear for a criminal proceeding;

(D) violates any condition of a supersedeas bond;

(E) is incarcerated;

(F) is under any form of a pretrial intervention or diversion program; or

(G) is under any form of court-imposed or post-prison release community supervision and commits an offense that results in conviction. Legal status violations receive a score of 4 sentence points and are scored when the offense committed while under legal status is before the court for sentencing. Points for a legal status violation must only be assessed once regardless of the existence of more than 1 form of legal status at the time an offense is committed or the number of offenses committed while under any form of legal status.

(16) Community sanction violation points occur when the offender is found to have violated a condition of:

(A) probation;

(B) community control; or

(C) pretrial intervention or diversion.

Community sanction violation points are assessed when a community sanction violation is before the court for sentencing. Six community sanction violation points must be assessed for each violation or if the violation results from a new felony conviction, 12 community sanction violation points must be assessed. For violations occurring on or after March 12, 2007, if the community sanction violation that is not based upon a failure to pay fines, costs, or restitution is committed by a violent felony offender of special concern as defined in section 948.06, Florida Statutes, 12 community sanction violation points must be assessed or if the violation results from a new felony conviction, 24 community sanction points must be assessed. Where there are multiple violations, points may be assessed only for each successive violation that follows a continuation of supervision, or modification or revocation of the community sanction before the court for sentencing and are not to be assessed for violation of several conditions of a single community sanction. Multiple counts of community sanction violations before the sentencing court may not be the basis for multiplying the assessment of community sanction violation points.

(17) Possession of a firearm, semiautomatic firearm, or a machine gun during the commission or attempt to commit a crime will result in additional sentence points. Eighteen sentence points are assessed if the offender is convicted of committing, or attempting to commit, any felony other than those enumerated in subsection 775.087(2), Florida Statutes, while having in his or her possession a firearm as defined in subsection 790.001(6), Florida Statutes. Twenty-five sentence points are assessed if the offender is convicted of committing or attempting to commit any felony other than those enumerated in subsection 775.087(3), Florida Statutes, while having in his or her possession a semiautomatic firearm as defined in subsection 775.087(3), Florida Statutes, or a machine gun as defined in subsection 790.001(9), Florida Statutes. Only 1 assessment of either 18 or 25 points can be made.

(18) "Subtotal sentence points" are the sum of the primary offense points, the total additional offense points, the total victim injury points, the total prior record points, any legal status points, community sanction points, prior serious felony points, prior capital felony points, and points for possession of a firearm or semiautomatic weapon.

(19) If the primary offense is drug trafficking under section 893.135, Florida Statutes, ranked in offense severity level 7 or 8, the subtotal sentence points may be multiplied, at the discretion of the sentencing court, by a factor of 1.5.

(20) If the primary offense is a violation of subsection 775.0823(2), (3), or (4), Florida Statutes, the subtotal sentence points are multiplied by 2.5. If the primary offense is a violation of subsection 775.0823(5), (6), (7), (8), or (9), Florida Statutes, the subtotal sentence points are multiplied by 2.0. If the primary offense is a violation of subsection 784.07(3) or 775.0875(1), Florida Statutes, or subsection 775.0823(10) or (11), Florida Statutes, the subtotal sentence points are multiplied by 1.5.

(21) If the primary offense is grand theft of the third degree of a motor vehicle and the offender's prior record includes 3 or more grand thefts of the third degree of a motor vehicle, the subtotal sentence points are multiplied by 1.5.

(22) If the offender is found to have committed the offense for the purpose of benefiting, promoting, or furthering the interests of a criminal street gang under section 874.04, Florida Statutes, at the time of the commission of the primary offense, the subtotal sentence points are multiplied by 1.5.

(23) If the primary offense is a crime of domestic violence as defined in section 741.28, Florida Statutes, which was committed in the presence of a child under 16 years of age who is a family household member as defined in section 741.28(2), Florida Statutes, with the victim or perpetrator, the subtotal sentence points are multiplied by 1.5.

(24)

   (A) Adult on minor sex offense. The subtotal sentence points are multiplied by 2.0 if:

      (i) the offender was 18 years of age or older and the victim was younger than 18 years of age at the time the offender committed the primary offense; and

      (ii) the primary offense was committed on or after October 1, 2014, and is a violation of:

         a. section 787.01(2) (kidnapping) or 787.02(2) (false imprisonment), Florida Statutes, if in the course of committing the kidnapping or false imprisonment the defendant committed a sexual battery under chapter 794, Florida Statutes, or a lewd act under section 800.04 or 847.0135(5), Florida Statutes, against the victim;

         b. section 787.01(3)(a)2. or (3)(a)3., Florida Statutes, (kidnapping of a child under 13 with a sexual battery or lewd act);

  c. section 787.02(3)(a)2. or (3)(a)3., Florida Statutes, (false imprisonment of a child under 13 with a sexual battery or lewd act);

  d. section 794.011, Florida Statutes, (sexual battery), excluding section 794.011(10);

  e. section 800.04, Florida Statutes, (lewd or lascivious offenses); or

  f. section 847.0135(5), Florida Statutes, (lewd or lascivious exhibition using a computer).

(B) Notwithstanding subdivision (d)(24)(A), the court may not apply the multiplier and must sentence the defendant to the statutory maximum sentence if applying the multiplier results in the lowest permissible sentence exceeding the statutory maximum sentence for the primary offense under chapter 775, Florida Statutes.

(25) "Total sentence points" are the subtotal sentence points or the enhanced subtotal sentence points.

(26) The lowest permissible sentence is the minimum sentence that may be imposed by the trial court, absent a valid reason for departure. The lowest permissible sentence is any nonstate prison sanction in which the total sentence points equals or is less than 44 points, unless the court determines within its discretion that a prison sentence, which may be up to the statutory maximums for the offenses committed, is appropriate. When the total sentence points exceeds 44 points, the lowest permissible sentence in prison months must be calculated by subtracting 28 points from the total sentence points and decreasing the remaining total by 25 percent. The total sentence points must be calculated only as a means of determining the lowest permissible sentence. The maximum sentence for each individual felony offense is the statutory maximum as provided in s. 775.082, Florida Statutes, unless the lowest permissible sentence exceeds the statutory maximum for that offense. If the lowest permissible sentence exceeds the statutory maximum for an individual felony offense, the lowest permissible sentence replaces the statutory maximum and must be imposed for that offense. Sentences for multiple felony offenses may be imposed concurrently or consecutively. However, any sentence to state prison must exceed 1 year. If the total sentence points are greater than or equal to 363, the court may sentence the offender to life imprisonment.

Rule 3.703. Sentencing Guidelines (1994 as amended).

(27) The sentence imposed must be entered on the scoresheet.

(28) For those offenses having a mandatory minimum sentence, a scoresheet must be completed and the lowest permissible sentence under the Code calculated. If the lowest permissible sentence is less than the mandatory minimum sentence, the mandatory minimum sentence takes precedence. If the lowest permissible sentence exceeds the mandatory sentence, the requirements of the Criminal Punishment Code and any mandatory minimum penalties apply. Mandatory minimum sentences must be recorded on the scoresheet.

(29) Any downward departure from the lowest permissible sentence, as calculated according to the total sentence points under section 921.0024, Florida Statutes, is prohibited unless there are circumstances or factors that reasonably justify the downward departure. Circumstances or factors that can be considered include, but are not limited to, those listed in subsection 921.0026(2), Florida Statutes.

(A) If a sentencing judge imposes a sentence that is below the lowest permissible sentence, it is a departure sentence and must be accompanied by a written statement by the sentencing court delineating the reasons for the departure, filed within 7 days after the date of sentencing. A written transcription of orally stated reasons for departure articulated at the time sentence was imposed is sufficient if it is filed by the court within 7 days after the date of sentencing. The sentencing judge may also list the written reasons for departure in the space provided on the Criminal Punishment Code scoresheet.

(B) The written statement delineating the reasons for departure must be made a part of the record. The written statement, if it is a separate document, must accompany the scoresheet required to be provided to the Department of Corrections under subsection 921.0024(6), Florida Statutes. If a split sentence is imposed, the total sanction (incarceration and community control or probation) must not exceed the term provided by general law or the maximum sentence under the Criminal Punishment Code.

(30) If the lowest permissible sentence under the criminal punishment code is a state prison sanction but the total sentencing points do not exceed 48 points (or 54 points if 6 of those points are for a violation of probation, community control, or other community supervision that does not involve a new crime), the court may sentence the defendant to probation, community control, or community supervision with mandatory participation in a prison diversion program, as provided for in section 921.00241, Florida Statutes, if the defendant meets the requirements for that program as set forth in section 921.00241, Florida Statutes.

(31) If the total sentence points equal 22 or less, the court must sentence the offender to a nonstate prison sanction unless it makes written findings that a nonstate prison sanction could present a danger to the public. Unless there is a stipulation, there must be a finding by the jury that a nonstate prison sanction could present a danger to the public before the court may sentence a defendant to prison under section 775.082(10), Florida Statutes.

(32) Sentences imposed after revocation of probation or community control must be imposed according to the sentencing law applicable at the time of the commission of the original offense.

Committee Notes

1996 Amendments (a) This portion was amended to show that the earliest offense date to which this rule applies is October 1, 1995 and that all subsequent changes are incorporated. It is intended that Committee Notes will be used to indicate effective dates of changes.

(c) This amendment applies to offenses committed on or after October 1, 1996.

(d)(9) The 1996 Legislature created two crimes for which sexual penetration or sexual contact points are not scored. That exception applies to offenses committed on or after October 1, 1996 pursuant to section 872.06, Florida Statutes or section 944.35(3)(b)2, Florida Statutes.

(d)(12) The amendment applies to offenses committed on or after October 1, 1996.

(d)(13) The amendment applies on or after October 1, 1996.

(d)(17) This amendment, which applies on or after October 1, 1996, clarifies when points may be assessed for multiple violations. It also incorporates legislative changes that indicate that multiple assessments may not be made for multiple counts of community sanction violations.

(d)(24) The amendment applies to crimes committed on or after October 1, 1996.

Committee Note to Form at Rule 3.991(b) 1996 Amendment:

Effective January 1, 1997, the fact that a defendant committed an offense involving sexual contact or sexual penetration and as a direct result of the offense, the victim contracted a sexually transmissible disease, is an aggravating circumstance justifying an upward departure sentence.

1997 Amendments. (d)(25) The amendment applies to crimes committed on or after October 1, 1997.

Rule 3.704. The Criminal Punishment Code.

(a) Use. This rule is to be used in conjunction with the forms located at rule 3.992. This rule implements the 1998 Criminal Punishment Code, in compliance with chapter 921, Florida Statutes. This rule applies to offenses committed on or after October 1, 1998, or as otherwise required by law.

(b) Purpose and Construction. The purpose of the 1998 Criminal Punishment Code, and the principles it embodies, are set out in subsection 921.002(1), Florida Statutes. Existing case law construing the application of sentencing guidelines will continue as precedent unless in conflict with the provisions of this rule or the 1998 Criminal Punishment Code.

(c) Offense Severity Ranking.

(1) Felony offenses subject to the 1998 Criminal Punishment Code are listed in a single offense severity ranking chart located at section 921.0022, Florida Statutes. The offense severity ranking chart employs 10 offense levels, ranked from least severe to most severe. Each felony offense is assigned to a level according to the severity of the offense, commensurate with the harm or potential for harm to the community that is caused by the offense, as determined by statute. The numerical statutory reference in the left column of the chart and the felony degree designations in the middle column of the chart determine whether felony offenses are specifically listed in the offense severity ranking chart and the appropriate severity level. The language in the right column is merely descriptive.

(2) Felony offenses not listed in section 921.0022 are assigned a severity level in accordance with section 921.0023, Florida Statutes, as follows:

(A) a felony of the third degree within offense level 1;

(B) a felony of the second degree within offense level 4;

(C) a felony of the first degree within offense level 7;

(D) a felony of the first degree punishable by life within offense level 9; or

(E) a life felony within offense level 10.

An offense does not become unlisted and subject to the provisions of section 921.0023 because of a reclassification of the degree of felony under section 775.0845, section 775.087, section 775.0875, or section 794.023, Florida Statutes, or any other law that provides an enhanced penalty for a felony offense.

(d) General Rules and Definitions.

(1) One or more Criminal Punishment Code scoresheets must be prepared for each offender covering all offenses pending before the court for sentencing, including offenses for which the offender may qualify as an habitual felony offender, an habitual violent felony offender, a violent career criminal, or a prison releasee reoffender. The office of the prosecuting attorney must prepare the scoresheets and present them to defense counsel for review as to accuracy. If sentences are imposed under section 775.084, or section 775.082(9), Florida Statutes, and the Criminal Punishment Code, a scoresheet listing only those offenses sentenced under the Criminal Punishment Code must be filed in addition to any sentencing documents filed under section 775.084 or section 775.082(9).

(2) One scoresheet must be prepared for all offenses committed under any single version or revision of the guidelines or Criminal Punishment Code pending before the court for sentencing.

(3) If an offender is before the court for sentencing for more than 1 felony and the felonies were committed under more than 1 version or revision of the guidelines or Criminal Punishment Code, separate scoresheets must be prepared and used at sentencing. The sentencing court may impose such sentence concurrently or consecutively.

(4) The sentencing judge must review the scoresheet for accuracy and sign it.

(5) Felonies, except capital felonies, with continuing dates of enterprise are to be sentenced under the guidelines or Criminal Punishment Code in effect on the beginning date of the criminal activity.

Rule 3.704. The Criminal Punishment Code.

(6) "Conviction" means a determination of guilt that is the result of a plea or trial, regardless of whether adjudication is withheld.

(7) "Primary offense" means the offense at conviction pending before the court for sentencing for which the total sentence points recommend a sanction that is as severe as, or more severe than, the sanction recommended for any other offense committed by the offender and pending before the court at sentencing. Only 1 count of 1 offense before the court for sentencing may be classified as the primary offense.

(8) "Additional offense" means any offense other than the primary offense for which an offender is convicted and which is pending before the court for sentencing at the time of the primary offense.

(9) "Victim injury" is scored for physical injury or death suffered by a person as a direct result of any offense pending before the court for sentencing. Except as otherwise provided by law, the sexual penetration and sexual contact points will be scored as follows. Sexual penetration points are scored if an offense pending before the court for sentencing involves sexual penetration. Sexual contact points are scored if an offense pending before the court for sentencing involves sexual contact, but no penetration. If the victim of an offense involving sexual penetration or sexual contact without penetration suffers any physical injury as a direct result of an offense pending before the court for sentencing, that physical injury must be scored in addition to any points scored for the sexual contact or sexual penetration.

Victim injury must be scored for each victim physically injured and for each offense resulting in physical injury whether there are 1 or more victims. However, victim injury must not be scored for an offense for which the offender has not been convicted.

Victim injury resulting from 1 or more capital offenses before the court for sentencing must not be included upon any scoresheet prepared for non-capital offenses also pending before the court for sentencing. This does not prohibit the scoring of victim injury as a result of the non-capital offense or offenses before the court for sentencing.

(10) Unless specifically provided otherwise by statute, attempts, conspiracies, and solicitations must be indicated in the space provided on the Criminal Punishment Code scoresheet and must be scored at 1 severity level below the completed offense.

Attempts, solicitations, and conspiracies of third-degree felonies located in offense severity levels 1 and 2 must be scored as misdemeanors. Attempts, solicitations, and conspiracies of third-degree felonies located in offense severity levels 3, 4, 5, 6, 7, 8, 9, and 10 must be scored as felonies 1 offense level beneath the incomplete or inchoate offense.

(11) An increase in offense severity level may result from a reclassification of felony degrees under sections 775.0845, 775.087, 775.0875, or 794.023, Florida Statutes. Any such increase must be indicated in the space provided on the Criminal Punishment Code scoresheet.

(12) A single assessment of 30 prior serious felony points is added if the offender has a primary offense or any additional offense ranked in level 8, 9, or 10 and 1 or more prior serious felonies. A 'prior serious felony' is an offense in the offender's prior record ranked in level 8, 9, or 10 and for which the offender is serving a sentence of confinement, supervision, or other sanction or for which the offender's date of release from confinement, supervision, or other sanction, whichever is later, is within 3 years before the date the primary offense or any additional offenses were committed. Out of state convictions wherein the analogous or parallel Florida offenses are located in offense severity level 8, 9, or 10 must be considered prior serious felonies.

(13) If the offender has 1 or more prior capital felonies, points must be added to the subtotal sentence points of the offender equal to twice the number of points the offender receives for the primary offense and any additional offense. Out-of-state convictions wherein the analogous or parallel Florida offenses are capital offenses must be considered capital offenses for purposes of operation of this section.

(14) "Prior record" refers to any conviction for an offense committed by the offender prior to the commission of the primary offense. Prior record includes convictions for offenses committed by the offender as an adult or as a juvenile, convictions by federal, out of state, military, or foreign courts and convictions for violations of county or municipal ordinances that incorporate by reference a penalty under state law. Federal, out of state, military or foreign convictions are scored

Rule 3.704. The Criminal Punishment Code.

at the severity level at which the analogous or parallel Florida crime is located.

(A) Convictions for offenses committed more than 10 years before the date of the commission of the primary offense must not be scored as prior record if the offender has not been convicted of any other crime for a period of 10 consecutive years from the most recent date of release from confinement, supervision, or other sanction, whichever is later, to the date of the commission of the primary offense.

(B) Juvenile dispositions of offenses committed by the offender within 5 years before the date of the commission of the primary offense must be scored as prior record if the offense would have been a crime if committed by an adult. Juvenile dispositions of sexual offenses committed by the offender more than 5 years before the date of the primary offense must be scored as prior record if the offender has not maintained a conviction-free record, either as an adult or as a juvenile, for a period of 5 consecutive years from the most recent date of release from confinement, supervision, or sanction, whichever is later, to the date of commission of the primary offense.

(C) Entries in criminal histories that show no disposition, disposition unknown, arrest only, or a disposition other than conviction must not be scored. Criminal history records expunged or sealed under section 943.058, Florida Statutes, or other provisions of law, including former sections 893.14 and 901.33, Florida Statutes, must be scored as prior record where the offender whose record has been expunged or sealed is before the court for sentencing.

(D) Any uncertainty in the scoring of the offender's prior record must be resolved in favor of the offender and disagreement as to the propriety of scoring specific entries in the prior record must be resolved by the sentencing judge.

(E) When unable to determine whether the conviction to be scored as prior record is a felony or a misdemeanor, the conviction must be scored as a misdemeanor. When the degree of felony is ambiguous or the severity level cannot be determined, the conviction must be scored at severity level 1.

(15) "Legal status points" are assessed when an offender:

(A) escapes from incarceration;

(B) flees to avoid prosecution;

(C) fails to appear for a criminal proceeding;

(D) violates any condition of a supersedeas bond;

(E) is incarcerated;

(F) is under any form of a pretrial intervention or diversion program; or

(G) is under any form of court-imposed or post-prison release community supervision and commits an offense that results in conviction. Legal status violations receive a score of 4 sentence points and are scored when the offense committed while under legal status is before the court for sentencing. Points for a legal status violation must only be assessed once regardless of the existence of more than 1 form of legal status at the time an offense is committed or the number of offenses committed while under any form of legal status.

(16) Community sanction violation points occur when the offender is found to have violated a condition of:

(A) probation;

(B) community control; or

(C) pretrial intervention or diversion.

Community sanction violation points are assessed when a community sanction violation is before the court for sentencing. Six community sanction violation points must be assessed for each violation or if the violation results from a new felony conviction, 12 community sanction violation points must be assessed. For violations occurring on or after March 12, 2007, if the community sanction violation that is not based upon a failure to pay fines, costs, or restitution is committed by a violent felony offender of special concern as defined in section 948.06, Florida Statutes, 12 community sanction violation points must be assessed or if the violation results from a new felony conviction, 24 community sanction points must be assessed. Where there are multiple violations, points may be assessed only for each successive violation that follows a continuation of supervision, or modification or revocation of the community sanction before the court for sentencing and are not to be assessed for violation of several conditions of a single community sanction. Multiple counts of community sanction violations before the sentencing court may not be the basis for multiplying the assessment of community sanction violation points.

Rule 3.704. The Criminal Punishment Code.

(17) Possession of a firearm, semiautomatic firearm, or a machine gun during the commission or attempt to commit a crime will result in additional sentence points. Eighteen sentence points are assessed if the offender is convicted of committing, or attempting to commit, any felony other than those enumerated in subsection 775.087(2), Florida Statutes, while having in his or her possession a firearm as defined in subsection 790.001(6), Florida Statutes. Twenty-five sentence points are assessed if the offender is convicted of committing or attempting to commit any felony other than those enumerated in subsection 775.087(3), Florida Statutes, while having in his or her possession a semiautomatic firearm as defined in subsection 775.087(3), Florida Statutes, or a machine gun as defined in subsection 790.001(9), Florida Statutes. Only 1 assessment of either 18 or 25 points can be made.

(18) "Subtotal sentence points" are the sum of the primary offense points, the total additional offense points, the total victim injury points, the total prior record points, any legal status points, community sanction points, prior serious felony points, prior capital felony points, and points for possession of a firearm or semiautomatic weapon.

(19) If the primary offense is drug trafficking under section 893.135, Florida Statutes, ranked in offense severity level 7 or 8, the subtotal sentence points may be multiplied, at the discretion of the sentencing court, by a factor of 1.5.

(20) If the primary offense is a violation of subsection 775.0823(2), (3), or (4), Florida Statutes, the subtotal sentence points are multiplied by 2.5. If the primary offense is a violation of subsection 775.0823(5), (6), (7), (8), or (9), Florida Statutes, the subtotal sentence points are multiplied by 2.0. If the primary offense is a violation of subsection784.07(3) or 775.0875(1), Florida Statutes, or subsection 775.0823(10) or (11), Florida Statutes, the subtotal sentence points are multiplied by 1.5.

(21) If the primary offense is grand theft of the third degree of a motor vehicle and the offender's prior record includes 3 or more grand thefts of the third degree of a motor vehicle, the subtotal sentence points are multiplied by 1.5.

(22) If the offender is found to have committed the offense for the purpose of benefiting, promoting, or furthering the interests of a criminal street gang under section 874.04, Florida Statutes, at the time of the commission of the primary offense, the subtotal sentence points are multiplied by 1.5.

(23) If the primary offense is a crime of domestic violence as defined in section 741.28, Florida Statutes, which was committed in the presence of a child under 16 years of age who is a family household member as defined in section 741.28(2), Florida Statutes, with the victim or perpetrator, the subtotal sentence points are multiplied by 1.5.

(24)

(A) Adult on minor sex offense. The subtotal sentence points are multiplied by 2.0 if:

(i) the offender was 18 years of age or older and the victim was younger than 18 years of age at the time the offender committed the primary offense; and

(ii) the primary offense was committed on or after October 1, 2014, and is a violation of:

a. section 787.01(2) (kidnapping) or 787.02(2) (false imprisonment), Florida Statutes, if in the course of committing the kidnapping or false imprisonment the defendant committed a sexual battery under chapter 794, Florida Statutes, or a lewd act under section 800.04 or 847.0135(5), Florida Statutes, against the victim;

b. section 787.01(3)(a)2. or (3)(a)3., Florida Statutes, (kidnapping of a child under 13 with a sexual battery or lewd act);

c. section 787.02(3)(a)2. or (3)(a)3., Florida Statutes, (false imprisonment of a child under 13 with a sexual battery or lewd act);

d. section 794.011, Florida Statutes, (sexual battery), excluding section 794.011(10);

e. section 800.04, Florida Statutes, (lewd or lascivious offenses); or

f. section 847.0135(5), Florida Statutes, (lewd or lascivious exhibition using a computer).

(B) Notwithstanding subdivision (d)(24)(A), the court may not apply the multiplier and must sentence the defendant to the statutory maximum sentence if applying the multiplier results in the lowest permissible sentence exceeding the statutory maximum sentence for the primary offense under chapter 775, Florida Statutes.

(25) "Total sentence points" are the subtotal sentence points or the enhanced subtotal sentence points.

Rule 3.704. The Criminal Punishment Code.

(26) The lowest permissible sentence is the minimum sentence that may be imposed by the trial court, absent a valid reason for departure. The lowest permissible sentence is any nonstate prison sanction in which the total sentence points equals or is less than 44 points, unless the court determines within its discretion that a prison sentence, which may be up to the statutory maximums for the offenses committed, is appropriate. When the total sentence points exceeds 44 points, the lowest permissible sentence in prison months must be calculated by subtracting 28 points from the total sentence points and decreasing the remaining total by 25 percent. The total sentence points must be calculated only as a means of determining the lowest permissible sentence. The maximum sentence for each individual felony offense is the statutory maximum as provided in s. 775.082, Florida Statutes, unless the lowest permissible sentence exceeds the statutory maximum for that offense. If the lowest permissible sentence exceeds the statutory maximum for an individual felony offense, the lowest permissible sentence replaces the statutory maximum and must be imposed for that offense. Sentences for multiple felony offenses may be imposed concurrently or consecutively. However, any sentence to state prison must exceed 1 year. If the total sentence points are greater than or equal to 363, the court may sentence the offender to life imprisonment.

(27) The sentence imposed must be entered on the scoresheet.

(28) For those offenses having a mandatory minimum sentence, a scoresheet must be completed and the lowest permissible sentence under the Code calculated. If the lowest permissible sentence is less than the mandatory minimum sentence, the mandatory minimum sentence takes precedence. If the lowest permissible sentence exceeds the mandatory sentence, the requirements of the Criminal Punishment Code and any mandatory minimum penalties apply. Mandatory minimum sentences must be recorded on the scoresheet.

(29) Any downward departure from the lowest permissible sentence, as calculated according to the total sentence points under section 921.0024, Florida Statutes, is prohibited unless there are circumstances or factors that reasonably justify the downward departure. Circumstances or factors that can be considered include, but are not limited to, those listed in subsection 921.0026(2), Florida Statutes.

(A) If a sentencing judge imposes a sentence that is below the lowest permissible sentence, it is a departure sentence and must be accompanied by a written statement by the sentencing court delineating the reasons for the departure, filed within 7 days after the date of sentencing. A written transcription of orally stated reasons for departure articulated at the time sentence was imposed is sufficient if it is filed by the court within 7 days after the date of sentencing. The sentencing judge may also list the written reasons for departure in the space provided on the Criminal Punishment Code scoresheet.

(B) The written statement delineating the reasons for departure must be made a part of the record. The written statement, if it is a separate document, must accompany the scoresheet required to be provided to the Department of Corrections under subsection 921.0024(6), Florida Statutes. If a split sentence is imposed, the total sanction (incarceration and community control or probation) must not exceed the term provided by general law or the maximum sentence under the Criminal Punishment Code.

(30) If the lowest permissible sentence under the criminal punishment code is a state prison sanction but the total sentencing points do not exceed 48 points (or 54 points if 6 of those points are for a violation of probation, community control, or other community supervision that does not involve a new crime), the court may sentence the defendant to probation, community control, or community supervision with mandatory participation in a prison diversion program, as provided for in section 921.00241, Florida Statutes, if the defendant meets the requirements for that program as set forth in section 921.00241, Florida Statutes.

(31) If the total sentence points equal 22 or less, the court must sentence the offender to a nonstate prison sanction unless it makes written findings that a nonstate prison sanction could present a danger to the public. Unless there is a stipulation, there must be a finding by the jury that a nonstate prison sanction could present a danger to the public before the court may sentence a defendant to prison under section 775.082(10), Florida Statutes.

(32) Sentences imposed after revocation of probation or community control must be imposed according to the sentencing

law applicable at the time of the commission of the original offense.

Committee Notes

The terms must and shall, as used in this rule, are mandatory and not permissive.

2001 Amendment. 3.704(d)(14)(B). The definition of "prior record" was amended to include juvenile dispositions of offenses committed within 5 years prior to the date of the commission of the primary offense. "Prior record" was previously defined to include juvenile disposition of offenses committed within 3 years prior to the date of the commission of the primary offense. This amendment reflects the legislative change to section 921.0021, Florida Statutes, effective July 1, 2001. This new definition of prior record applies to primary offenses committed on or after July 1, 2001.

2023 Amendment. The Committee proposed the amendments to subdivision (d)(26) based on the Court's opinion in State v. Gabriel, 314 So. 3d 1243 (Fla. 2021).

Rule 3.710. Presentence Report.

(a) Cases In Which Court Has Discretion. In all cases in which the court has discretion as to what sentence may be imposed, the court may refer the case to the Department of Corrections for investigation and recommendation. No sentence or sentences other than probation or the statutorily required mandatory minimum may be imposed on any defendant found guilty of a first felony offense or found guilty of a felony while under the age of 18 years, until after such investigation has first been made and the recommendations of the Department of Corrections received and considered by the sentencing judge. The requirements of this subdivision are not applicable to a subsequent violation of probation proceeding.

(b) Capital Defendant Who Refuses To Present Mitigation Evidence. Should a defendant in a capital case choose not to challenge the death penalty and refuse to present mitigation evidence, the court shall refer the case to the Department of Corrections for the preparation of a presentence report. The report shall be comprehensive and should include information such as previous mental health problems (including hospitalizations), school records, and relevant family background.

Committee Notes

1972 Adoption. The rule provides for the utilization of a presentence report as part of the sentencing process. While use of the report is discretionary in all cases, it is mandatory in two instances, the sentencing of a first felony offender and of a defendant under 18 years of age. Of course, no report is necessary where the specific sentence is mandatory, e.g., the sentence of death or life imprisonment in a verdict of first degree murder.

1988 Amendment. This amendment changes wording to conform with current responsibility of the Department of Corrections to prepare the presentence investigation and report.

2004 Amendment. The amendment adds subdivision (b). Section 948.015, Florida Statutes, is by its own terms inapplicable to those cases described in this new subdivision. Nonetheless, subdivision (b) requires a report that is "comprehensive." Accordingly, the report should include, if reasonably available, in addition to those matters specifically listed in Muhammad v. State, 782 So.2d 343, 363 (Fla. 2000), a description of the status of all of the charges in the indictment as well as any other pending offenses; the defendant's medical history; and those matters listed in section 948.015(3)-(8) and (13), Florida Statutes. The Department of Corrections should not recommend a sentence.

2018 Amendment. The amendment modifies subdivision (a). The rule makes clear that a report is not required prior to sentencing in violation of probation proceedings following the ruling in Barber v. State, 293 So. 2d 710 (Fla. 1974).

Rule 3.711. Presentence Report: When Prepared.

(a) Except as provided in subdivision (b), the sentencing court shall not authorize the commencement of the presentence investigation until there has been a finding of guilt.

(b) The sentencing court may authorize the commencement of the presentence investigation prior to finding of guilt if:

(1) the defendant has consented to such action; and

(2) nothing disclosed by the presentence investigation comes to the attention of the prosecution, the court, or the jury prior to an adjudication of guilt. Upon motion of the defense and prosecution, the court may examine the presentence investigation prior to the entry of a plea.

Committee Notes

1972 Adoption. The rule permits presentence investigations to be initiated prior to finding of guilt. Its purpose is to reduce unwarranted jail time by a defendant who expects to plead guilty and who may well merit probation or commitment to facilities other than prison.

Rule 3.712. Presentence Report: Disclosure.

The presentence investigation shall not be a public record and shall be available only to the following persons under the following stated conditions:

(a) To the sentencing court to assist it in determining an appropriate sentence.

(b) To persons or agencies having a legitimate professional interest in the information that it would contain.

(c) To reviewing courts if relevant to an issue on which an appeal has been taken.

(d) To the parties as rule 3.713 provides.

Committee Notes

1972 Amendment. Provides for disclosure of the report to the trial court, appropriate agencies of the state, and appellate courts, if needed.

Rule 3.713. Presentence Investigation Disclosure: Parties.

(a) The trial judge may disclose any of the contents of the presentence investigation to the parties prior to sentencing. Any information so disclosed to one party shall be disclosed to the opposing party.

(b) The trial judge shall disclose all factual material, including but not limited to the defendant's education, prior occupation, prior arrests, prior convictions, military service and the like, to the defendant and the state a reasonable time prior to sentencing. If any physical or mental evaluations of the defendant have been made and are to be considered for the purposes of sentencing or release, such reports shall be disclosed to counsel for both parties.

(c) On motion of the defendant or the prosecutor or on its own motion, the sentencing court may order the defendant to submit to a mental or physical examination that would be relevant to the sentencing decision. Copies of the examination or any other examination to be considered for the purpose of sentencing shall be disclosed to counsel for the parties subject to the limitation of rule 3.713(b).

Committee Notes

1972 Adoption. This rule represents a compromise between the philosophy that presentence investigations should be fully disclosed to a defendant and the objection that such disclosure would dry up sources of confidential information and render such report virtually useless. (a) gives the trial judge discretion to disclose any or all of the report to the parties. (b) makes mandatory the disclosure of factual and physical and mental evaluation material only. In this way, it is left to the discretion of the trial judge to disclose to a defendant or defendant's counsel any other evaluative material. The judicial discretion should amply protect the confidentiality of those sources who do not wish to be disclosed, while the availability of all factual material will permit the defendant to discover and make known to the sentencing court any errors that may appear in the report.

Rule 3.720. Sentencing Hearing.

As soon as practicable after the determination of guilt and after the examination of any presentence reports, the sentencing court shall order a sentencing hearing. At the hearing:

(a) The court shall inform the defendant of the finding of guilt against the defendant and of the judgment and ask the defendant whether there is any legal cause to show why sentence should not be pronounced. The defendant may allege and show as legal cause why sentence should not be pronounced only:

(1) that the defendant is insane;

(2) that the defendant has been pardoned of the offense for which he or she is about to be sentenced;

(3) that the defendant is not the same person against whom the verdict or finding of the court or judgment was rendered; or

(4) if the defendant is a woman and sentence of death is to be pronounced, that she is pregnant.

(b) The court shall entertain submissions and evidence by the parties that are relevant to the sentence.

(c) In cases where guilt was determined by plea, the court shall inform itself, if not previously informed, of the existence of plea discussions or agreements and the extent to which they involve recommendations as to the appropriate sentence.

(d)

(1) If the accused was represented by a public defender or other court appointed counsel, the court shall notify the accused of the imposition of a lien pursuant to section 938.29, Florida Statutes. The amount of the lien shall be given and a judgment entered in that amount against the accused. Notice of the accused's right to a hearing to contest the amount of the lien shall be given at the time of sentence.

(2) If the accused requests a hearing to contest the amount of the lien, the court shall set a hearing date within 30 days of the date of sentencing.

Committee Notes

1968 Adoption (of Rule 3.730). A revamped version of section 921.08, Florida Statutes.

1972 Amendment. 3.720(a): Substantially the same as former rule 3.730. 3.720(b): The defendant is to be permitted to challenge factual bases for the sentence that the defendant believes to be incorrect. When possible, submissions should be done informally, but the rule does not preclude an evidentiary hearing if it should be necessary. 3.720(c): Provides for plea discussions to be made a part of the record.

1980 Amendment. Modification of the rule by the addition of (d)(1) and (d)(2) requires a trial judge to adequately inform a defendant of the imposition of a lien for public defender services. A uniform procedure for scheduling hearings to contest liens would reduce the number of postsentence petitions from incarcerated defendants at times remote from sentencing. The procedure is designed to complete all lien requirements established by section 27.56, Florida Statutes, before defendants are removed from the jurisdiction of the trial court.

Rule 3.721. Record of the Proceedings.

The sentencing court shall ensure that a record of the entire sentencing proceeding is made and preserved in such a manner that it can be transcribed as needed.

Committee Notes

1972 Adoption. New, providing for a record of the sentencing proceeding.

Rule 3.730. Issuance of Capias When Necessary to Bring Defendant Before Court.

Whenever the court deems it necessary to do so in order to procure the presence of the defendant before it for the adjudication of guilt or the pronouncement of sentence, or both, when the defendant is not in custody, it shall direct the clerk to issue immediately or when directed by the prosecuting attorney a capias for the arrest of the defendant. Subsequent capiases may be issued from time to time by direction of the court or the prosecuting attorney.

Committee Notes

1968 Adoption (of Rule 3.710). A revamped version of section 921.06, Florida Statutes, adding provision that defendant be required to be present at the adjudication of guilt.

1972 Amendment. Same as prior rule 3.710.

Rule 3.750. Procedure When Pardon Is Alleged as Cause for Not Pronouncing Sentence.

When the cause alleged for not pronouncing sentence is that the defendant has been pardoned for the offense for which the defendant is about to be sentenced, the court, if necessary, shall postpone the pronouncement of sentence for the purpose of hearing evidence on the allegation. If the court decides that the allegation is true, it shall discharge the defendant from custody unless the defendant is in custody on some other charge. If, however, it decides that the allegation is not true, it shall proceed to pronounce sentence.

Committee Notes

1968 Adoption. A revamped version of section 921.10, Florida Statutes.

1972 Amendment. Same as prior rule.

Rule 3.760. Procedure When Nonidentity Is Alleged as Cause for Not Pronouncing Sentence.

When the cause alleged for not pronouncing sentence is that the person brought before the court to be sentenced is not the same person against whom the verdict, finding of the court, or judgment was rendered, the court, if necessary, shall postpone the pronouncement of sentence for the purpose of hearing evidence on the allegation. If the court decides that the allegation is true, it shall discharge the person from custody unless the person is in custody on some other charge. If, however, it decides that the allegation is not true, it shall proceed to pronounce sentence.

Committee Notes
1968 Adoption. A revamped version of section 921.11, Florida Statutes.
1972 Amendment. Same as prior rule.

Rule 3.770. Procedure When Pregnancy Is Alleged as Cause for Not Pronouncing Death Sentence.

When pregnancy of a defendant is alleged as the cause for not pronouncing the death sentence, the court shall postpone the pronouncement of sentence until after it has decided the truth of that allegation. If necessary in order to arrive at such a decision, it shall immediately fix a time for a hearing to determine whether the defendant is pregnant and shall appoint not exceeding 3 competent disinterested physicians to examine the defendant as to the defendant's alleged pregnancy and to testify at the hearing as to whether the defendant is pregnant. Other evidence regarding whether the defendant is pregnant may be introduced at the hearing by either party. If the court decides that the defendant is not pregnant, it shall proceed to pronounce sentence. If it decides that the defendant is pregnant, it shall commit the defendant to prison until it appears that the defendant is not pregnant and shall then pronounce sentence.

Committee Notes

1968 Adoption. A revamped version of section 921.12, Florida Statutes.

Note that the rule omits the statutory provisions for the payment of fees to the examining physicians. The supreme court probably does not have the power to make rules governing such matters.

1972 Amendment. Same as prior rule.

Rule 3.780. Sentencing Hearing for Capital Cases.

(a) Evidence. In capital sentencing proceedings the state and defendant will be permitted to present evidence of an aggravating or mitigating nature, consistent with the requirements of the statutes and the notice requirements of Florida Rule of Criminal Procedure 3.181. Each side will be permitted to cross-examine the witnesses presented by the other side. The state will present evidence first.

(b) Rebuttal. The trial judge shall permit rebuttal testimony.

(c) Opening Statement and Closing Argument. Both the state and the defendant will be given an equal opportunity for one opening statement and one closing argument. The state will proceed first.

Committee Notes

1977 Adoption. This is a new rule designed to create a uniform procedure that will be consistent with both section 921.141, Florida Statutes, and State v. Dixon, 283 So.2d 1 (Fla. 1973).

Rule 3.781. Sentencing Hearing to Consider the Imposition of a Life Sentence for Juvenile Offenders.

(a) Application. The courts shall use the following procedures in sentencing a juvenile offender for an offense which was committed after July 1, 2014, if the conviction may result in a sentence of life imprisonment or a term of years equal to life imprisonment, or for resentencing any juvenile offender whose sentence is determined to be unconstitutional pursuant to the United States Supreme Court's decision in Miller v. Alabama, 132 S. Ct. 2455, 2469 (2012) or Graham v. Florida, 560 U.S. 48 (2010).

Rule 3.781. Sentencing Hearing to Consider the Imposition of a Life Sentence for Juvenile Offenders.

(b) Procedure; Evidentiary Hearing. After a determination of guilt for an offense punishable under sections 775.082(1)(b), 775.082(3)(a)5., 775.082(3)(b)2., or 775.082(3)(c), Florida Statutes, and after the examination of any presentence reports, the sentencing court shall order a sentencing hearing to be held pursuant to rules 3.720 and 3.721. The sentencing court shall allow the state and the juvenile offender to present evidence relevant to the offense, the juvenile offender's youth, and attendant circumstances, including, but not limited to those enumerated in section 921.1401(2), Florida Statutes. Additionally, the court shall allow the state and the juvenile offender to present evidence relevant to whether or not the juvenile offender killed, intended to kill, or attempted to kill the victim.

(c) Findings.

(1) The court shall make specific findings on the record that all relevant factors have been reviewed and considered by the court prior to imposing a sentence of life imprisonment or a term of years equal to life imprisonment. The court shall make written findings as to whether the juvenile offender is eligible for a sentence review hearing under subsections (2)(a), (2)(b), or (2)(c) of section 921.1402, Florida Statutes, based on whether the juvenile offender killed, attempted to kill, or intended to kill the victim. If the juvenile offender is found eligible for a sentence review hearing, the court shall issue a written order specifying:

A. which subsection of section 921.1402(2), Florida Statutes, applies;

B. when the juvenile offender is eligible to apply for a sentence review hearing; and

C. that subsection 921.1402(3), Florida Statutes, requires the Department of Corrections to notify the juvenile offender when he or she will be eligible to apply for a sentence review hearing.

(2) A juvenile offender who is convicted of an offense punishable under section 775.082(1)(b)1., Florida Statutes, shall not be eligible for a sentence review hearing if the trial court finds that the juvenile offender has previously been convicted of one of the enumerated offenses, or conspiracy to commit one of the enumerated offenses, found in section 921.1402(2)(a), Florida Statutes.

(3) A copy of the written findings shall be made a part of the commitment packet for the Department of Corrections.

Rule 3.790. Probation and Community Control.

(a) Suspension of the Pronouncement and Imposition of Sentence; Probation or Community Control. Pronouncement and imposition of sentence of imprisonment shall not be made on a defendant who is to be placed on probation, regardless of whether the defendant has been adjudicated guilty. An order of the court placing a person on probation or community control shall place the probationer under the authority of the Department of Corrections to be supervised as provided by law. The court shall specify the length of time during which the defendant is to be supervised.

(b) Revocation of Probation or Community Control; Judgment; Sentence.

(1) **Generally.** Except as otherwise provided in subdivisions (b)(2) and (b)(3) below, when a probationer or a community controllee is brought before a court of competent jurisdiction charged with a violation of probation or community control, the court shall advise the person of the charge and, if the charge is admitted to be true, may immediately enter an order revoking, modifying, or continuing the probation or community control. If the violation of probation or community control is not admitted by the probationer or community controllee, the court may commit the person or release the person with or without bail to await further hearing or it may dismiss the charge of violation of probation or community control. If the charge is not admitted by the probationer or community controllee and if it is not dismissed, the court, as soon as practicable, shall give the probationer or community controllee an opportunity to be fully heard in person, by counsel, or both. After the hearing, the court may enter an order revoking, modifying, or continuing the probation or community control. Following a revocation of probation or community control, the trial court shall adjudicate the defendant guilty of the crime forming the basis of the probation or community control if no such adjudication has been made previously. Pronouncement and imposition of sentence then shall be made on the defendant.

(2) **Lunsford Act Proceedings.** When a probationer or community controllee is arrested for violating his or her probation or community control in a material respect and is

Rule 3.790. Probation and Community Control.

under supervision for any criminal offense proscribed in chapter 794, Florida Statutes, section 800.04(4), Florida Statutes, section 800.04(5), Florida Statutes, section 800.04(6), Florida Statutes, section 827.071, Florida Statutes, or section 847.0145, Florida Statutes, or is a registered sexual predator or a registered sexual offender, or is under supervision for a criminal offense for which, but for the effective date, he or she would meet the registration criteria of section 775.21, Florida Statutes, section 943.0435, Florida Statutes, or section 944.607, Florida Statutes, the court must make a finding that the probationer or community controllee is not a danger to the public prior to release with or without bail.

(A) The hearing to determine whether the defendant is a danger to the public shall be conducted by a court of competent jurisdiction no sooner than 24 hours after arrest. The time for conducting the hearing may be extended at the request of the accused, or at the request of the state upon a showing of good cause.

(B) At the hearing, the defendant shall have the right to be heard in person or through counsel, to present witnesses and evidence, and to cross-examine witnesses.

(C) In determining the danger posed by the defendant's release, the court may consider:

(i) the nature and circumstances of the violation and any new offenses charged;

(ii) the defendant's past and present conduct, including convictions of crimes;

(iii) any record of arrests without conviction for crimes involving violence or sexual crimes;

(iv) any other evidence of allegations of unlawful sexual conduct or the use of violence by the defendant;

(v) the defendant's family ties, length of residence in the community, employment history, and mental condition;

(vi) the defendant's history and conduct during the probation or community control supervision from which the violation arises and any other previous supervisions, including disciplinary records of previous incarcerations;

(vii) the likelihood that the defendant will engage again in a criminal course of conduct;

(viii) the weight of the evidence against the defendant; and

(ix) any other facts the court considers relevant.

(3) Anti-Murder Act Proceedings. The provisions of this subdivision shall control over any conflicting provisions in subdivision (b)(2). When a probationer or community controllee is arrested for violating his or her probation or community control in a material respect and meets the criteria for a violent felony offender of special concern, or for certain other related categories of offender, as set forth in section 948.06(8), Florida Statutes, the defendant shall be brought before the court that granted the probation or community control and, except when the alleged violation is based solely on the defendant's failure to pay costs, fines, or restitution, shall not be granted bail or any other form of pretrial release prior to the resolution of the probation or community control violation hearing.

(A) The court shall not dismiss the probation or community control violation warrant pending against the defendant without holding a recorded violation hearing at which both the state and the accused are represented.

(B) If, after conducting the hearing, the court determines that the defendant has committed a violation of probation or community control other than a failure to pay costs, fines, or restitution, the court shall make written findings as to whether the defendant poses a danger to the community. In determining the danger to the community posed by the defendant's release, the court shall base its findings on one or more of the following:

(i) The nature and circumstances of the violation and any new offenses charged;

(ii) The defendant's present conduct, including criminal convictions;

(iii) The defendant's amenability to nonincarcerative sanctions based on his or her history and conduct during the probation or community control supervision from which the violation hearing arises and any other previous supervisions, including disciplinary records of previous incarcerations;

(iv) The weight of the evidence against the defendant; and

Rule 3.790. Probation and Community Control.

(v) Any other facts the court considers relevant.

(C) If the court finds that the defendant poses a danger to the community, the court shall revoke probation or community control and sentence the defendant up to the statutory maximum, or longer if permitted by law.

(D) If the court finds that the defendant does not pose a danger to the community, the court may revoke, modify, or continue the probation or community control or may place the probationer into community control as provided in section 948.06, Florida Statutes.

Committee Notes

1968 Adoption. Subdivisions (a) and (b) contain the procedural aspects of section 948.01(1), (2), and (3), Florida Statutes. It should be noted that in (b) provision is made for no pronouncements in addition to no imposition of sentence prior to the granting of probation. The terminology in section 948.01(3), Florida Statutes, is that the trial court shall "withhold the imposition of sentence." The selected terminology is deemed preferable to the present statutory language since the latter is apparently subject to misconstruction whereby a sentence may be pronounced and merely the execution of the sentence is suspended.

The Third District Court of Appeal has indicated that the proper procedure to be followed is that probation be granted prior to sentencing. A sentence, therefore, is not a prerequisite of probation. See Yates v. Buchanan, 170 So.2d 72 (Fla. 3d DCA 1964); also see Bateh v. State, 101 So.2d 869 (Fla. 1st DCA 1958), decided by the First District Court of Appeal to the same effect.

While a trial court initially can set a probationary period at less than the maximum allowed by law, this period may be extended to the maximum prior to the expiration of the initially-set probationary period. Pickman v. State, 155 So.2d 646 (Fla. 1st DCA 1963). This means, therefore, that any specific time set by the court as to the probationary period is not binding if the court acts timely in modifying it. It is clear, in view of the foregoing, that if a trial judge pronounces a definite sentence and then purports to suspend its execution and place the defendant on probation for the period of time specified in the sentence, matters may become unduly complicated.

If such procedure is considered to be nothing more than an informal manner of suspending the imposition of sentence and thus adhering to present statutory requirements, it should be noted that the time specified in the "sentence" is not binding on the court with reference to subsequent modification, if timely action follows. On the other hand, if the action of the trial court is considered strictly, it would be held to be void as not in conformity with statutory requirements.

A probationary period is not a sentence, and any procedure that tends to mix them is undesirable, even if this mixture is accomplished by nothing more than the terminology used by the trial court in its desire to place a person on probation. See sections 948.04 and 948.06(1), Florida Statutes, in which clear distinctions are drawn between the period of a sentence and the period of probation.

(c) Contains the procedural aspects of section 948.06(1), Florida Statutes.

1972 Amendment. (a) of former rule deleted, as its substance is now contained in rules 3.710, 3.711, and 3.713. Former subdivisions (b) and (c) are now renumbered (a) and (b) respectively.

1988 Amendment. This amendment changes wording to conform with current responsibilities of the Department of Corrections to supervise a person placed on either probation or community control and brings community control within the scope of the rule.

Rule 3.800. Correction, Reduction, and Modification of Sentences.

(a) Correction.

(1) Generally. A court may at any time correct an illegal sentence imposed by it, or an incorrect calculation made by it in a sentencing scoresheet, when it is affirmatively alleged that the court records demonstrate on their face an entitlement to that relief, provided that a party may not file a motion to correct an illegal sentence under this subdivision during the time allowed for the filing of a motion under subdivision (b)(1) or during the pendency of a direct appeal.

(2) Successive Motions. A court may dismiss a second or successive motion if the court finds that the motion fails to allege new or different grounds for relief and the prior determination was on the merits. When a motion is dismissed under this subdivision, a copy of that portion of the files and

Rule 3.800. Correction, Reduction, and Modification of Sentences.

records necessary to support the court's ruling must accompany the order dismissing the motion.

(3) Sexual Predator Designation. A defendant may seek correction of an allegedly erroneous sexual predator designation under this subdivision, but only when it is apparent from the face of the record that the defendant did not meet the criteria for designation as a sexual predator.

(4) Appeals. All orders denying or dismissing motions under subdivision (a) must include a statement that the defendant has the right to appeal within 30 days of rendition of the order.

(b) Motion to Correct Sentencing Error. A motion to correct any sentencing error, including an illegal sentence or incorrect jail credit, may be filed as allowed by this subdivision. This subdivision shall not be applicable to those cases in which the death sentence has been imposed and direct appeal jurisdiction is in the supreme court under article V, section 3(b)(1) of the Florida Constitution. The motion must identify the error with specificity and provide a proposed correction. A response to the motion may be filed within 15 days, either admitting or contesting the alleged error. Motions may be filed by the state under this subdivision only if the correction of this sentencing error would benefit the defendant or to correct a scrivener's error.

(1) Motion Before Appeal. During the time allowed for the filing of a notice of appeal of a sentence, a defendant or the state may file a motion to correct a sentencing error.

(A) This motion shall stay rendition under Florida Rule of Appellate Procedure 9.020(h).

(B) Unless the trial court determines that the motion can be resolved as a matter of law without a hearing, it shall hold a calendar call no later than 20 days from the filing of the motion, with notice to all parties, for the express purpose of either ruling on the motion or determining the need for an evidentiary hearing. If an evidentiary hearing is needed, it shall be set no more than 20 days from the date of the calendar call. Within 60 days from the filing of the motion, the trial court shall file an order ruling on the motion. A party may file a motion for rehearing of any signed, written order entered under subdivisions (a) and (b) of this rule within 15 days of the date of service of the order or within 15 days of the expiration of the time period for filing an order if no order is filed. A response may be filed within 10 days of service of the motion. The trial court's order disposing of the motion for rehearing shall be filed within 15 days of the response but not later than 40 days from the date of the order of which rehearing is sought. A timely filed motion for rehearing shall toll rendition of the order subject to appellate review and the order shall be deemed rendered upon the filing of a signed, written order denying the motion for rehearing.

(2) Motion Pending Appeal. If an appeal is pending, a defendant or the state may file in the trial court a motion to correct a sentencing error. The motion may be filed by appellate counsel and must be served before the party's first brief is served. A notice of pending motion to correct sentencing error shall be filed in the appellate court, which notice automatically shall extend the time for the filing of the brief until 10 days after the clerk of circuit court transmits the supplemental record under Florida Rule of Appellate Procedure 9.140(f)(6).

(A) The motion shall be served on the trial court and on all trial and appellate counsel of record. Unless the motion expressly states that appellate counsel will represent the movant in the trial court, trial counsel will represent the movant on the motion under Florida Rule of Appellate Procedure 9.140(d). If the state is the movant, trial counsel will represent the defendant unless appellate counsel for the defendant notifies trial counsel and the trial court that he or she will represent the defendant on the state's motion.

(B) The trial court shall resolve this motion in accordance with the procedures in subdivision (b)(1)(B), except that if the trial court does not file an order ruling on the motion within 60 days, the motion shall be deemed denied. Similarly, if the trial court does not file an order ruling on a timely motion for rehearing within 40 days from the date of the order of which rehearing is sought, the motion for rehearing shall be deemed denied.

(C) In accordance with Florida Rule of Appellate Procedure 9.140(f)(6), the clerk of circuit court shall supplement the appellate record with the motion, the order, any amended sentence, and, if designated, a transcript of any additional portion of the proceedings.

(c) Reduction and Modification. A court may reduce or modify to include any of the provisions of chapter 948, Florida Statutes, a

Rule 3.800. Correction, Reduction, and Modification of Sentences.

legal sentence imposed by it, sua sponte, or upon motion filed, within 60 days after the imposition, or within 60 days after receipt by the court of a mandate issued by the appellate court on affirmance of the judgment and/or sentence on an original appeal, or within 60 days after receipt by the court of a certified copy of an order of the appellate court dismissing an original appeal from the judgment and/or sentence, or, if further appellate review is sought in a higher court or in successively higher courts, within 60 days after the highest state or federal court to which a timely appeal has been taken under authority of law, or in which a petition for certiorari has been timely filed under authority of law, has entered an order of affirmance or an order dismissing the appeal and/or denying certiorari. If review is upon motion, the trial court shall have 90 days from the date the motion is filed or such time as agreed by the parties or as extended by the trial court to enter an order ruling on the motion. This subdivision shall not be applicable to those cases in which the death sentence is imposed or those cases in which the trial judge has imposed the minimum mandatory sentence or has no sentencing discretion.

Committee Notes

1968 Adoption. Same as sections 921.24 and 921.25, Florida Statutes. Similar to Federal Rule of Criminal Procedure 35.

1972 Amendment. Same as prior rule.

1977 Amendment. This amendment provides a uniform time within which a defendant may seek a reduction in sentence and excludes death and minimum mandatory sentences from its operation.

1980 Amendment. Permits the sentencing judge, within the 60-day time period, to modify as well as to reduce the sentence originally imposed. Such modification would permit the judge to impose, in the modification, any sentence which could have been imposed initially, including split sentence or probation. The trial judge may not, in such modification, increase the original sentence.

1996 Amendments. Subdivision (b) was added and existing subdivision (b) was renumbered as subdivision (c) in order to authorize the filing of a motion to correct a sentence or order of probation, thereby providing a vehicle to correct sentencing errors in the trial court and to preserve the issue should the motion be denied. A motion filed under subdivision (b) is an authorized motion which tolls the time for filing the notice of appeal. The presence of a defendant who is represented by counsel would not be required at the hearing on the disposition of such a motion if it only involved a question of law.

2000 Amendment. The amendment to subdivision (a) is intended to conform the rule with State v. Mancino, 714 So.2d 429 (Fla. 1998).

2015 Amendments. The amendment to rule 3.800(a)(2) is not intended to render inapplicable the "manifest injustice" exception as described in State v. McBride, 848 So. 2d 287 (Fla. 2003).

Court Commentary

1999 Amendments. Rule 3.800(b) was substantially rewritten to accomplish the goals of the Criminal Appeal Reform Act of 1996 (Ch. 96-248, Laws of Fla.). As revised, this rule permits the filing of a motion during the initial stages of an appeal. A motion pursuant to this rule is needed only if the sentencing error has not been adequately preserved for review at an earlier time in the trial court.

The State may file a motion to correct a sentencing error pursuant to rule 3.800(b) only if the correction of that error will benefit the defendant or correct a scrivener's error. This amendment is not intended to alter the substantive law of the State concerning whether a change to the defendant's sentence violates the constitutional prohibition against double jeopardy. See, e.g., Cheshire v. State, 568 So.2d 908 (Fla. 1990); Goene v. State, 577 So.2d 1306, 1309 (Fla. 1991); Troupe v. Rowe, 283 So.2d 857, 859 (Fla. 1973).

A scrivener's error in this context describes clerical or ministerial errors in a criminal case that occur in the written sentence, judgment, or order of probation or restitution. The term scrivener's error refers to a mistake in the written sentence that is at variance with the oral pronouncement of sentence or the record but not those errors that are the result of a judicial determination or error. See, e.g., Allen v. State, 739 So.2d 166 (Fla. 3rd DCA 1999) (correcting a "scrivener's error" in the written order that adjudicated the appellant in contempt for "jailing polygraph exam"); Pressley v. State, 726 So.2d 403 (Fla. 2d DCA 1999) (correcting scrivener's error in the sentencing documents that identified the defendant as a habitual offender when he was notsentenced as a habitual offender); Ricks v. State, 725 So.2d 1205 (Fla. 2d DCA 1999) (correcting scrivener's error that resulted from the written sentence not identifying the defendant as a habitual offender although the court had orally pronounced a habitual offender sentence), review denied, 732 So.2d 328 (Fla. 1999); McKee v. State, 712 So.2d 837 (Fla. 2d DCA 1998) (remanding for the trial court to determine whether a scrivener's error occurred where the written order of probation imposed six years' probation, which conflicted with the written sentence and the trial court minutes that reflected only five years' probation had been imposed); Florczak v. State, 712 So.2d 467, 467 (Fla. 4th DCA 1998) (correcting a scrivener's error in the judgment of conviction where the defendant was acquitted of grand theft but the written judgment stated otherwise); Stombaugh v. State, 704 So.2d 723, 725-26 (Fla. 5th DCA 1998) (finding a scrivener's error occurred where the State had nol prossed a count of the information as part of plea bargain but the written sentence reflected that the defendant was sentenced under that count). But see Carridine v. State, 721 So.2d 818, 819 (Fla. 4th DCA 1998) (trial court's failure to sign written reasons for imposing an upward departure sentence did not constitute a scrivener's error that could be corrected nunc pro tunc by the trial court), and cases cited therein.

When a trial court determines that an evidentiary hearing is necessary to resolve a factual issue, it is possible that the court will need to utilize the entire 60-day period authorized by this rule. However, trial courts and counsel are strongly encouraged to cooperate to resolve these motions as expeditiously as possible because they delay the appellate process. For purposes of this rule, sentencing errors include harmful errors in orders entered as a result of the sentencing process. This includes errors in orders of probation, orders of community control, cost and restitution orders, as well as errors within the sentence itself.

Rule 3.801. Correction of Jail Credit.

(a) Correction of Jail Credit. A court may correct a final sentence that fails to allow a defendant credit for all of the time he or she spent in the county jail before sentencing as provided in section 921.161, Florida Statutes.

(b) Time Limitations. No motion shall be filed or considered pursuant to this rule if filed more than 1 year after the sentence becomes final.

(c) Contents of Motion. The motion shall be under oath and include:

> (1) a brief statement of the facts relied on in support of the motion;

(2) the dates, location of incarceration, and total time for credit already provided;

(3) the dates, location of incarceration, and total time for credit the defendant contends was not properly awarded;

(4) whether any other criminal charges were pending at the time of the incarceration noted in subdivision (c)(3), and if so, the location, case number, and resolution of the charges; and

(5) whether the defendant waived any county jail credit at the time of sentencing, and if so, the number of days waived.

(d) Successive Motions. No successive motions for jail credit will be considered.

(e) Incorporation of Portions of Florida Rule of Criminal Procedure 3.850. The following subdivisions of Florida Rule of Criminal Procedure 3.850 apply to proceedings under this rule: 3.850(e), (f), (j), (k), and (n).

Committee Notes

2013 Adoption. All jail credit issues must be handled pursuant to this rule. The rule is intended to require that jail credit issues be dealt with promptly, within 1 year of the sentence becoming final. No successive motions for jail credit will be allowed.

2016 Amendment. The 2016 amendment clarifies that rule 3.801 applies to final sentences. Prior to the sentence being final, defendants may avail themselves of all appropriate proceedings to litigate a jail credit issue, including direct appeal if properly preserved, a motion for rehearing, or a motion pursuant to rule 3.800(b).

Rule 3.802. Review of Sentences for Juvenile Offenders.

(a) Application. A juvenile offender, as defined in section 921.1402(1), Florida Statutes, may seek a modification of sentence pursuant to section 921.1402, Florida Statutes, by submitting an application to the trial court requesting a sentence review hearing.

(b) Time for Filing. An application for sentence review may not be filed until the juvenile offender becomes eligible pursuant to section 921.1402(2), Florida Statutes. A juvenile offender becomes eligible:

(1) after 25 years, if the juvenile offender is sentenced to life under section 775.082(1)(b)1., Florida Statutes, or to a term of

Rule 3.802. Review of Sentences for Juvenile Offenders.

more than 25 years under sections 775.082(3)(a)5.a. or 775.082(3)(b)2.a., Florida Statutes; or

(2) after 20 years, if the juvenile offender is sentenced to a term of 20 years or more under section 775.082(3)(c), Florida Statutes; or

(3) after 15 years, if the juvenile offender is sentenced to a term of more than 15 years under sections 775.082(1)(b)2., 775.082(3)(a)5.b., or 775.082(3)(b)2.b., Florida Statutes.

(c) Contents of Application. The application must state that the juvenile offender is eligible for sentence review and include:

(1) a copy of the judgment and sentence, or a statement containing the following:

(A) the date of sentencing;

(B) the offense for which the juvenile offender was sentenced; and

(C) the sentence imposed; and

(2) whether a previous application has been filed, the date of filing of the application, and the disposition of that application.

(d) Procedure; Evidentiary Hearing; Disposition. Upon application from an eligible juvenile offender, the trial court shall hold a sentence review hearing to determine whether the juvenile offender's sentence should be modified. If the application, files, and records in the case conclusively show that the applicant does not qualify as a juvenile offender under section 921.1402(1), Florida Statutes, or that the application is premature, the court may deny the application without a hearing, and shall attach such documents to the order. If an application is denied as premature, the denial shall be without prejudice.

(1) At the sentence review hearing, the court shall consider the following factors when determining if it is appropriate to modify the juvenile offender's sentence:

(A) whether the juvenile offender demonstrates maturity and rehabilitation;

(B) whether the juvenile offender remains at the same level of risk to society as he or she did at the time of the initial sentencing;

(C) the opinion of the victim or the victim's next of kin;

(D) whether the juvenile offender was a relatively minor participant in the criminal offense or acted under extreme duress or the domination of another person;

(E) whether the juvenile offender has shown sincere and sustained remorse for the criminal offense;

(F) whether the juvenile offender's age, maturity, and psychological development at the time of the offense affected his or her behavior;

(G) whether the juvenile offender has successfully obtained a general educational development certificate or completed another educational, technical, work, vocational, or self-rehabilitation program, if such a program is available;

(H) whether the juvenile offender was a victim of sexual, physical, or emotional abuse before he or she committed the offense;

(I) the results of any mental health assessment, risk assessment, or evaluation of the juvenile offender as to rehabilitation; and

(J) any other factor the court deems appropriate.

(2) If the court determines at a sentence review hearing that the juvenile offender has been rehabilitated and is reasonably believed to be fit to reenter society, the court shall modify the sentence and impose a term of probation of at least 5 years. If the court determines that the juvenile offender has not demonstrated rehabilitation, or is not fit to reenter society, the court shall issue a written order stating the reasons why the sentence is not being modified.

(e) Successive Applications. A second or successive application shall be denied without a hearing, except under the following circumstances:

(1) the initial application was denied as premature; or

(2) pursuant to section 921.1402(2)(d), Florida Statutes, the initial application was submitted by a juvenile offender sentenced to a term of 20 years or more under section 775.082(3)(c), Florida Statutes, and more than 10 years has elapsed since the initial sentence review hearing.

(f) Jurisdiction. The sentencing court shall retain original jurisdiction for the duration of the sentence for the purpose of a sentence review hearing.

(g) Right to Counsel. A juvenile offender who is eligible for a sentence review hearing under section 921.1402(5), Florida Statutes, is entitled to be represented by counsel, and the court shall appoint a public defender to represent the juvenile offender if the juvenile offender cannot afford an attorney.

XV. Execution of Sentence

Rule 3.810. Commitment of Defendant; Duty of Sheriff.

On pronouncement of a sentence imposing a penalty other than a fine only or death, the court shall, unless the execution of the sentence is suspended or stayed, and, in such case, on termination of the suspension or stay, immediately commit the defendant to the custody of the sheriff. The commitment documents must include certified copies of the sentence, the judgment of conviction, and the indictment or information. If the sheriff is not the proper official to execute the sentence, the sheriff will transfer the prisoner, with certified copies of the commitment documents to the custody of the official whose duty it is to execute the sentence and shall take from that person a receipt for the defendant that will be returned to the court.

Committee Notes

1968 Adoption. Substantially the same as section 922.01, Florida Statutes. There has been added to the rule the requirement that, if the commitment is to the state prison, it shall be accompanied by a certified copy of the judgment of conviction and a certified copy of the indictment or information. (Section 944.18, Florida Statutes, requires a certified copy of the indictment or information to be transmitted to the Division of Corrections; the Division of Corrections should also have a certified copy of the judgment.)

1972 Amendment. Same as prior rule.

Rule 3.811. Insanity At Time of Execution: Capital Cases.

(a) Insanity to Be Executed. A person under sentence of death shall not be executed while insane to be executed.

(b) Insanity Defined. A person under sentence of death is insane for purposes of execution if the person lacks the mental capacity to understand the fact of the impending execution and the reason for it.

(c) Stay of Execution. No motion for a stay of execution pending hearing, based on grounds of the prisoner's insanity to be executed, shall be entertained by any court until such time as the Governor of Florida shall have held appropriate proceedings for determining the issue pursuant to the appropriate Florida Statutes.

(d) Motion for Stay after Governor's Determination of Sanity to Be Executed. On determination of the Governor of Florida, subsequent to the signing of a death warrant for a prisoner under sentence of death and pursuant to the applicable Florida Statutes relating to insanity at time of execution, that the prisoner is sane to be executed, counsel for the prisoner may move for a stay of execution and a hearing based on the prisoner's insanity to be executed.

(1) The motion shall be filed in the circuit court of the circuit in which the execution is to take place and shall be heard by one of the judges of that circuit or such other judge as shall be assigned by the chief justice of the supreme court to hear the motion. The state attorney of the circuit shall represent the State of Florida in any proceedings held on the motion.

(2) The motion shall be in writing and shall contain a certificate of counsel that the motion is made in good faith and on reasonable grounds to believe that the prisoner is insane to be executed.

(3) Counsel for the prisoner shall file, along with the motion, all reports of experts that were submitted to the governor pursuant to the statutory procedure for executive determination of sanity to be executed. If any of the evidence is not available to counsel for the prisoner, counsel shall attach to the motion an affidavit so stating, with an explanation of why the evidence is unavailable.

(4) Counsel for the prisoner and the state may submit such other evidentiary material and written submissions including reports of experts on behalf of the prisoner as shall be relevant to determination of the issue.

(5) A copy of the motion and all supporting documents shall be served on the Florida Department of Legal Affairs and the state attorney of the circuit in which the motion has been filed.

(e) Order Granting. If the circuit judge, upon review of the motion and submissions, has reasonable grounds to believe that the prisoner is insane to be executed, the judge shall grant a stay of execution and may order further proceedings which may include a hearing pursuant to rule 3.812.

Committee Notes

1988 Adoption. This rule is not intended to preclude the Office of the Attorney General or the state attorney of the circuit in which the trial was held from appearing on behalf of the State of Florida under circumstances when permitted by law.

Rule 3.812. Hearing on Insanity At Time of Execution: Capital Cases.

(a) Hearing on Insanity to Be Executed. The hearing on the prisoner's insanity to be executed shall not be a review of the governor's determination, but shall be a hearing de novo.

(b) Issue at Hearing. At the hearing the issue shall be whether the prisoner presently meets the criteria for insanity at time of execution, that is, whether the prisoner lacks the mental capacity to understand the fact of the pending execution and the reason for it.

(c) Procedure. The court may do any of the following as may be appropriate and adequate for a just resolution of the issues raised:

    (1) require the presence of the prisoner at the hearing;

    (2) appoint no more than 3 disinterested mental health experts to examine the prisoner with respect to the criteria for insanity to be executed and to report their findings and conclusions to the court; or

    (3) enter such other orders as may be appropriate to effectuate a speedy and just resolution of the issues raised.

(d) Evidence. At hearings held pursuant to this rule, the court may admit such evidence as the court deems relevant to the issues, including but not limited to the reports of expert witnesses, and the court shall not be strictly bound by the rules of evidence.

(e) Order. If, at the conclusion of the hearing, the court shall find, by clear and convincing evidence, that the prisoner is insane to be executed, the court shall enter its order continuing the stay of the death warrant; otherwise, the court shall deny the motion and enter its order dissolving the stay of execution.

Rule 3.820. Habeas Corpus.

(a) Custody Pending Appeal of Order of Denial. When a defendant has been sentenced, and is actually serving the sentence, and has not appealed from the judgment or sentence, but seeks a release from imprisonment by habeas corpus proceedings, and the writ has been discharged after it has been issued, the custody of the prisoner shall not be disturbed, pending review by the appellate court.

(b) Custody Pending Appeal of Order Granting. Pending review of a decision discharging a prisoner on habeas corpus, the prisoner shall be discharged on bail, with sureties to be approved as other bail bonds are approved for the prisoner's appearance to answer and abide by the judgment of the appellate court.

Committee Notes

1968 Adoption. Same as section 922.03, Florida Statutes.

1972 Amendment. Same as prior rule, but some terminology has been changed.

XVI. Criminal Contempt

Rule 3.830. Direct Criminal Contempt.

A criminal contempt may be punished summarily only if the court saw or heard the conduct constituting the contempt committed in the actual presence of the court. The court shall strictly comply with the following five procedural requirements.

    (a) Prior to the adjudication of guilt the judge shall inform the defendant of the accusation against the defendant and inquire as to whether the defendant has any cause to show why he or she should not be adjudged guilty of contempt by the court and sentenced therefor.

    (b) The court shall provide the defendant the opportunity to present evidence of excusing or mitigating circumstances.

    (c) The judgment of guilt of contempt shall include a recital of those facts on which the adjudication of guilt is based, and confirm compliance with the five procedural requirements of this rule.

(d) The judgment shall be signed by the judge and entered of record.

(e) Sentence shall be pronounced in open court.

If necessary to ensure safety of individuals in the courtroom, the court may order the defendant be temporarily detained and removed from the courtroom; however once the danger to individuals in the courtroom has abated, the defendant should be returned to the courtroom to allow for the procedures set forth in this rule.

Committee Notes

1968 Adoption. This proposal is consistent with present Florida practice in authorizing summary proceedings in direct criminal contempt cases. See Ballengee v. State, 144 So.2d 68 (Fla. 2d DCA 1962); Baumgartner v. Joughin, 105 Fla. 334, 141 So. 185 (1932); also see State v. Lehman, 100 Fla. 481, 129 So. 818 (1930), holding that the defendant is not entitled to notice of the accusation or a motion for attachment. Fairness dictates that the defendant be allowed to present excusing or mitigating evidence even in direct criminal contempt cases.

Much of the terminology of the proposal is patterned after Federal Rule of Criminal Procedure 42(a) with variations for purposes of clarity. What may be considered a significant change from the terminology of the federal rule is that the proposal provides for a "judgment" of contempt, whereas the term "order" of contempt is used in the federal rule. Both terms have been used in Florida appellate cases. The term "judgment" is preferred here since it is consistent with the procedure of adjudicating guilt and is more easily reconciled with a "conviction" of contempt, common terminology on the trial and appellate levels in Florida. It also is consistent with appeals in contempt cases. See, e.g., State ex rel. Shotkin v. Buchanan, 149 So.2d 574, 98 A.L.R.2d 683 (Fla. 3d DCA 1963), for the use of the term "judgment."

1972 Amendment. Same as prior rule.

Rule 3.840. Indirect Criminal Contempt.

A criminal contempt, except as provided in rule 3.830 concerning direct contempts, shall be prosecuted in the following manner:

(a) Order to Show Cause. The judge, on the judge's own motion or on affidavit of any person having knowledge of the facts, may issue and sign an order directed to the defendant, stating the essential facts constituting the criminal contempt charged and requiring the defendant to appear before the court to show cause why the defendant should not be held in contempt of court. The order shall specify the time and place of the hearing, with a reasonable time allowed for preparation of the defense after service of the order on the defendant.

(b) Motions; Answer. The defendant, personally or by counsel, may move to dismiss the order to show cause, move for a statement of particulars, or answer the order by way of explanation or defense. All motions and the answer shall be in writing unless specified otherwise by the judge. A defendant's omission to file motions or answer shall not be deemed as an admission of guilt of the contempt charged.

(c) Order of Arrest; Bail. The judge may issue an order of arrest of the defendant if the judge has reason to believe the defendant will not appear in response to the order to show cause. The defendant shall be admitted to bail in the manner provided by law in criminal cases.

(d) Arraignment; Hearing. The defendant may be arraigned at the time of the hearing, or prior thereto at the defendant's request. A hearing to determine the guilt or innocence of the defendant shall follow a plea of not guilty. The judge may conduct a hearing without assistance of counsel or may be assisted by the prosecuting attorney or by an attorney appointed for that purpose. The defendant is entitled to be represented by counsel, have compulsory process for the attendance of witnesses, and testify in his or her own defense. All issues of law and fact shall be heard and determined by the judge.

(e) Disqualification of Judge. If the contempt charged involves disrespect to or criticism of a judge, the judge shall disqualify himself or herself from presiding at the hearing. Another judge shall be designated by the chief justice of the supreme court.

(f) Verdict; Judgment. At the conclusion of the hearing the judge shall sign and enter of record a judgment of guilty or not guilty. There should be included in a judgment of guilty a recital of the facts constituting the contempt of which the defendant has been found and adjudicated guilty.

(g) Sentence; Indirect Contempt. Prior to the pronouncement of sentence, the judge shall inform the defendant of the accusation and judgment against the defendant and inquire as to whether the

Rule 3.840. Indirect Criminal Contempt.

defendant has any cause to show why sentence should not be pronounced. The defendant shall be afforded the opportunity to present evidence of mitigating circumstances. The sentence shall be pronounced in open court and in the presence of the defendant.

Committee Notes

1968 Adoption.

(a)(1) Order to Show Cause. The courts have used various and, at times, misleading terminology with reference to this phase of the procedure, viz. "citation," "rule nisi," "rule," "rule to show cause," "information," "indicted," and "order to show cause." Although all apparently have been used with the same connotation the terminology chosen probably is more readily understandable than the others. This term is used in Federal Rule of Criminal Procedure 42(b) dealing with indirect criminal contempts.

In proceedings for indirect contempt, due process of law requires that the accused be given notice of the charge and a reasonable opportunity to meet it by way of defense or explanation. State ex rel. Giblin v. Sullivan, 157 Fla. 496, 26 So.2d 509 (1946); State ex rel. Geary v. Kelly, 137 So.2d 262, 263 (Fla. 3d DCA 1962).

The petition (affidavit is used here) must be filed by someone having actual knowledge of the facts and must be under oath. Phillips v. State, 147 So.2d 163 (Fla. 3d DCA 1962); see also Croft v. Culbreath, 150 Fla. 60, 6 So.2d 638 (1942); Ex parte Biggers, 85 Fla. 322, 95 So. 763 (1923).

(2) Motions; Answer. The appellate courts of Florida, while apparently refraining from making motions and answers indispensable parts of the procedure, seem to regard them with favor in appropriate situations. Regarding motions to quash and motion for bill of particulars, see Geary v. State, 139 So.2d 891 (Fla. 3d DCA 1962); regarding the answer, see State ex rel. Huie v. Lewis, 80 So.2d 685 (Fla. 1955).

Elsewhere in these rules is a recommended proposal that a motion to dismiss replace the present motion to quash; hence, the motion to dismiss is recommended here.

The proposal contains no requirement that the motions or answer be under oath. Until section 38.22, Florida Statutes, was amended in 1945 there prevailed in Florida the common law rule that denial under oath is conclusive and requires discharge of the defendant in indirect contempt cases; the discharge was considered as justified because the defendant could be convicted of perjury if the defendant had sworn falsely in the answer or in a motion denying the charge. The amendment of section 38.22, Florida Statutes, however, has been construed to no longer justify the discharge of the defendant merely because the defendant denies the charge under oath. See Ex parte Earman, 85 Fla. 297, 95 So. 755 (1923), re the common law; see Dodd v. State, 110 So.2d 22 (Fla. 3d DCA 1959) re the construction of section 38.22, Florida Statutes, as amended. There appears, therefore, no necessity of requiring that a pleading directed to the order to show cause be under oath, except as a matter of policy of holding potential perjury prosecutions over the heads of defendants. It is recommended, therefore, that no oath be required at this stage of the proceeding.

Due process of law in the prosecution for indirect contempt requires that the defendant have the right to assistance by counsel. Baumgartner v. Joughin, 105 Fla. 335, 141 So. 185 (1932), adhered to, 107 Fla. 858, 143 So. 436 (1932).

(3) Order of Arrest; Bail. Arrest and bail, although apparently used only rarely, were permissible at common law and, accordingly, are unobjectionable under present Florida law. At times each should serve a useful purpose in contempt proceedings and should be included in the rule. As to the common law, see Ex parte Biggers, supra.

(4) Arraignment; Hearing. Provision is made for a pre-hearing arraignment in case the defendant wishes to plead guilty to the charge prior to the date set for the hearing. The defendant has a constitutional right to a hearing under the due process clauses of the state and federal constitutions. State ex rel. Pipia v. Buchanan, 168 So.2d 783 (Fla. 3d DCA 1964). This right includes the right to assistance of counsel and the right to call witnesses. Baumgartner v. Joughin, supra. The defendant cannot be compelled to testify against himself. Demetree v. State, ex rel. Marsh, 89 So.2d 498 (Fla. 1956).

Section 38.22, Florida Statutes, as amended in 1945, provides that all issues of law or fact shall be heard and determined by the judge. Apparently under this statute the defendant is not only precluded from considering a jury trial as a right but also the judge has no discretion to allow the defendant a jury trial. See State ex rel. Huie v. Lewis, supra, and Dodd v. State, supra, in which the court seems to assume this, such assumption seemingly being warranted by the terminology of the statute.

Rule 3.840. Indirect Criminal Contempt.

There is no reason to believe that the statute is unconstitutional as being in violation of section 11 of the Declaration of Rights of the Florida Constitution which provides, in part, that the accused in all criminal prosecutions shall have the right to a public trial by an impartial jury. Criminal contempt is not a crime; consequently, no criminal prosecution is involved. Neering v. State, 155 So.2d 874 (Fla. 1963); State ex rel. Saunders v. Boyer, 166 So.2d 694 (Fla. 2d DCA 1964); Ballengee v. State, 144 So.2d 68 (Fla. 2d DCA 1962).

Section 3 of the Declaration of Rights, providing that the right of trial by jury shall be secured to all and remain inviolate forever, also apparently is not violated. This provision has been construed many times as guaranteeing a jury trial in proceedings at common law, as practiced at the time of the adoption of the constitution (see, e.g., Hawkins v. Rellim Inv. Co., 92 Fla. 784, 110 So. 350 (1926)), i.e., it is applicable only to cases in which the right existed before the adoption of the constitution (see, e.g., State ex rel. Sellers v. Parker, 87 Fla. 181, 100 So. 260 (1924)). Section 3 was never intended to extend the right of a trial by jury beyond this point. Boyd v. Dade County, 123 So.2d 323 (Fla. 1960).

There is some authority that trial by jury in indirect criminal contempt existed in the early common law, but this practice was eliminated by the Star Chamber with the result that for centuries the common law courts have punished indirect contempts without a jury trial. See 36 Mississippi Law Journal 106. The practice in Florida to date apparently has been consistent with this position. No case has been found in this state in which a person was tried by a jury for criminal contempt. See Justice Terrell's comment adverse to such jury trials in State ex rel. Huie v. Lewis, supra.

The United States Supreme Court has assumed the same position with reference to the dictates of the common law. Quoting from Eilenbecker v. District Court, 134 U.S. 31, 36, 10 S.Ct. 424, 33 L.Ed. 801 (1890), the Court stated, "If it has ever been understood that proceedings according to the common law for contempt of court have been subject to the right of trial by jury, we have been unable to find any instance of it." United States v. Barnett, 376 U.S. 681, 696, 84 S.Ct. 984, 12 L.Ed.2d 23 (1964). In answer to the contention that contempt proceedings without a jury were limited to trivial offenses, the Court stated, "[W]e find no basis for a determination that, at the time the Constitution was adopted, contempt was generally regarded as not extending to cases of serious misconduct." 376 U.S. at 701. There is little doubt, therefore, that a defendant in a criminal contempt case in Florida has no constitutional right to a trial by jury.

Proponents for such trials seemingly must depend on authorization by the legislature or Supreme Court of Florida to attain their objective. By enacting section 38.22, Florida Statutes, which impliedly prohibits trial by jury the legislature exhibited a legislative intent to remain consistent with the common law rule. A possible alternative is for the Supreme Court of Florida to promulgate a rule providing for such trials and assume the position that under its constitutional right to govern practice and procedure in the courts of Florida such rule would supersede section 38.22, Florida Statutes. It is believed that the supreme court has such authority. Accordingly, alternate proposals are offered for the court's consideration; the first provides for a jury trial unless waived by the defendant and the alternate is consistent with present practice.

(5) Disqualification of Judge. Provision for the disqualification of the judge is made in federal rule 42(b). The proposal is patterned after this rule.

Favorable comments concerning disqualification of judges in appropriate cases may be found in opinions of the Supreme Court of Florida. See Pennekamp v. State, 156 Fla. 227, 22 So.2d 875 (1945), and concurring opinion in State ex rel Huie v. Lewis, supra.

(6) Verdict; Judgment. "Judgment" is deemed preferable to the term "order," since the proper procedure involves an adjudication of guilty. The use of "judgment" is consistent with present Florida practice. E.g., Dinnen v. State, 168 So.2d 703 (Fla. 2d DCA 1964); State ex rel. Byrd v. Anderson, 168 So.2d 554 (Fla. 1st DCA 1964).

The recital in the judgment of facts constituting the contempt serves to preserve for postconviction purposes a composite record of the offense by the person best qualified to make such recital: the judge. See Ryals v. United States, 69 F.2d 946 (5th Cir. 1934), in which such procedure is referred to as "good practice."

(7) Sentence; Indirect Contempt. The substance of this subdivision is found in present sections 921.05(2), 921.07 and 921.13, Florida Statutes. While these sections are concerned with sentences in criminal cases, the First District Court of Appeal in 1964 held that unless a defendant convicted of criminal contempt is paid the same deference the defendant is not being accorded due process of law as provided in section 12 of the Declaration of Rights of the Florida Constitution and the Fourteenth Amendment of the Constitution of

the United States. Neering v. State, 164 So.2d 29 (Fla. 1st DCA 1964).

Statement concerning the effect the adoption of this proposed rule will have on contempt statutes:

This rule is not concerned with the source of the power of courts to punish for contempt. It is concerned with desirable procedure to be employed in the implementation of such power. Consequently, its adoption will in no way affect the Florida statutes purporting to be legislative grants of authority to the courts to punish for contempt, viz., sections 38.22 (dealing with "all" courts), 932.03 (dealing with courts having original jurisdiction in criminal cases), and 39.13 (dealing with juvenile courts). This is true regardless of whether the source of power is considered to lie exclusively with the courts as an inherent power or is subject, at least in part, to legislative grant.

The adoption of the rule also will leave unaffected the numerous Florida statutes concerned with various situations considered by the legislature to be punishable as contempt (e.g., section 38.23, Florida Statutes), since these statutes deal with substantive rather than procedural law.

Section 38.22, Florida Statutes, as discussed in the preceding notes, is concerned with procedure in that it requires the court to hear and determine all questions of law or fact. Insofar, therefore, as criminal contempts are concerned the adoption of the alternate proposal providing for a jury trial will mean that the rule supersedes this aspect of the statute and the statute should be amended accordingly.

1972 Amendment. Same as prior rule.

XVII. Postconviction Relief

Rule 3.850. Motion To Vacate; Set Aside; Or Correct Sentence.

(a) Grounds for Motion. The following grounds may be claims for relief from judgment or release from custody by a person who has been tried and found guilty or has entered a plea of guilty or nolo contendere before a court established by the laws of Florida:

(1) the judgment was entered or sentence was imposed in violation of the Constitution or laws of the United States or the State of Florida;

(2) the court did not have jurisdiction to enter the judgment;

(3) the court did not have jurisdiction to impose the sentence;

(4) the sentence exceeded the maximum authorized by law;

(5) the plea was involuntary; or

(6) the judgment or sentence is otherwise subject to collateral attack.

(b) Time Limitations. A motion to vacate a sentence that exceeds the limits provided by law may be filed at any time. No other motion shall be filed or considered pursuant to this rule if filed more than 2 years after the judgment and sentence become final unless it alleges that:

(1) the facts on which the claim is predicated were unknown to the movant or the movant's attorney and could not have been ascertained by the exercise of due diligence, and the claim is made within 2 years of the time the new facts were or could have been discovered with the exercise of due diligence;

(2) the fundamental constitutional right asserted was not established within the period provided for herein and has been held to apply retroactively, and the claim is made within 2 years of the date of the mandate of the decision announcing the retroactivity; or

(3) the defendant retained counsel to timely file a 3.850 motion and counsel, through neglect, failed to file the motion. A claim based on this exception shall not be filed more than 2 years after the expiration of the time for filing a motion for postconviction relief.

(c) Contents of Motion. The motion must be under oath stating that the defendant has read the motion or that it has been read to him or her, that the defendant understands its content, and that all of the facts stated therein are true and correct. The motion must include the certifications required by subdivision (n) of this rule and must also include an explanation of:

(1) the judgment or sentence under attack and the court that rendered the same;

(2) whether the judgment resulted from a plea or a trial;

(3) whether there was an appeal from the judgment or sentence and the disposition thereof;

Rule 3.850. Motion To Vacate; Set Aside; Or Correct Sentence.

(4) whether a previous postconviction motion has been filed, and if so, how many;

(5) if a previous motion or motions have been filed, the reason or reasons the claim or claims in the present motion were not raised in the former motion or motions;

(6) the nature of the relief sought; and

(7) a brief statement of the facts and other conditions relied on in support of the motion.

This rule does not authorize relief based on grounds that could have or should have been raised at trial and, if properly preserved, on direct appeal of the judgment and sentence. If the defendant is filing a newly discovered evidence claim based on recanted trial testimony or on a newly discovered witness, the defendant shall include an affidavit from that person as an attachment to his or her motion. For all other newly discovered evidence claims, the defendant shall attach an affidavit from any person whose testimony is necessary to factually support the defendant's claim for relief. If the affidavit is not attached to the motion, the defendant shall provide an explanation why the required affidavit could not be obtained.

(d) Form of Motion. Motions shall be typewritten or hand-written in legible printed lettering, in blue or black ink, double-spaced, with margins no less than 1 inch on white 8½ by 11 inch paper. No motion, including any memorandum of law, shall exceed 50 pages without leave of the court upon a showing of good cause.

(e) Amendments to Motion. When the court has entered an order under subdivision (f)(2) or (f)(3), granting the defendant an opportunity to amend the motion, any amendment to the motion must be served within 60 days. A motion may otherwise be amended at any time prior to either the entry of an order disposing of the motion or the entry of an order pursuant to subdivision (f)(5) or directing that an answer to the motion be filed pursuant to (f)(6), whichever occurs first. Leave of court is required for the filing of an amendment after the entry of an order pursuant to subdivision (f)(5) or (f)(6). Notwithstanding the timeliness of an amendment, the court need not consider new factual assertions contained in an amendment unless the amendment is under oath. New claims for relief contained in an amendment need not be considered by the court unless the amendment is filed within the time frame specified in subdivision (b).

(f) Procedure; Evidentiary Hearing; Disposition. On filing of a motion under this rule, the clerk shall forward the motion and file to the court. Disposition of the motion shall be in accordance with the following procedures, which are intended to result in a single, final, appealable order that disposes of all claims raised in the motion.

(1) Untimely and Insufficient Motions. If the motion is insufficient on its face, and the time to file a motion under this rule has expired prior to the filing of the motion, the court shall enter a final appealable order summarily denying the motion with prejudice.

(2) Timely but Insufficient Motions. If the motion is insufficient on its face, and the motion is timely filed under this rule, the court shall enter a nonfinal, nonappealable order allowing the defendant 60 days to amend the motion. If the amended motion is still insufficient or if the defendant fails to file an amended motion within the time allowed for such amendment, the court, in its discretion, may permit the defendant an additional opportunity to amend the motion or may enter a final, appealable order summarily denying the motion with prejudice.

(3) Timely Motions Containing Some Insufficient Claims. If the motion sufficiently states 1 or more claims for relief and it also attempts but fails to state additional claims, and the motion is timely filed under this rule, the court shall enter a nonappealable order granting the defendant 60 days to amend the motion to sufficiently state additional claims for relief. Any claim for which the insufficiency has not been cured within the time allowed for such amendment shall be summarily denied in an order that is a nonfinal, nonappealable order, which may be reviewed when a final, appealable order is entered.

(4) Motions Partially Disposed of by the Court Record. If the motion sufficiently states 1 or more claims for relief but the files and records in the case conclusively show that the defendant is not entitled to relief as to 1 or more claims, the claims that are conclusively refuted shall be summarily denied on the merits without a hearing. A copy of that portion of the files and records in the case that conclusively shows that the defendant is not entitled to relief as to 1 or more claims shall be attached to the order summarily denying these claims. The files and records in the case are the documents and exhibits

Rule 3.850. Motion To Vacate; Set Aside; Or Correct Sentence.

previously filed in the case and those portions of the other proceedings in the case that can be transcribed. An order that does not resolve all the claims is a nonfinal, nonappealable order, which may be reviewed when a final, appealable order is entered.

(5) Motions Conclusively Resolved by the Court Record. If the motion is legally sufficient but all grounds in the motion can be conclusively resolved either as a matter of law or by reliance upon the records in the case, the motion shall be denied without a hearing by the entry of a final order. If the denial is based on the records in the case, a copy of that portion of the files and records that conclusively shows that the defendant is entitled to no relief shall be attached to the final order.

(6) Motions Requiring a Response from the State Attorney. Unless the motion, files, and records in the case conclusively show that the defendant is entitled to no relief, the court shall order the state attorney to file, within the time fixed by the court, an answer to the motion. The answer shall respond to the allegations contained in the defendant's sufficiently pleaded claims, describe any matters in avoidance of the sufficiently pleaded claims, state whether the defendant has used any other available state postconviction remedies including any other motion under this rule, and state whether the defendant has previously been afforded an evidentiary hearing.

(7) Appointment of Counsel. The court may appoint counsel to represent the defendant under this rule. The factors to be considered by the court in making this determination include: the adversary nature of the proceeding, the complexity of the proceeding, the complexity of the claims presented, the defendant's apparent level of intelligence and education, the need for an evidentiary hearing, and the need for substantial legal research.

(8) Disposition by Evidentiary Hearing.

(A) If an evidentiary hearing is required, the court shall grant a prompt hearing and shall cause notice to be served on the state attorney and the defendant or defendant's counsel, and shall determine the issues, and make findings of fact and conclusions of law with respect thereto.

(B) At an evidentiary hearing, the defendant shall have the burden of presenting evidence and the burden of proof in support of his or her motion, unless otherwise provided by law.

(C) The order issued after the evidentiary hearing shall resolve all the claims raised in the motion and shall be considered the final order for purposes of appeal.

(g) Defendant's Presence Not Required. The defendant's presence shall not be required at any hearing or conference held under this rule except at the evidentiary hearing on the merits of any claim.

(h) Successive Motions.

(1) A second or successive motion must be titled: "Second or Successive Motion for Postconviction Relief."

(2) A second or successive motion is an extraordinary pleading. Accordingly, a court may dismiss a second or successive motion if the court finds that it fails to allege new or different grounds for relief and the prior determination was on the merits or, if new and different grounds are alleged, the judge finds that the failure of the defendant or the attorney to assert those grounds in a prior motion constituted an abuse of the procedure or there was no good cause for the failure of the defendant or defendant's counsel to have asserted those grounds in a prior motion. When a motion is dismissed under this subdivision, a copy of that portion of the files and records necessary to support the court's ruling shall accompany the order denying the motion.

(i) Service on Parties. The clerk of the court shall promptly serve on the parties a copy of any order entered under this rule, noting thereon the date of service by an appropriate certificate of service.

(j) Rehearing. Any party may file a motion for rehearing of any order addressing a motion under this rule within 15 days of the date of service of the order. A motion for rehearing is not required to preserve any issue for review in the appellate court. A motion for rehearing must be based on a good faith belief that the court has overlooked a previously argued issue of fact or law or an argument based on a legal precedent or statute not available prior to the court's ruling. A response may be filed within 10 days of service of the motion. The trial court's order disposing of the motion for rehearing shall be filed within 15 days of the response but not later than 40 days from the date of the order of which rehearing is sought.

(k) Appeals. An appeal may be taken to the appropriate appellate court only from the final order disposing of the motion. All final

Rule 3.850. Motion To Vacate; Set Aside; Or Correct Sentence.

orders denying motions for postconviction relief shall include a statement that the defendant has the right to appeal within 30 days of the rendition of the order. All nonfinal, nonappealable orders entered pursuant to subdivision (f) should include a statement that the defendant has no right to appeal the order until entry of the final order.

(l) Belated Appeals and Discretionary Review. Pursuant to the procedures outlined in Florida Rule of Appellate Procedure 9.141, a defendant may seek a belated appeal or discretionary review.

(m) Habeas Corpus. An application for writ of habeas corpus on behalf of a prisoner who is authorized to apply for relief by motion pursuant to this rule shall not be entertained if it appears that the applicant has failed to apply for relief, by motion, to the court that sentenced the applicant or that the court has denied the applicant relief, unless it also appears that the remedy by motion is inadequate or ineffective to test the legality of the applicant's detention.

(n) Certification of Defendant; Sanctions. No motion may be filed pursuant to this rule unless it is filed in good faith and with a reasonable belief that it is timely, has potential merit, and does not duplicate previous motions that have been disposed of by the court.

(1) By signing a motion pursuant to this rule, the defendant certifies that: the defendant has read the motion or that it has been read to the defendant and that the defendant understands its content; the motion is filed in good faith and with a reasonable belief that it is timely filed, has potential merit, and does not duplicate previous motions that have been disposed of by the court; and, the facts contained in the motion are true and correct.

(2) The defendant shall either certify that the defendant can understand English or, if the defendant cannot understand English, that the defendant has had the motion translated completely into a language that the defendant understands. The motion shall contain the name and address of the person who translated the motion and that person shall certify that he or she provided an accurate and complete translation to the defendant. Failure to include this information and certification in a motion shall be grounds for the entry of an order dismissing the motion pursuant to subdivision (f)(1), (f)(2), or (f)(3).

(3) Conduct prohibited under this rule includes, but is not limited to, the following: the filing of frivolous or malicious claims; the filing of any motion in bad faith or with reckless disregard for the truth; the filing of an application for habeas corpus subject to dismissal pursuant to subdivision (m); the willful violation of any provision of this rule; and the abuse of the legal process or procedures governed by this rule.

The court, upon its own motion or on the motion of a party, may determine whether a motion has been filed in violation of this rule. The court shall issue an order setting forth the facts indicating that the defendant has or may have engaged in prohibited conduct. The order shall direct the defendant to show cause, within a reasonable time limit set by the court, why the court should not find that the defendant has engaged in prohibited conduct under this rule and impose an appropriate sanction. Following the issuance of the order to show cause and the filing of any response by the defendant, and after such further hearing as the court may deem appropriate, the court shall make a final determination of whether the defendant engaged in prohibited conduct under this subdivision.

(4) If the court finds by the greater weight of the evidence that the defendant has engaged in prohibited conduct under this rule, the court may impose one or more sanctions, including:

(A) contempt as otherwise provided by law;

(B) assessing the costs of the proceeding against the defendant;

(C) dismissal with prejudice of the defendant's motion;

(D) prohibiting the filing of further pro se motions under this rule and directing the clerk of court to summarily reject any further pro se motion under this rule;

(E) requiring that any further motions under this rule be signed by a member in good standing of The Florida Bar, who shall certify that there is a good faith basis for each claim asserted in the motion; and/or

(F) if the defendant is a prisoner, a certified copy of the order be forwarded to the appropriate institution or facility for consideration of disciplinary action against the defendant, including forfeiture of gain time pursuant to Chapter 944, Florida Statutes.

(5) If the court determines there is probable cause to believe that a sworn motion contains a false statement of fact

Rule 3.850. Motion To Vacate; Set Aside; Or Correct Sentence.

constituting perjury, the court may refer the matter to the state attorney.

Committee Notes

1972 Amendment. Same as prior rule. Former rule 3.860, previously deleted, now found in article 18, The Florida Bar Integration Rules.

1977 Amendment. Nothing has been taken from proposed rule 3.850. Additions have been made. The committee proceeded on the theory that generally the motions coming under the purview of the rule were filed by prisoners and will be considered ex parte.

The proposed amendment contemplates that in those cases where the trial court found the movant entitled to some relief, the state attorney would be noticed and given an opportunity to be heard. The rule further contemplates that if the appellate court reverses, it would do so with directions to conduct a hearing with notice to all parties.

(a), (b), (c), (d), (e)

The committee was of the opinion that the motion should contain the minimum prerequisites indicated in the lettered portions to permit the trial court to quickly ascertain whether or not the motion was entitled to consideration and, if not, provide for its return to the movant as unacceptable. This procedure is similar to federal rules dealing with post conviction motions.

The committee perceives that denial of a motion will either be based on the insufficiency of the motion itself or on the basis of the file or record which the trial court will have before it. The proposal provides for a simplified expeditious disposition of appeals in such cases. It is to be noted, however, that in those cases where the record is relied on as a basis for denial of the motion, it may in exceptional cases involve a substantial record, but the advantages of this procedure seem to justify coping with the unusual or exceptional case. It is the opinion of the committee that, in any order of denial based on the insufficiency of the motion or on the face of the record, trial courts will set forth specifically the basis of the court's ruling with sufficient specificity to delineate the issue for the benefit of appellate courts.

The committee thought that the provision permitting ex parte denial of a motion based on the face of the record was appropriate inasmuch as the movant was granted an opportunity for rehearing in which to point out any errors the court may have made, thus providing sufficient safeguards to ensure consideration of the prisoner's contentions.

The prisoner or movant's motion for rehearing will be a part of the record on appeal, thereby alerting the appellate court to the movant's dissatisfaction with the trial court's ruling.

1984 Amendment. The committee felt that provisions should be added to allow the court to consider why a subsequent motion was being filed and whether it was properly filed, similar to Federal Rule of Criminal Procedure 9(b) or 35.

The committee also felt that the court should have the authority to order the state to respond to a 3.850 motion by answer or other pleading as the court may direct.

The committee felt that even if a motion filed under rule 3.850 does not substantially comply with the requirements of the rule, the motion should still be filed and ruled on by the court. Hence the former provision authorizing the court to refuse to receive such a nonconforming motion has been removed and words allowing the presiding judge to summarily deny a noncomplying motion have been satisfied.

1992 Amendment. Pursuant to State v. District Court of Appeal of Florida, First District, 569 So. 2d 439 (Fla. 1990), motions seeking a belated direct appeal based on the ineffective assistance of counsel should be filed in the trial court under rule 3.850. Also, see rule 3.111(e) regarding trial counsel's duties before withdrawal after judgment and sentence.

Court Commentary

1993 Commentary. This amendment is necessary to make this rule consistent with rule 3.851.

1996 Court Commentary. Florida Rule of Judicial Administration 2.071(b) allows for telephonic and teleconferencing communication equipment to be utilized "for a motion hearing, a pretrial conference, or a status conference." Teleconferencing sites have been established by the Department of Management Services, Division of Communications at various metropolitan locations in the state. The "Shevin Study"[1] examined, at this Court's request, the issue of delays in capital postconviction relief proceedings and noted that travel problems of counsel cause part of those delays. The Court strongly encourages the use of the new telephonic and

Rule 3.850. Motion To Vacate; Set Aside; Or Correct Sentence.

teleconferencing technology for postconviction relief proceedings that do not require evidentiary hearings.

1 Letter from Robert L. Shevin "Re: Study of the Capital Collateral Representative" to Chief Justice Stephen H. Grimes (Feb. 26, 1996) (on file with the Supreme Court of Florida in No. 87,688).

2013 Amendment. Rule 3.850 has been revised to address several issues identified by the Postconviction Rules Workgroup in 2006 and by the Criminal Court Steering Committee and the Subcommittee on Postconviction Relief in 2011.

Rule 3.850(d). New subdivision (d) is derived from the final two sentences formerly contained in subdivision (c).

Rule 3.850(e). Subdivision (e) was added to codify existing case law on amendments to postconviction motions and to comport with subdivision (f).

Rule 3.850(f). Subdivision (f) attempts to set out each of the different options that a trial judge has when considering a motion under this rule. It reflects the timeframe requirement of subdivision (b) and codifies existing case law regarding timely but facially insufficient motions, partial orders of denial, and the appointment of counsel. See, e.g., Spera v. State, 971 So. 2d 754 (Fla. 2007).

Rule 3.850(g). Subdivision (g) was previously contained in subdivision (e), but the language is largely derived from rule 3.851(c)(3).

Rule 3.850(h). Subdivision (h), formerly rule 3.850(f), was substantially rewritten.

Rule 3.850(i). Subdivision (i) is substantially the same as former subdivision (g).

Rule 3.850(j). Subdivision (j) allows both the state and the defendant the right to rehearing and is intended to allow the court to correct an obvious error without the expense and delay of a state appeal. See King v. State, 870 So. 2d 69 (Fla. 2d DCA 2003). The statement regarding finality is consistent with Florida Rule of Appellate Procedure 9.020(i) and is intended to clarify the date of rendition of the final order disposing of any motion under this rule.

Rule 3.850(k). Subdivision (k), formerly rule 3.850(i), was substantially rewritten to simplify the review process in both the trial and appellate courts and to provide for the efficient disposition of all claims in both courts. The requirement of a statement indicating whether the order is a nonfinal or final order subject to appeal is intended to ensure that all claims will be disposed of by the trial court and addressed in a single appeal.

Rule 3.850(l). Subdivision (l), formerly rule 3.850(j), reflects the consolidation of the subdivision with former rule 3.850(k).

Rule 3.850(n). Subdivision (n) is a substantial rewrite of former subdivision (m).

Rule 3.851. Collateral Relief After Death Sentence Has Been Imposed and Affirmed on Direct Appeal.

(a) Scope. This rule shall apply to all postconviction proceedings that commence upon issuance of the appellate mandate affirming the death sentence to include all motions and petitions for any type of postconviction or collateral relief brought by a defendant in state custody who has been sentenced to death and whose conviction and death sentence have been affirmed on direct appeal. It shall apply to all postconviction motions filed on or after January 1, 2015, by defendants who are under sentence of death. Motions pending on that date are governed by the version of this rule in effect immediately prior to that date.

(b) Appointment of Postconviction Counsel.

(1) Upon the issuance of the mandate affirming a judgment and sentence of death on direct appeal, the Supreme Court of Florida shall at the same time issue an order appointing the appropriate office of the Capital Collateral Regional Counsel or directing the trial court to immediately appoint counsel from the Registry of Attorneys maintained by the Justice Administrative Commission. The name of Registry Counsel shall be filed with the Supreme Court of Florida.

(2) Within 30 days of the issuance of the mandate, the Capital Collateral Regional Counsel or Registry Counsel shall file either a notice of appearance or a motion to withdraw in the trial court. Motions to withdraw filed more than 30 days after the issuance of the mandate shall not be entertained unless based on a conflict of interest as set forth in section 27.703, Florida Statutes.

(3) Within 15 days after Capital Collateral Regional Counsel or Registry Counsel files a motion to withdraw, the chief judge or assigned judge shall rule on the motion and appoint new postconviction counsel if necessary. The appointment of new collateral counsel shall be from the Registry of attorneys

Rule 3.851. Collateral Relief After Death Sentence Has Been Imposed and Affirmed on Direct Appeal.

maintained by the Justice Administrative Commission unless the case is administratively transferred to another Capital Collateral Regional Counsel.

(4) In every capital postconviction case, one lawyer shall be designated as lead counsel for the defendant. The lead counsel shall be the defendant's primary lawyer in all state court litigation. No lead counsel shall be permitted to appear for a limited purpose on behalf of a defendant in a capital postconviction proceeding.

(5) After the filing of a notice of appearance, Capital Collateral Regional Counsel, Registry Counsel, or a private attorney shall represent the defendant in the state courts until a judge allows withdrawal or until the sentence is reversed, reduced, or carried out, regardless of whether another attorney represents the defendant in a federal court.

(6) A defendant who has been sentenced to death may not represent himself or herself in a capital postconviction proceeding in state court. The only bases for a defendant to seek to dismiss postconviction counsel in state court shall be pursuant to statute due to actual conflict or subdivision (i) of this rule.

(c) Preliminary Procedures.

(1) Judicial Assignment and Responsibilities. Within 30 days of the issuance of mandate affirming a judgment and sentence of death on direct appeal, the chief judge shall assign the case to a judge qualified under the Rules of General Practice and Judicial Administration to conduct capital proceedings. The assigned judge is responsible for case management to ensure compliance with statutes, rules, and administrative orders that impose processing steps, time deadlines, and reporting requirements for capital postconviction litigation. From the time of assignment, the judge must issue case management orders for every step of the capital postconviction process, including at the conclusion of all hearings and conferences.

(2) Status Conferences. The assigned judge shall conduct a status conference not later than 90 days after the judicial assignment, and shall hold status conferences at least every 90 days thereafter until the evidentiary hearing has been completed or the motion has been ruled on without a hearing. The attorneys, with leave of the trial court, may appear electronically at the status conferences. Requests to appear electronically shall be liberally granted. Pending motions, disputes involving public records, or any other matters ordered by the court shall be heard at the status conferences.

(3) Defendant's Presence Not Required. The defendant's presence shall not be required at any hearing or conference held under this rule, except at the evidentiary hearing on the merits of any claim and at any hearing involving conflict with or removal of collateral counsel.

(4) Duties of Defense Counsel. Within 45 days of appointment of postconviction counsel, the defendant's trial counsel shall provide to postconviction counsel a copy of the original file including all work product not otherwise subject to a protective order and information pertaining to the defendant's capital case which was created and obtained during the representation of the defendant. Postconviction counsel shall maintain the confidentiality of all confidential information received. Postconviction counsel shall bear the costs of any copying. The defendant's trial counsel must retain the defendant's original file.

(5) Record on Direct Appeal. The Clerk of the Circuit Court shall retain a copy of the record for the direct appeal when the record is transmitted to the Supreme Court of Florida. The Clerk of the Supreme Court of Florida shall deliver the record on appeal to the records repository within 30 days after the appointment of postconviction counsel.

(d) Time Limitation.

(1) Any motion to vacate judgment of conviction and sentence of death shall be filed by the defendant within 1 year after the judgment and sentence become final. For the purposes of this rule, a judgment is final:

> **(A)** on the expiration of the time permitted to file in the United States Supreme Court a petition for writ of certiorari seeking review of the Supreme Court of Florida decision affirming a judgment and sentence of death (90 days after the opinion becomes final); or
>
> **(B)** on the disposition of the petition for writ of certiorari by the United States Supreme Court, if filed.

(2) No motion shall be filed or considered pursuant to this rule if filed beyond the time limitation provided in subdivision (d)(1) unless it alleges:

(A) the facts on which the claim is predicated were unknown to the movant or the movant's attorney and could not have been ascertained by the exercise of due diligence, or

(B) the fundamental constitutional right asserted was not established within the period provided for in subdivision (d)(1) and has been held to apply retroactively, or

(C) postconviction counsel, through neglect, failed to file the motion.

(3) All petitions for extraordinary relief in which the Supreme Court of Florida has original jurisdiction, including petitions for writs of habeas corpus, shall be filed simultaneously with the initial brief filed on behalf of the death-sentenced defendant in the appeal of the circuit court's order on the initial motion for postconviction relief filed under this rule.

(4) If the governor signs a death warrant before the expiration of the time limitation in subdivision (d)(1), the Supreme Court of Florida, on a defendant's request, will grant a stay of execution to allow any postconviction relief motions to proceed in a timely and orderly manner.

(5) An extension of time may be granted by the Supreme Court of Florida for the filing of postconviction pleadings if the defendant's counsel makes a showing that due to exceptional circumstances, counsel was unable to file the postconviction pleadings within the 1-year period established by this rule.

(e) Contents of Motion.

(1) Initial Motion. A motion filed under this rule is an initial postconviction motion if no state court has previously ruled on a postconviction motion challenging the same judgment and sentence. An initial motion and memorandum of law filed under this rule shall not exceed 75 pages exclusive of the attachments. Each claim or subclaim shall be separately pled and shall be sequentially numbered beginning with claim number 1. If upon motion or upon the court's own motion, a judge determines that this portion of the rule has not been followed, the judge shall give the movant 30 days to amend. If no amended motion is filed, the judge shall deem the non-compliant claim, subclaim, and/or argument waived. Attachments shall include, but are not limited to, the judgment and sentence. The memorandum of law shall set forth the applicable case law supporting the granting of relief as to each separately pled claim. This rule does not authorize relief based upon claims that could have or should have been raised at trial and, if properly preserved, on direct appeal of the judgment and sentence. If claims that were raised on appeal or should have or could have been raised on appeal are contained in the motion, the memorandum of law shall contain a brief statement explaining why these claims are being raised on postconviction relief. The motion need not be under oath or signed by the defendant but shall include:

(A) a description of the judgment and sentence under attack and the court that rendered the same;

(B) a statement of each issue raised on appeal and the disposition thereof;

(C) the nature of the relief sought;

(D) a detailed allegation of the factual basis for any claim for which an evidentiary hearing is sought;

(E) a detailed allegation as to the basis for any purely legal or constitutional claim for which an evidentiary hearing is not required and the reason that this claim could not have been or was not raised on direct appeal; and

(F) a certification from the attorney that he or she has discussed the contents of the motion fully with the defendant, that he or she has complied with Rule 4-1.4 of the Rules of Professional Conduct, and that the motion is filed in good faith.

(2) Successive Motion. A motion filed under this rule is successive if a state court has previously ruled on a postconviction motion challenging the same judgment and sentence. A claim raised in a successive motion shall be dismissed if the trial court finds that it fails to allege new or different grounds for relief and the prior determination was on the merits; or, if new and different grounds are alleged, the trial court finds that the failure to assert those grounds in a prior motion constituted an abuse of the procedure; or, if the trial court finds there was no good cause for failing to assert those grounds in a prior motion; or, if the trial court finds the claim fails to meet the time limitation exceptions set forth in subdivision (d)(2)(A), (d)(2)(B), or (d)(2)(C).

A successive motion shall not exceed 25 pages, exclusive of attachments, and shall include:

(A) all of the pleading requirements of an initial motion under subdivision (e)(1);

(B) the disposition of all previous claims raised in postconviction proceedings and the reason or reasons the claim or claims raised in the present motion were not raised in the former motion or motions;

(C) if based upon newly discovered evidence, Brady v. Maryland, 373 U.S. 83 (1963), or Giglio v. United States, 405 U.S. 150 (1972), the following:

(i) the names, addresses, and telephone numbers of all witnesses supporting the claim;

(ii) a statement that the witness will be available, should an evidentiary hearing be scheduled, to testify under oath to the facts alleged in the motion or affidavit;

(iii) if evidentiary support is in the form of documents, copies of all documents shall be attached, including any affidavits obtained; and

(iv) as to any witness or document listed in the motion or attachment to the motion, a statement of the reason why the witness or document was not previously available.

(f) Procedure; Evidentiary Hearing; Disposition.

(1) Filing and Service. All pleadings in the postconviction proceeding shall be filed with the clerk of the trial court and served on the assigned judge, opposing party, and the attorney general. Upon the filing of any original court document in the postconviction proceeding, the clerk of the trial court shall determine that the assigned judge has received a copy. All motions other than the postconviction motion itself shall be accompanied by a notice of hearing.

(2) Duty of Clerk. A motion filed under this rule shall be immediately delivered to the chief judge or the assigned judge along with the court file.

(3) Answer.

(A) Answer to the Initial Motion. Within 60 days of the filing of an initial motion, the state shall file its answer. The answer and accompanying memorandum of law shall not exceed 75 pages, exclusive of attachments and exhibits. The answer shall address the legal insufficiency of any claim in the motion, respond to the allegations of the motion, and address any procedural bars. The answer shall use the same claim numbering system contained in the defendant's initial motion. As to any claims of legal insufficiency or procedural bar, the state shall include a short statement of any applicable case law.

(B) Answer to a Successive Motion. Within 20 days of the filing of a successive motion, the state shall file its answer. The answer shall not exceed 25 pages, exclusive of attachments and exhibits. The answer shall use the same claim numbering system contained in the defendant's motion. The answer shall specifically respond to each claim in the motion and state the reason(s) that an evidentiary hearing is or is not required.

(4) Amendments. A motion filed under this rule may not be amended unless good cause is shown. A copy of the claim sought to be added. must be attached to the motion to amend. The trial court may in its discretion grant a motion to amend provided that the motion to amend was filed at least 45 days before the scheduled evidentiary hearing. Granting a motion under this subdivision shall not be a basis for granting a continuance of the evidentiary hearing unless a manifest injustice would occur if a continuance was not granted. If amendment is allowed, the state shall file an amended answer within 20 days after the judge allows the motion to be amended.

(5) Case Management Conference; Evidentiary Hearing.

(A) Initial Postconviction Motion. No later than 90 days after the state files its answer to an initial motion, the trial court shall hold a case management conference. At the case management conference, the defendant shall disclose all documentary exhibits that he or she intends to offer at the evidentiary hearing and shall file and serve an exhibit list of all such exhibits and a witness list with the names and addresses of any potential witnesses. All expert witnesses shall be specifically designated on the witness list and copies of all expert reports shall be attached. Within 60 days after the case management conference, the state shall disclose all documentary exhibits that it intends to offer at the evidentiary hearing and shall file and serve an exhibit list of all such exhibits and a witness list with the names and addresses of any potential witnesses. All expert witnesses shall be specifically designated on the witness list and copies of all expert reports shall be attached. At the case management conference, the trial court shall:

> **(i)** schedule an evidentiary hearing, to be held within 150 days, on claims listed by the defendant as requiring a factual determination;
>
> **(ii)** hear argument on any purely legal claims not based on disputed facts; and
>
> **(iii)** resolve disputes arising from the exchange of information under this subdivision.

(B) Successive Postconviction Motion. Within 30 days after the state files its answer to a successive motion for postconviction relief, the trial court shall hold a case management conference. At the case management conference, the trial court also shall determine whether an evidentiary hearing should be held and hear argument on any purely legal claims not based on disputed facts. If the motion, files, and records in the case conclusively show that the movant is entitled to no relief, the motion may be denied without an evidentiary hearing. If the trial court determines that an evidentiary hearing should be held, the court shall schedule the hearing to be held within 90 days. If a death warrant has been signed, the trial court shall expedite these time periods in accordance with subdivision (h) of this rule.

(C) Extension of Time to Hold Evidentiary Hearing. The trial court also may for good cause extend the time for holding an evidentiary hearing for up to 90 days.

(D) Taking Testimony. Upon motion, or upon its own motion and without the consent of any party, the court may permit a witness to testify at the evidentiary hearing by contemporaneous video communication equipment that makes the witness visible to all parties during the testimony. There must be appropriate safeguards for the court to maintain sufficient control over the equipment and the transmission of the testimony so the court may stop the communication to accommodate objections or prevent prejudice. If testimony is taken through video communication equipment, there must be a notary public or other person authorized to administer oaths in the witness's jurisdiction who is present with the witness and who administers the oath consistent with the laws of the jurisdiction where the witness is located. The cost for the use of video communication equipment is the responsibility of either the requesting party or, if upon its own motion, the court.

(E) Procedures After Evidentiary Hearing. Immediately following an evidentiary hearing, the trial court shall order a transcript of the hearing, which shall be filed within 10 days if real-time transcription was utilized, or within 45 days if real-time transcription was not utilized. The trial judge may permit written closing arguments instead of oral closing arguments. If the trial court permits the parties to submit written closing arguments, the arguments shall be filed by both parties within 30 days of the filing of the transcript of the hearing. No answer or reply arguments shall be allowed. Written arguments shall be in compliance with the requirements for briefs in rule 9.210(a)(1) and (a)(2), shall not exceed 60 pages without leave of court, and shall include proposed findings of facts and conclusions of law, with citations to authority and to appropriate portions of the transcript of the hearing.

(F) Rendition of the Order. If the court does not permit written closing arguments, the court shall render its order within 30 days of the filing of the transcript of the hearing. If the court permits written closing arguments, the court shall render its order within 30 days of the filing of the last written closing argument and no later than 60 days from the filing of the transcript of the hearing. The court shall rule on each claim considered at the evidentiary hearing and all other claims raised in the motion, making detailed findings of fact and conclusions of law with respect to each claim, and attaching or referencing such portions of the record as are necessary to allow for meaningful appellate review. The order issued after the evidentiary hearing shall resolve all the claims raised in the motion and shall be considered the final order for purposes of appeal. The clerk of the trial court shall promptly serve upon the parties and the attorney general a copy of the final order, with a certificate of service.

(6) Experts and Other Witnesses. All expert witnesses who will testify at the evidentiary hearing must submit written reports, which shall be disclosed to opposing counsel as provided in subdivision (f)(5)(A). If the defendant intends to offer expert testimony of his or her mental status, the state shall be entitled to have the defendant examined by its own mental health expert. If the defendant fails to cooperate with the state's expert, the trial court may, in its discretion, proceed as provided in rule 3.202(e).

(7) Rehearing. Motions for rehearing shall be filed within 15 days of the rendition of the trial court's order and a response thereto filed within 10 days thereafter. A motion for rehearing shall be based on a good faith belief that the court has overlooked a previously argued issue of fact or law or an argument based on a legal precedent or statute not available prior to the court's ruling. The trial court's order disposing of the motion for rehearing shall be rendered not later than 30 days from the filing of the motion for rehearing. If no order is filed within 30 days from the filing of the motion for rehearing, the motion is deemed denied. A motion for rehearing is not required to preserve any issue for review.

(8) Appeals. Any party may appeal a final order entered on a defendant's motion for rule 3.851 relief by filing a notice of appeal with the clerk of the lower tribunal within 30 days of the rendition of the order to be reviewed. Pursuant to the procedures outlined in Florida Rule of Appellate Procedure 9.142, a defendant under sentence of death may petition for a belated appeal.

(g) Incompetence to Proceed in Capital Collateral Proceedings.

(1) A death-sentenced defendant pursuing collateral relief under this rule who is found by the court to be mentally incompetent shall not be proceeded against if there are factual matters at issue, the development or resolution of which require the defendant's input. However, all collateral relief issues that involve only matters of record and claims that do not require the defendant's input shall proceed in collateral proceedings notwithstanding the defendant's incompetency.

(2) Collateral counsel may file a motion for competency determination and an accompanying certificate of counsel that the motion is made in good faith and on reasonable grounds to believe that the death-sentenced defendant is incompetent to proceed.

(3) If, at any stage of a postconviction proceeding, the court determines that there are reasonable grounds to believe that a death-sentenced defendant is incompetent to proceed and that factual matters are at issue, the development or resolution of which require the defendant's input, a judicial determination of incompetency is required.

(4) The motion for competency examination shall be in writing and shall allege with specificity the factual matters at issue and the reason that competent consultation with the defendant is necessary with respect to each factual matter specified. To the extent that it does not invade the lawyer-client privilege with collateral counsel, the motion shall contain a recital of the specific observations of, and conversations with, the death-sentenced defendant that have formed the basis of the motion.

(5) If the court finds that there are reasonable grounds to believe that a death-sentenced defendant is incompetent to proceed in a postconviction proceeding in which factual matters are at issue, the development or resolution of which require the defendant's input, the court shall order the defendant examined by no more than 3, nor fewer than 2, experts before setting the matter for a hearing. The court may seek input from the death-sentenced defendant's counsel and the state attorney before appointment of the experts.

(6) The order appointing experts shall:

(A) identify the purpose of the evaluation and specify the area of inquiry that should be addressed;

(B) specify the legal criteria to be applied; and

(C) specify the date by which the report shall be submitted and to whom it shall be submitted.

(7) Counsel for both the death-sentenced defendant and the state may be present at the examination, which shall be conducted at a date and time convenient for all parties and the Department of Corrections.

(8) On appointment by the court, the experts shall examine the death-sentenced defendant with respect to the issue of

Rule 3.851. Collateral Relief After Death Sentence Has Been Imposed and Affirmed on Direct Appeal.

competence to proceed, as specified by the court in its order appointing the experts to evaluate the defendant, and shall evaluate the defendant as ordered.

(A) The experts first shall consider factors related to the issue of whether the death-sentenced defendant meets the criteria for competence to proceed, that is, whether the defendant has sufficient present ability to consult with counsel with a reasonable degree of rational understanding and whether the defendant has a rational as well as factual understanding of the pending collateral proceedings.

(B) In considering the issue of competence to proceed, the experts shall consider and include in their report:

(i) the defendant's capacity to understand the adversary nature of the legal process and the collateral proceedings;

(ii) the defendant's ability to disclose to collateral counsel facts pertinent to the postconviction proceeding at issue; and

(iii) any other factors considered relevant by the experts and the court as specified in the order appointing the experts.

(C) Any written report submitted by an expert shall:

(i) identify the specific matters referred for evaluation;

(ii) describe the evaluative procedures, techniques, and tests used in the examination and the purpose or purposes for each;

(iii) state the expert's clinical observations, findings, and opinions on each issue referred by the court for evaluation, and indicate specifically those issues, if any, on which the expert could not give an opinion; and

(iv) identify the sources of information used by the expert and present the factual basis for the expert's clinical findings and opinions.

(9) If the experts find that the death-sentenced defendant is incompetent to proceed, the experts shall report on any recommended treatment for the defendant to attain competence to proceed. In considering the issues relating to treatment, the experts shall report on:

(A) the mental illness or intellectual disability causing the incompetence;

(B) the treatment or treatments appropriate for the mental illness or intellectual disability of the defendant and an explanation of each of the possible treatment alternatives in order of choices; and

(C) the likelihood of the defendant attaining competence under the treatment recommended, an assessment of the probable duration of the treatment required to restore competence, and the probability that the defendant will attain competence to proceed in the foreseeable future.

(10) Within 30 days after the experts have completed their examinations of the death-sentenced defendant, the court shall schedule a hearing on the issue of the defendant's competence to proceed.

(11) If, after a hearing, the court finds the defendant competent to proceed, or, after having found the defendant incompetent, finds that competency has been restored, the court shall enter its order so finding and shall proceed with a postconviction motion. The defendant shall have 60 days to amend his or her rule 3.851 motion only as to those issues that the court found required factual consultation with counsel.

(12) If the court does not find the defendant incompetent, the order shall contain:

(A) findings of fact relating to the issues of competency;

(B) copies of the reports of the examining experts; and

(C) copies of any other psychiatric, psychological, or social work reports submitted to the court relative to the mental state of the death-sentenced defendant.

(13) If the court finds the defendant incompetent or finds the defendant competent subject to the continuation of appropriate treatment, the court shall follow the procedures set forth in rule 3.212(c), except that, to the extent practicable, any treatment shall take place at a custodial facility under the direct supervision of the Department of Corrections.

(h) **After Death Warrant Signed.**

(1) **Judicial Assignment.** The chief judge of the circuit shall assign the case to a judge qualified under the Rules of General Practice and Judicial Administration to conduct capital cases as soon as notification of the death warrant is received.

(2) Calendar Advancement. Proceedings after a death warrant has been issued shall take precedence over all other cases. The assigned judge shall make every effort to resolve scheduling conflicts with other cases including cancellation or rescheduling of hearings or trials and requesting senior judge assistance.

(3) Schedule of Proceedings. The time limitations in this rule shall not apply after a death warrant has been signed. All motions shall be heard expeditiously considering the time limitations set by the date of execution and the time required for appellate review.

(4) Location of Hearings. The location of hearings after a death warrant is signed shall be determined by the trial judge considering the availability of witnesses or evidence, the security problems involved in the case, and any other factor determined by the trial court.

(5) Postconviction Motions. All motions filed after a death warrant is issued shall be considered successive motions and subject to the content requirement of subdivision (e)(2) of this rule.

(6) Case Management Conference. The assigned judge shall schedule a case management conference as soon as reasonably possible after receiving notification that a death warrant has been signed. During the case management conference the court shall set a time for filing a postconviction motion and shall schedule a hearing to determine whether an evidentiary hearing should be held and hear argument on any purely legal claims not based on disputed facts. If the motion, files, and records in the case conclusively show that the movant is entitled to no relief, the motion may be denied without an evidentiary hearing. If the trial court determines that an evidentiary hearing should be held, the court shall schedule the hearing to be held as soon as reasonably possible considering the time limitations set by the date of execution and the time required for appellate review.

(7) Reporting. The assigned judge shall require the proceedings conducted under death warrant to be reported using the most advanced and accurate technology available in general use at the location of the hearing. The proceedings shall be transcribed expeditiously considering the time limitations set by the execution date.

(8) Procedures After Hearing. The court shall obtain a transcript of all proceedings and shall render its order in as soon as possible after the hearing is concluded. A copy of the final order shall be electronically transmitted to the Supreme Court of Florida and to the attorneys of record.

(9) Transmittal of Record. The record shall be immediately delivered to the clerk of the Supreme Court of Florida by the clerk of the trial court or as ordered by the assigned judge. The record shall also be electronically transmitted if the technology is available. A notice of appeal shall not be required to transmit the record.

(i) Dismissal of Postconviction Proceedings.

(1) This subdivision applies only when a defendant seeks both to dismiss pending postconviction proceedings and to discharge collateral counsel.

(2) If the defendant files the motion pro se, the Clerk of the Court shall serve copies of the motion on counsel of record for both the defendant and the state. Counsel of record may file responses within 10 days.

(3) The trial judge shall review the motion and the responses and schedule a hearing. The defendant, collateral counsel, and the state shall be present at the hearing.

(4) The judge shall examine the defendant at the hearing and shall hear argument of the defendant, collateral counsel, and the state. No fewer than 2 or more than 3 qualified experts shall be appointed to examine the defendant if the judge concludes that there are reasonable grounds to believe the defendant is not mentally competent for purposes of this rule. The experts shall file reports with the court setting forth their findings. Thereafter, the court shall conduct an evidentiary hearing and enter an order setting forth findings of competency or incompetency.

(5) If the defendant is found to be incompetent for purposes of this rule, the court shall deny the motion without prejudice.

(6) If the defendant is found to be competent for purposes of this rule, the court shall conduct a complete (Durocher/Faretta) inquiry to determine whether the defendant knowingly, freely

and voluntarily wants to dismiss pending postconviction proceedings and discharge collateral counsel.

(7) If the court determines that the defendant has made the decision to dismiss pending postconviction proceedings and discharge collateral counsel knowingly, freely, and voluntarily, the court shall enter an order dismissing all pending postconviction proceedings and discharging collateral counsel. But if the court determines that the defendant has not made the decision to dismiss pending postconviction proceedings and discharge collateral counsel knowingly, freely, and voluntarily, the court shall enter an order denying the motion without prejudice.

(8) If the court grants the motion:

(A) a copy of the motion, the order, and the transcript of the hearing or hearings conducted on the motion shall be forwarded to the Clerk of the Supreme Court of Florida within 30 days; and

(B) discharged counsel shall, within 10 days after issuance of the order, file with the clerk of the circuit court 2 copies of a notice seeking review in the Supreme Court of Florida, and shall, within 20 days after the filing of the transcript, serve an initial brief. Both the defendant and the state may serve responsive briefs. Briefs shall be served as prescribed by rule 9.210.

(9) If the court denies the motion, the defendant may seek review as prescribed by Florida Rule of Appellate Procedure 9.142(b).

(j) Attorney General Notification to Clerk. The Office of the Attorney General shall notify the clerk of the supreme court when it believes the defendant has completed his or her direct appeal, initial postconviction proceeding in state court, and habeas corpus proceeding and appeal therefrom in federal court. The Office of the Attorney General shall serve a copy of the notification on defendant's counsel of record.

Court Commentary

1993 Adoption. This rule is consistent with the recommendation of the Supreme Court Committee on Postconviction Relief in Capital

Cases, which was created because of the substantial delays in the death penalty postconviction relief process. The committee was created because of the inability of the capital collateral representative to properly represent all death penalty inmates in postconviction relief cases and because of the resulting substantial delays in those cases. That committee recognized that, to make the process work properly, each death row prisoner should have counsel available to represent him or her in postconviction relief proceedings. The committee found that one of the major problems with the process was that the triggering mechanism to start or assure movement of the postconviction relief proceedings was the signing of a death warrant. In a number of instances, the courts were not aware of the problems concerning representation of a defendant until a death warrant was signed. In other instances, the committee found that, when postconviction relief motions had been filed, they clearly had not moved at an orderly pace and the signing of a death warrant was being used as a means to expedite the process. The committee recommended that specific named counsel should be designated to represent each prisoner not later than 30 days after the defendant's judgment and sentence of death becomes final. To assure that representation, the committee's report noted that it was essential that there be adequate funding of the capital collateral representative and sought temporary assistance from The Florida Bar in providing pro bono representation for some inmates.

There is a justification for the reduction of the time period for a capital prisoner as distinguished from a noncapital prisoner, who has two years to file a postconviction relief proceeding. A capital prisoner will have counsel immediately available to represent him or her in a postconviction relief proceeding, while counsel is not provided or constitutionally required for noncapital defendants to whom the two-year period applies.

In the event the capital collateral representative is not fully funded and available to provide proper representation for all death penalty defendants, the reduction in the time period would not be justified and would necessarily have to be repealed, and this Court will forthwith entertain a petition for the repeal of the rule. In this context, it is important to emphasize that the governor agrees that absent the circumstance where a competent death-sentenced individual voluntarily requests that a death warrant be signed, no death warrants will be issued during the initial round of federal and state review, provided that counsel for death penalty defendants is

Rule 3.851. Collateral Relief After Death Sentence Has Been Imposed and Affirmed on Direct Appeal.

proceeding in a timely and diligent manner. This Court agrees that the initial round of postconviction proceedings should proceed in a deliberate but timely manner without the pressure of a pending death warrant. Subdivision 3.851(b)(4) above addresses concerns of The Florida Bar and The Florida Bar Foundation.

The provisions of the present rule 3.851 providing for time periods where a 60-day warrant is signed by the governor are abolished because they are unnecessary if the guidelines are followed. The proceedings and grounds for postconviction relief remain as provided under Florida Rule of Criminal Procedure 3.850, which include, as one of the grounds, the opportunity for a defendant to present newly discovered evidence in accordance with Scott v. Dugger, 604 So. 2d 465 (Fla. 1992), Jones v. State, 591 So. 2d 911 (Fla. 1991), and Richardson v. State, 546 So. 2d 1037 (Fla. 1989).

1996 Amendment. Subdivision (c) is added to make the Court's decision in Huff v. State, 622 So. 2d 982 (Fla. 1993), applicable to all rule 3.850 motions filed by a prisoner who has been sentenced to death. Florida Rule of Judicial Administration 2.071(b) allows for telephonic and teleconferencing communication equipment to be utilized "for a motion hearing, pretrial conference, or a status conference." Teleconferencing sites have been established by the Department of Management Services, Division of Communications at various metropolitan locations in the state. The "Shevin Study" examined, at this Court's request, the issue of delays in capital postconviction relief proceedings and noted that travel problems of counsel cause part of those delays. The Court strongly encourages the use of the new telephonic and teleconferencing technology for postconviction relief proceedings that do not require evidentiary hearings, such as the hearing required under subdivision (c) of this rule. Only the attorneys need be involved in a hearing held under subdivision (c) of this rule; attendance of the postconviction defendant is not required.

2001 Amendment. Several new procedures are added to rule 3.851. New subdivision (b), Appointment of Postconviction Counsel, is added to ensure appointment of postconviction counsel upon the Supreme Court of Florida's issuance of mandate on direct appeal. New subdivision (c), Preliminary Procedures, provides for, among other things, the assignment of a qualified judge within 30 days after mandate issues on direct appeal and status conferences every 90 days after the assignment until the evidentiary hearing has been completed or the motion has been ruled on without a hearing. These status conferences are intended to provide a forum for the timely resolution of public records issues and other preliminary matters. New subdivision (f), Procedure; Evidentiary Hearing; Disposition, sets forth general procedures. Most significantly, that subdivision requires an evidentiary hearing on claims listed in an initial motion as requiring a factual determination. The Court has identified the failure to hold evidentiary hearings on initial motions as a major cause of delay in the capital postconviction process and has determined that, in most cases, requiring an evidentiary hearing on initial motions presenting factually based claims will avoid this cause of delay. See Amendments to Florida Rules of Criminal Procedure 3.851, 3.852 and 3.993, 772 So. 2d 488, 491 (Fla. 2000).

2006 Amendment. The amendments provide for the appointment of Registry Counsel in areas of the state that are not served by a Capital Collateral Regional Counsel. Counsel are allowed to appear at status conferences electronically to authorize both telephonic and video appearances.

2013 Amendment. Only minor amendments are made to rule 3.851.

Rule 3.852. Capital Postconviction Public Records Production.

(a) Applicability and Scope.

(1) This rule is applicable only to the production of public records for capital postconviction defendants and does not change or alter the time periods specified in Florida Rules of Criminal Procedure 3.851. Furthermore, this rule does not affect, expand, or limit the production of public records for any purposes other than use in a proceeding held pursuant to rule 3.850 or rule 3.851.

(2) This rule shall not be a basis for renewing requests that have been initiated previously or for relitigating issues pertaining to production of public records upon which a court has ruled prior to October 1, 1998.

(3) This rule is to be used in conjunction with the forms found at Florida Rule of Criminal Procedure 3.993.

(b) Definitions.

(1) "Public records" has the meaning set forth in section 119.011, Florida Statutes.

Rule 3.852. Capital Postconviction Public Records Production.

(2) "Trial court" means:

(A) the judge who entered the judgment and imposed the sentence of death; or

(B) the judge assigned by the chief judge.

(3) "Records repository" means the location designated by the secretary of state pursuant to section 27.7081, Florida Statutes, for archiving capital postconviction public records.

(4) "Collateral counsel" means a capital collateral regional counsel from one of the three regions in Florida; a private attorney who has been appointed to represent a capital defendant for postconviction litigation; or a private attorney who has been hired by the capital defendant or who has agreed to work pro bono for a capital defendant for postconviction litigation.

(5) "Agency" means an entity or individual as defined in section 119.011, Florida Statutes, that is subject to the requirements of producing public records for inspection under section 119.07, Florida Statutes.

(6) "Index" means a list of the public records included in each container of public records sent to the records repository.

(c) Filing and Service.

(1) The original of all notices, requests, or objections filed under this rule must be filed with the clerk of the trial court. Copies must be served on the trial court, the attorney general, the state attorney, collateral counsel, and any affected person or agency, unless otherwise required by this rule.

(2) Service shall be made pursuant to Florida Rule of Criminal Procedure 3.030.

(3) In all instances requiring written notification or request, the party who has the obligation of providing a notification or request shall provide proof of receipt.

(4) Persons and agencies receiving postconviction public records notifications or requests pursuant to this rule are not required to furnish records filed in a trial court prior to the receipt of the notice.

(d) Action Upon Issuance of Mandate.

(1) Within 15 days after receiving written notification of the Supreme Court of Florida's mandate affirming the sentence of death, the attorney general shall file with the trial court a

written notice of the mandate and serve a copy of it upon the state attorney who prosecuted the case, the Department of Corrections, and the defendant's trial counsel. The notice to the state attorney shall direct the state attorney to submit public records to the records repository within 90 days after receipt of written notification and to notify each law enforcement agency involved in the investigation of the capital offense, with a copy to the trial court, to submit public records to the records repository within 90 days after receipt of written notification. The notice to the Department of Corrections shall direct the department to submit public records to the records repository within 90 days after receipt of written notification. The attorney general shall make a good faith effort to assist in the timely production of public records and written notices of compliance by the state attorney and the Department of Corrections with copies to the trial court.

(2) Within 90 days after receiving written notification of issuance of the Supreme Court of Florida's mandate affirming a death sentence, the state attorney shall provide written notification to the attorney general and to the trial court of the name and address of any additional person or agency that has public records pertinent to the case.

(3) Within 90 days after receiving written notification of issuance of the Supreme Court of Florida's mandate affirming a death sentence, the defendant's trial counsel shall provide written notification to the attorney general and to the trial court of the name and address of any person or agency with information pertinent to the case which has not previously been provided to collateral counsel.

(4) Within 15 days after receiving written notification of any additional person or agency pursuant to subdivision (d)(2) or (d)(3) of this rule, the attorney general shall notify all persons or agencies identified pursuant to subdivisions (d)(2) or (d)(3), with a copy to the trial court, that these persons or agencies are required by law to copy, index, and deliver to the records repository all public records pertaining to the case that are in their possession. The person or agency shall bear the costs related to copying, indexing, and delivering the records. The attorney general shall make a good faith effort to assist in the timely production of public records and a written notice of

Rule 3.852. Capital Postconviction Public Records Production.

compliance by each additional person or agency with a copy to the trial court.

(e) Action Upon Receipt of Notice of Mandate.

(1) Within 15 days after receipt of a written notice of the mandate from the attorney general, the state attorney shall provide written notification to each law enforcement agency involved in the specific case to submit public records to the records repository within 90 days after receipt of written notification. A copy of the notice shall be served upon the defendant's trial counsel and the trial court. The state attorney shall make a good faith effort to assist in the timely production of public records and a written notice of compliance by each law enforcement agency with a copy to the trial court.

(2) Within 90 days after receipt of a written notice of the mandate from the attorney general, the state attorney shall copy, index, and deliver to the records repository all public records, in a current, nonproprietary technology format, that were produced in the state attorney's investigation or prosecution of the case. The state attorney shall bear the costs. The state attorney shall also provide written notification to the attorney general and the trial court of compliance with this section, including certifying that, to the best of the state attorney's knowledge or belief, all public records in the state attorney's possession have been copied, indexed, and delivered to the records repository as required by this rule.

(3) Within 90 days after receipt of written notification of the mandate from the attorney general, the Department of Corrections shall copy, index, and deliver to the records repository all public records, in a current, nonproprietary technology format, determined by the department to be relevant to the subject matter of a proceeding under rule 3.851, unless such copying, indexing, and delivering would be unduly burdensome. To the extent that the records determined by the department to be relevant to the subject matter of a proceeding under rule 3.851 are the defendant's medical, psychological, substance abuse, or psychiatric records, upon receipt of express consent by the defendant or pursuant to the authority of a court of competent jurisdiction, the department shall provide a copy of the defendant's medical, psychological, substance abuse, and psychiatric records to the defendant's counsel of record. The department shall bear the costs. The secretary of the department shall provide written notification to the attorney general and the trial court of compliance with this section certifying that, to the best of the secretary of the department's knowledge or belief, all such public records in the possession of the secretary of the department have been copied, indexed, and delivered to the records repository.

(4) Within 90 days after receipt of written notification of the mandate from the state attorney, a law enforcement agency shall copy, index, and deliver to the records repository all public records, in a current, nonproprietary technology format, which were produced in the investigation or prosecution of the case. Each agency shall bear the costs. The chief law enforcement officer of each law enforcement agency shall provide written notification to the attorney general and the trial court of compliance with this section including certifying that, to the best of the chief law enforcement officer's knowledge or belief, all such public records in possession of the agency or in possession of any employee of the agency, have been copied, indexed, and delivered to the records repository.

(5) Within 90 days after receipt of written notification of the mandate from the attorney general, each additional person or agency identified pursuant to subdivision (d)(2) or (d)(3) of this rule shall copy, index, and deliver to the records repository all public records, in a current, nonproprietary technology format, which were produced during the prosecution of the case. The person or agency shall bear the costs. The person or agency shall provide written notification to the attorney general and the trial court of compliance with this subdivision and shall certify, to the best of the person or agency's knowledge and belief, all such public records in the possession of the person or agency have been copied, indexed, and delivered to the records repository.

(f) Exempt or Confidential Public Records.

(1) Any public records delivered to the records repository pursuant to these rules that are confidential or exempt from the requirements of section 119.07, Florida Statutes, or article I, section 24(a), Florida Constitution, must be separately contained, without being redacted, and sealed. The outside of the container must clearly identify that the public record is confidential or exempt and that the seal may not be broken without an order of the trial court. The outside of the container

Rule 3.852. Capital Postconviction Public Records Production.

must identify the nature of the public records and the legal basis for the exemption.

(2) Upon the entry of an appropriate court order, sealed containers subject to an inspection by the trial court shall be shipped to the clerk of court. The containers may be opened only for inspection by the trial court in camera. The moving party shall bear all costs associated with the transportation and inspection of such records by the trial court. The trial court shall perform the unsealing and inspection without ex parte communications and in accord with procedures for reviewing sealed documents.

(3) Collateral counsel must file a motion for in camera inspection within 30 days of receipt of the notice of delivery of the sealed records to the central records repository, or the in camera inspection will be deemed waived.

(g) Demand for Additional Public Records.

(1) Within 240 days after collateral counsel is appointed, retained, or appears pro bono, such counsel shall send a written demand for additional public records to each person or agency submitting public records or identified as having information pertinent to the case under subdivision (d) of this rule, with a copy to the trial court. However, if collateral counsel was appointed prior to October 1, 2001, then within 90 days after collateral counsel is appointed, retained, or appears pro bono, such counsel shall send a written demand for additional public records to each person or agency submitting public records or identified as having information pertinent to the case under subdivision (d) of this rule.

(2) Within 90 days of receipt of the written demand, each person or agency notified under this subdivision shall deliver to the records repository any additional public records in the possession of the person or agency that pertain to the case and shall certify to the best of the person or agency's knowledge and belief that all additional public records have been delivered to the records repository or, if no additional public records are found, shall recertify that the public records previously delivered are complete. To the extent that the additional public records are the defendant's Department of Corrections' medical, psychological, substance abuse, or psychiatric records, upon receipt of express consent by the defendant or pursuant to the authority of a court of competent jurisdiction, the department shall provide a copy of the defendant's medical, psychological, substance abuse, and psychiatric records to the defendant's counsel of record. A copy of each person's or agency's certification shall be provided to the trial court.

(3) Within 60 days of receipt of the written demand, any person or agency may file with the trial court an objection to the written demand described in subdivision (g)(1). The trial court shall hear and rule on any objection no later than the next 90-day status conference after the filing of the objection, ordering a person or agency to produce additional public records if the court determines each of the following exists:

(A) Collateral counsel has made a timely and diligent search as provided in this rule.

(B) Collateral counsel's written demand identifies, with specificity, those additional public records that are not at the records repository.

(C) The additional public records sought are relevant to the subject matter of a proceeding under rule 3.851, or appear reasonably calculated to lead to the discovery of admissible evidence.

(D) The additional public records request is not overly broad or unduly burdensome.

(h) Cases in Which Mandate was Issued Prior to Effective Date of Rule.

(1) If the mandate affirming a defendant's conviction and sentence of death was issued prior to October 1, 1998, and no initial public records requests have been made by collateral counsel by that date, the attorney general and the state attorney shall file notifications with the trial court as required by subdivisions (d) and (e) of this rule.

(2) If on October 1, 1998, a defendant is represented by collateral counsel and has initiated the public records process, collateral counsel shall, within 90 days after October 1, 1998, or within 90 days after the production of records which were requested prior to October 1, 1998, whichever is later, file with the trial court and serve a written demand for any additional public records that have not previously been the subject of a request for public records. The request for these records shall be treated the same as a request pursuant to subdivisions (d)(3) and (d)(4) of this rule, and the records shall be copied, indexed,

Rule 3.852. Capital Postconviction Public Records Production.

and delivered to the repository as required in subdivision (e)(5) of this rule.

(3) Within 10 days of the signing of a defendant's death warrant, collateral counsel may request in writing the production of public records from a person or agency from which collateral counsel has previously requested public records. A person or agency shall copy, index, and deliver to the repository any public record:

(A) that was not previously the subject of an objection;

(B) that was received or produced since the previous request; or

(C) that was, for any reason, not produced previously.

The person or agency providing the records shall bear the costs of copying, indexing, and delivering such records. If none of these circumstances exist, the person or agency shall file with the trial court and the parties an affidavit stating that no other records exist and that all public records have been produced previously. A person or agency shall comply with this subdivision within 10 days from the date of the written request or such shorter time period as is ordered by the court.

(4) In all instances in subdivision (h) which require written notification the receiving party shall provide proof of receipt by return mail or other carrier.

(i) Limitation on Postproduction Request for Additional Records.

(1) In order to obtain public records in addition to those provided under subdivisions (e), (f), (g), and (h) of this rule, collateral counsel shall file an affidavit in the trial court which:

(A) attests that collateral counsel has made a timely and diligent search of the records repository; and

(B) identifies with specificity those public records not at the records repository; and

(C) establishes that the additional public records are either relevant to the subject matter of the postconviction proceeding or are reasonably calculated to lead to the discovery of admissible evidence; and

(D) shall be served in accord with subdivision (c)(1) of this rule.

(2) Within 30 days after the affidavit of collateral counsel is filed, the trial court may order a person or agency to produce additional public records only upon finding each of the following:

(A) collateral counsel has made a timely and diligent search of the records repository;

(B) collateral counsel's affidavit identifies with specificity those additional public records that are not at the records repository;

(C) the additional public records sought are either relevant to the subject matter of a proceeding under rule 3.851 or appear reasonably calculated to lead to the discovery of admissible evidence; and

(D) the additional records request is not overly broad or unduly burdensome.

(j) Authority of the Court. In proceedings under this rule the trial court may:

(1) compel or deny disclosure of records;

(2) conduct an in-camera inspection;

(3) extend the times in this rule upon a showing of good cause;

(4) require representatives from government agencies to appear at status conferences to address public records issues;

(5) impose sanctions upon any party, person, or agency affected by this rule including initiating contempt proceedings, taxing expenses, extending time, ordering facts to be established, and granting other relief; and

(6) resolve any dispute arising under this rule unless jurisdiction is in an appellate court.

(k) Scope of Production and Resolution of Production Issues.

(1) Unless otherwise limited, the scope of production under any part of this rule shall be that the public records sought are not privileged or immune from production and are either relevant to the subject matter of the proceeding under rule 3.851 or are reasonably calculated to lead to the discovery of admissible evidence.

(2) Any objections or motions to compel production of public records pursuant to this rule shall be filed within 30 days after the end of the production time period provided by this rule. Counsel for the party objecting or moving to compel shall file a copy of the objection or motion directly with the trial court. The trial court shall hold a hearing on the objection or motion on an expedited basis.

(l) Destruction of Records Repository Records. Sixty days after a capital sentence is carried out, after a defendant is released from incarceration following the granting of a pardon or reversal of the sentence, or after a defendant has been resentenced to a term of years, the attorney general shall provide written notification of this occurrence to the secretary of state with service in accord with subdivision (c)(1). After the expiration of the 60 days, the secretary of state may then destroy the copies of the records held by the records repository that pertain to that case, unless an objection to the destruction is filed in the trial court and served upon the secretary of state and in accord with subdivision (c)(1). If no objection has been served within the 60-day period, the records may then be destroyed. If an objection is served, the records shall not be destroyed until a final disposition of the objection.

Rule 3.853. Motion for Postconviction DNA Testing.

(a) Purpose. This rule provides procedures for obtaining DNA (deoxyribonucleic acid) testing under sections 925.11 and 925.12, Florida Statutes.

(b) Contents of Motion. The motion for postconviction DNA testing must be under oath and must include the following:

(1) a statement of the facts relied upon in support of the motion, including a description of the physical evidence containing DNA to be tested and, if known, the present location or last known location of the evidence and how it originally was obtained;

(2) a statement that the evidence was not previously tested for DNA, or a statement that the results of previous DNA testing were inconclusive and that subsequent scientific developments in DNA testing techniques likely would produce a definitive result establishing that the movant is not the person who committed the crime;

(3) a statement that the movant is innocent and how the DNA testing requested by the motion will exonerate the movant of the crime for which the movant was sentenced, or a statement how the DNA testing will mitigate the sentence received by the movant for that crime;

(4) a statement that identification of the movant is a genuinely disputed issue in the case and why it is an issue or an explanation of how the DNA evidence would either exonerate the defendant or mitigate the sentence that the movant received;

(5) a statement of any other facts relevant to the motion; and

(6) a certificate that a copy of the motion has been served on the prosecuting authority.

(c) Procedure.

(1) Upon receipt of the motion, the clerk of the court shall file it and deliver the court file to the assigned judge.

(2) The court shall review the motion and deny it if it is facially insufficient. If the motion is facially sufficient, the prosecuting authority shall be ordered to respond to the motion within 30 days or such other time as may be ordered by the court.

(3) Upon receipt of the response of the prosecuting authority, the court shall review the response and enter an order on the merits of the motion or set the motion for hearing.

(4) In the event that the motion shall proceed to a hearing, the court may appoint counsel to assist the movant if the court determines that assistance of counsel is necessary and upon a determination of indigency pursuant to section 27.52, Florida Statutes.

(5) The court shall make the following findings when ruling on the motion:

(A) Whether it has been shown that physical evidence that may contain DNA still exists.

(B) Whether the results of DNA testing of that physical evidence likely would be admissible at trial and whether there exists reliable proof to establish that the evidence containing the tested DNA is authentic and would be admissible at a future hearing.

(C) Whether there is a reasonable probability that the movant would have been acquitted or would have received a lesser sentence if the DNA evidence had been admitted at trial.

(6) If the court orders DNA testing of the physical evidence, the cost of the testing may be assessed against the movant, unless the movant is indigent. If the movant is indigent, the state shall bear the cost of the DNA testing ordered by the court.

(7) The court-ordered DNA testing shall be ordered to be conducted by the Department of Law Enforcement or its designee, as provided by statute. However, the court, upon a showing of good cause, may order testing by another laboratory or agency certified by the American Society of Crime Laboratory Directors/Laboratory Accreditation Board (ASCLD/LAB) or Forensic Quality Services, Inc. (FQS) if requested by a movant who can bear the cost of such testing.

(8) The results of the DNA testing ordered by the court shall be provided in writing to the court, the movant, and the prosecuting authority.

(d) Time Limitations. The motion for postconviction DNA testing may be filed or considered at any time following the date that the judgment and sentence in the case becomes final.

(e) Rehearing. The movant may file a motion for rehearing of any order denying relief within 15 days after service of the order denying relief. The time for filing an appeal shall be tolled until an order on the motion for rehearing has been entered.

(f) Appeal. An appeal may be taken by any adversely affected party within 30 days from the date the order on the motion is rendered. All orders denying relief must include a statement that the movant has the right to appeal within 30 days after the order denying relief is rendered.

XVIII. Forms

[Editor's Note: Rules 3.984 - 3.996 omitted due to printing limitations.]

Made in United States
Orlando, FL
02 September 2025